RURAL MUSLIMS IN TRANSITION

Dedication

Dedicated to my Philosopher guide Professor S. Musi Raza who has always been a source of inspiration to me.

RURAL MUSLIMS IN TRANSITION

SARFARAZUDDIN AHMAD

Commonwealth Publishers
NEW DELHI-110002
(INDIA)

RURAL MUSLIMS IN TRANSITION

First Published 2024

ISBN 81-7169-170-6

Published by :
COMMONWEALTH PUBLISHERS (P) LTD.
4831/24, Govind Lane,
Ansari Road, Darya Ganj,
New Delhi - 110002
Ph. : 23242541, 23272541
e-mail : commonwealthpublishers2016@gmail.com

Distributed by :
ARJUN PUBLISHING HOUSE
4831/24, Govind Lane,
Ansari Road, Darya Ganj,
New Delhi - 110002
Ph. : 23242541, 23272541
e-mail : arjunbooks2001@gmail.com
arjunpubhouse@gmail.com

Laser Typesetting by :
Dimple Computers
Delhi

Printed at :
Milan Enterprises
Delhi

Preface

Village life in India has undergone a rapid change. But the forces influencing the rural life have not yielded identical changes because of different socio-economic and politico-religious factors such as diversities in faith, belief, rituals, traditions, local customary sanctions, social obligations, level of education, political awareness etc. For the comprehensive understanding of social life in rural India, all such factors need to be studied at micro-level. However some attempts have been made to study the various facets of rural social life but most of such studies are based on macro-level analyses and observations and little efforts have been made to study these phenomenon at micro-level. The present study is one of the efforts in this direction.

The very objective of this study is to present a comprehensive understanding of the changing patterns of social life of a village with predominanly Muslim population and non-Muslim population on its fringe areas. From this point of view, it is a very significant study to understand and conceptualise the social phenomenon of the changing Muslim village. This sociological analysis provides a systematic understanding of social structure of Muslims including their customs, rituals, attitudes, values and patterns of social interactions among themselves as well as with their non-Muslim neighbours.

I have every reason to believe that the book will inspire other scholars for making similar studies in different parts of the country to know more and more about the changing scenario of Indian villages.

I am deeply indebted to my Philosopher guide Professor S. Musi Raza, Sociology Department, Patna University who has always been a source of inspiration and encouragement from the very inception of my career. I also express my sincere thanks to Professor Mobin Raz, my teacher, guide and colleague for his constant help in this endeavour. I must also record my thanks to Professor Zeyauddin Ahmad, presently chairman, Department of Sociology, International Islamic University, Malaysia for his immense help in my career building. I also wish to record my deep sense of thanks to Dr. S.F. Rab, Librarian, A.N.S. Institute of Social Studies, Patna for his scholarly interest and support in this venture. Finally, my thanks are due to my wife Dr. (Ms) Talat Ara Ashrafi, lecturer in Sociology, S.G.G. College, Patna City for extending her cooperation and sharing my responsibilities at the time of writing this book.

SARFARAZUDDIN AHMAD

Contents

1

Introduction

In the recent time some attention is being paid to the study of social institutions and modes of social life prevailing among Muslims in different parts of the country. But such studies are scanty and insufficient in relation to the similar studies conducted by sociologists and social anthropologists on Hindu society and culture. Some of the studies conducted on Muslim community by Indian sociologists are yet to come out and those already done throw insufficient light on different aspects of life among Indian Muslims. Most of these published materials are concerned with the analysis of social institutions like, marriage, family, purdah, social hierarchy, political orientation, etc. But a comprehensive study of a Muslim community in India is still awaited and the sociologists are expected to explore this area of enquiry. The facts presented in these studies have, no doubt, helped in removing many of the stereotypes regarding Muslims in their social, religious, economic and political life. But these studies do not present a uniform and complete picture of Muslim society in India and their findings are also sometimes quite different from one another. Hence a systematic and well-crystallised picture is yet to emerge, and that is why more sociological studies are needed. Hence the necessity of the present study.

As regards village studies in India it can be said that the

sociological accounts given so far about rural communities mostly present different aspects of Hindu society and the social changes in the traditional institutions, such as, caste, Hindu joint family and Hindu kinship, etc., But little attention has, so far, been paid towards the study of Muslim community as a whole. The studies conducted in some of the Muslim villages are generally partial and superficial in nature. In different parts of the country there are, in fact, considerable number of villages which are either inhabited or dominantly inhabited by the Muslims. In many of these villages the non-Muslims are either insignificant or are found residing in the adjacent tolas of the villages. These groups are generally occupational castes or sub-castes of lower grades rendering services to the Muslims residing in the main villages. In such villages the Muslims have been traditionally dominant and playing an effective role in the traditional local power structure. These Muslims have their own customs, rituals, attitudes, values and patterns of social relationships among themselves as well as with their non-Muslim neighbours. Generally, these dominant Muslim villages have been inhabited by the Muslim zamindars and big farmers. Hence, a sociological study of such Muslim villages is of great importance for understanding the traditional modes of life, the social changes in modern times as well as the impact of Islamic sanctions on the traditional community life.

The village under study is a typical Muslim village named "Pinjrawan", located in Jehanabad sub-division of Gaya District in Bihar and is solely inhabited by Muslims. The non-Muslim families do not reside in the main village but they are living in the adjacent tolas which, in fact, constitute a part of the larger village. These non-Muslims belong to lower Hindu castes and have been serving the Muslims of the village since the early days. The social and economic condition of these Hindu service castes living in the adjacent tolas were miserable in the past and they entirely depended upon their Muslim masters. But today there are indications of certain changes in their traditional relations due to spread of literacy and economic independence. The changing relations between the Muslim and non-Muslim families in the villages are of greater sociological significance and require a systematic enquiry and investigation. Moreover, the abolition of Zamindari system, the spread of modern education, migration from rural to urban areas, changing political attitudes, etc. have produced far-reaching impact on the attitudes, life style, usages, customary practices and mode of economic life among the Muslims themselves. The study of such Muslim village presents a multi-dimensional problem for sociological enquiry and it is for this purpose that it has been selected for a detailed study.

As regards the objective of study it is not confined to any one aspect, rather it is a complete study of community covering all aspects of their life. The study aims at analysing the traditional patterns and the consequent changes taking place in various aspects of the community life. The major social institutions of Muslims, such as, purdah, family, marriage, social stratification, education, religious performances, trust institutions, economic activities and political orientations have been covered by the present study. Purdah has not only been a traditional practice but also an Islamic sanction and Muslim women have been observing purdah due to religious bindings. The present study has to find out the new trends in purdah system.

In the same way the institutions of marriage and family are guided by Islamic sanctions. The objective of the study is also to find out how the sanctions of 'Sharia' were being observed in the past and what changes are taking place in modern times. Moreover, it is also to be looked into whether there exists any ideological conflict between the traditionalists and the protagonists of change.

In Islam, acquiring knowledge and learning has been much valued. But in the traditional social order this Islamic spirit was not really translated into practice. By education the traditionalists meant only religious education, i.e., learning of Qur'an, traditions and fundamentals of Sharia. Moreover, there was no concept of female education in the traditional set up. But today we find that there has been a departure from this traditioual standpoint among Indian Muslims. Hence, in the present study an attempt has been made to find out what was the pattern of education in the past and also the new trends developing in the village in respect of education in general and female education in particular.

There has been a lengthy debate among scholars, intellectuals and academicians about the status of women in Islam as well as in the present day Muslim society. In the present study the position of Muslim women in the village has also been analysed and an attempt has been made to find out how far do the villagers themselves feel about the past and present status of Muslim women.

Economic life in general is changing very fast in the present age and the Muslims cannot remain isolated from the mainsteam of this change. The achievement of independence has brought many radical changes in the economic life. The abolition of zamindari, the rise of the lower castes, land reforms, growth of industries and employment opportunities in urban and industrial areas associated with the spread of literacy and education have produced profound impact on the mode of economic life. The present village was also dominated by Muslim zamindars and, with the abolition of zamindari system there has been a sudden change in the traditional economic relations and a collapse in the traditional power structure has taken place. Some of the ex-landlords have not reconciled themselves with the changing realities while others have accepted the changed climate and are struggling for finding out better avenues. Hence, economic relations are also undergoing significant change. The economic relations among the Muslim families themselves as well as between the Muslim and non-Muslim families have also started changing. This aspect of Muslim life in the village has also been covered in the present study.

Islam stands for equality among Muslims and does not discriminate between one another on the basis of race, birth or occupation. Only piety is the basis of distinction among Muslims and the Qur'anic sanctions also declare in clear words that he who is more pious is superior in the eyes of God. But under the impact of traditional Hindu society the Indian Muslims also developed a social hierarchy. The clear-cut division of the Muslim community between "Ashraf" and

"Atraf" categories representing Muslims of foreign origin and of indigenous population has been an established reality of traditional Muslim society in India. Hence, in the present study the analysis of the pattern of social hierarchy existing among Muslims of Pinjrawan village constitutes an important aspect of the present inquiry. Moreover, the present study also includes the changes taking place in the traditional hierarchy on account of the impact of a number of factors, such, as, zamindari abolition, secular Indian constitution, parliamentary democracy, spread of literacy and education and industrialization and urbanization. Therefore, the present study also includes an analysis of power structure as well as political socialization and political participation of the Muslims residing in the village. Hence, the study of the nature of political orientation and the magnitude of political participation along with the analysis of how the Muslims view the present political system, is an important aspect of the present research work.

Religion has always played a vital role in the community life of Indian Muslims. Individuals may violate Islamic sanctions in their personal life but as a community they are always adherents to the Islamic theology and Islamic sanctions. Even those Muslims who are not faith-oriented in their day-to-day life do not challenge the authenticity of Sharia and Islamic jurisprudence. In this state of affairs the religious life of the Muslims and their religious orientations have much relevance to the patterns of community life. Consequntly, therefore, a study of the religious life is essential for understanding other aspects of community life. Hence, such aspects have also been covered in the analysis of religious life of the Muslims living in Pinjrawan.

As the present study is concerned with the study of the structure of a Muslim community, it is desirable to describe briefly the very concept of social structure. In fact the idea of social structure has been derived in social sciences from physical and natural sciences. The concept of structure itself has borrowed from physics or from physiology to social sciences. In physics the structure of inorganic beings is analysed whereas physiology is concerned with the study of the structure of animals or human beings. Thus the idea of structure of an inorganic object in physics and of an organic object in biology or physiology facilitated the development of the idea of the structure of a superorganic aggregate, i e., society or communlty. In this way the concept of social structure developed in social sciences. Referring to this fact Eister[1] mentions, "the general concept of structure appears to have been borrowed and adapted from physics (especially classical mechanics) on one hand and, more extensively, from biology (especially the morphology and physiology of animals and plants) on the other. Although the comparison of social structure to machines or other inorganic structures or to organism was generally intended to be merely analogous, confusion concerning the precise denotation and the various connotations of the concept has resulted from this practice."

The social scientists have also discussed the concept of social structure in their own ways to analyse various social problems. A number of sociologists and social anthropologists have used this term. An analysis of their viewpoints suggests that a complete agreement does not exist among them. The social scientists and philosophers of 19th century also used this term as a distinctive arrangement of institutions. As pointed out by William Kolb, "In the sense in which Spencer and many more recent sociologists have used the concept, social structure refers to a more or loss distinctive arrangement (of which there may be more than one type) of specialized and mutually dependent institutions (q.v.) and the institutionalizational organisations of positions and/or of actors which they imply all evolved in the natural course of events as groups of human beings, with given needs and capacities have interacted with each other (in various types or modes of interaction) and sought to cope with their environment. The units of social structure in this case are themselves structures (either of culturally patterned practices, expectations, norms or of established relationships among

1. Allan, W. Eister, A dictionary of social sciences, edited by Julius Gold William L. Kolb, The Free Press, New York, 1967, p. 669.

given actors, or both) and the assumption is that integration and/or the survival as well being of the whole, if not also of all the durable parts severally, and especially the preservation of the generation from or arrangement of the whole, depend upon the adequate discharge or performance by each part of functions assigned to or associated with it under conditions laid down by nature."[2]

The facts mentioned above shows that according to Spencer and many other sociologists social structure is a manifestation of social institutions and social relations. But on the other hand authors like Hiller and Firth have presented a different meaning of social structure. According to Hiller "social structure is not an arrangement of institutions rather it may be viewed as an arrangement of positions or statuses variously created and maintained or it may be described as a network of relationship among persons or actors."[3]

In the same way the views expressed by Raymond Firth indicate that social structure includes basic relationship arising similarly from a class system. He is also of the opinion that other aspects of social structure arise through membership on other kinds of persistent groups like clans, castes and secret societies.[4]

Radcliffe Brown has also dealt with social structure in detail. According to him all natural sciences deal with structure and each science is concerned with a particular class or kind of structure. He declares that society has also got a structure commonly known as social structure which is as real as an individual organism. Hence, he holds that there should be a natural science dealing with social structure and according to him social anthropology, a natural science, should study social structure.

R. Brown has presented the concept of social structure and has included two basic things. In his own words "In

2. Hiller, E.T., Social Relation and Social Structure, Harper and Bros., New York, 1947, p. 330.
3. Ibid., p. 330.
4. Firth, R., Elements of Social Organisation, Watts, London, 1951, p. 32.

first place, I regard as a part of the social structure all social relations of person to person, for example, the kinship structure of any society consists of a number of such dyadic relations, as between a father and a son, or a brother's brothers and his sister's son. In an Australian tribe the whole social structure is based on a network of such relations of person to person established through geneological collection."[5]

He further continued, "Secondly I include under social structure the differentiations of individuals and of classes by their social roles. The differential social position of men and women of chiefs and of commoners, of employers and employees, are just as such determinants of social relation as belonging to different clans or different nations."[6]

It is evident from this discussion that in the opinion of R. Brown social structure of a group or society includes the relations among its members as well as their differentiated roles and positions. It means that R. Brown primarily recognizes the importance of social relations in determining social structure but in the second place he accepts the significance of differentiated roles and positions because they affect social relations. In this way the importance of role and status has also been recognized by R. Brown in conceptualising social structure. But the concept of social structure given by T. Parsons suggests that status and role are the basic determinants of social structure. According to him the roles are according to statuses. These roles, when get crystallised, form a social institution. He further declares that social structure is the organisation of social institutions. Parsons assumes that social structure is made up of institutions, institutions of roles, and roles of mutual expectations.[7]

It is obvious from these facts that Parsons regards social structure as an organisation of roles. In this way social role

5. Brown, A.R., Structure and Function in Primitive Society, Cohen and West Ltd., London, 1964, p. 191.
6. Ibid., pp. 191-92.
7. Martindale, Don, The Nature and Types of Sociological Theory, Routledge & Kegan Paul, London, 1961, p. 489.

has been accepted as the basic unit of social structure. The same viewpoint has been endorsed by Johnson when he says, "The structure of anything consists of the relatively stable interrelationships among its parts; moreover, the term 'parts' itself implies a certain degree of stability. Since a social system is composed of the interrelated acts of people, its structure must be sought in some degree of regularity or recurrence in these acts."[8]

Thus from Johnson's viewpoint also it is clear that social act or social roles are of basic importance in understanding and analysing social structure. In the present age the sociologists interested in the analysis of societies and social structure as a manifestation of the roles of the participants in the social system or sub-system.

In the light of the above discussions it appears that social structure has been defined in different ways by different sociologists and social scientists. The most appropriate and most acceptable definition of social structure appears to be that of Talcott Parsons. According to him the structure of any social system or sub-system refers to the institutions belonging to that system or sub-system. The institution itself refers to interrelationships and interrelated roles of the members of the system or sub-system. The analysis of regulative, integrative, relational and cultural institutions by Parsons also suggests the significance of the study of relations in the analysis of social structure. In the present study Parsonian concept of social structure has been adopted as the basis for analysing the social structure of the village under study. Hence the analysis of the social structure of the village under study requires the study of different types of relations found in the village and the institutions prevailing in the community life of the village. The main emphasis has been given on the analysis of relations—social, economic and political. Moreover, the institutions of purdah, religion and rituals and festivities also throw light on relational aspects and help in the analysis or social structure of a Muslim village.

8. Johnson, H.M., Sociology, Allied Publishers Pvt. Ltd., Bombay, 1967, p, 48.

Hence in the present study, these aspects of village life have also been included for analysing social structure.

For a systematic investigation into the objectives of study mentioned above, a research design was prepared by the present investigator. The nature of the problem required an exploratory research design for a systematic analysis of various aspects of community life. Before preparing the research design the investigator paid several visits to the village to collect preliminary information and also social, economic and religious background. During these visits the investigator met several residents of the community belonging to different age groups and of different social strata. The investigator tried to gather certain basic information regarding the community life and the problems faced by the residents. On the basis of the preliminary information it was decided that any single method for collecting data from the village would not be suitable in the present case. Hence it was found more profitable to combine the techniques of interview, observation and documentary sources for having a deeper and clearer insight into the problem. Even in case of interview it was decided to apply both the formal and informal interviewing techniques, though greater emphasis was to be laid on formal interviewing.

During the preliminary survey of the village through various visits it was found that the village is not very large in size. In all 159 Muslim families reside in the village. Each family resides in one household. Some of the families were found to be nuclear and smaller in size and some larger in size and joint in structure. It was decided not to take a sample of the families for the purpose of the present study. This decision was taken for two reasons. In the first place the smaller number of households or families did not justify drawing a sample for the present study. Secondly, a comprehensive study of the village was desired and in drawing a sample there was an apprehension of the exclusion of families belonging to a particular income-group or status group or lineage or any other such basic importance in the village life. Hence instead of sampling method the census method was adopted in the present study. Family was taken as the unit of study and all the families were covered. It was decided that the head of each family should be contacted for gathering information through formal and informal interviewing. In this way the present study is based on census method.

For conducting formal or structured interview in the present study, the first task before the investigator was to prepare an interview schedule. Keeping the above-stated objective in mind it was planned to divide the schedule into four broad sections concerning social, economic, political and religious aspects of community life. The section concerning social aspect was further divided into four sub-sections—education, family and marriage, social stratification and purdah. After this categorization questions were framed in respect of each major section and each of the four sub-sections. A large number of questions were framed to cover all aspects of problems in each section. In addition to these, certain questions were framed to collect preliminary information regarding personal identification of the respondents and the village under study. A copy of the schedule thus prepared is attached in the Appendix.

After the construction of the schedule the next task before the investigator was to decide who should be included in the list of the respondents and what should be the procedure for selcting these respondents. It was found from the survey of the village that the village community consisted of a large number of families and the units of village community were these families and not the individuals. Altogether there were 159 families of Muslims living in the village. It was decided that in the present study, family should be taken as the basic unit and from each family one person should be contacted for collecting information. As the number of families was not very large in the village, there was no question of drawing sample for the present study. All the families were covered by the study and thus the method of census was adopted. It was also found from experiences in the field that the female members were not available for conducting interview. The rigidity of purdah, the domination of traditional outlook in the village, the educational backwardness of women in particular and of the villagers in general were the main factors that stood in the way of women being interviewed. Neither the male members were willing to permit the investigator to ask questions from the women nor did the women move outside freely; and hence there was no possibility of any direct communication with the investigator. Thus it was decided to interview male members only. While conducting the interview it was experienced that the head of the family was not available in each case due to one reason or the other. In some cases the family heads were away from the village in connection with their economic pursuit. In other cases the family heads remained outside the village either for earning livelihood or in connection with litigation or some other family matter. In the same way some of the family heads were unwilling to respond and desired that some younger member of the family should be interviewed. Hence the respondents interviewed in the present study belong to different age groups. In case of one family no male respondent could be contacted in spite of several attempts and it was found that only children were living with the female members. Hence 158 respondents were interviewed from 158 families.

In addition to the mode of formal interview, informal interviews were also conducted with a few residents of the village. The purpose of this interview was to collect information regarding inter-family, inter-caste and inter-sect relations, etc. In the village community. sectarian division of the residents, waqf estates and waqf properties, management of these waqfs and the views of the people regarding the condition of waqf estates and the performances of the mutawallis or trustees of these waqfs or trusts, etc. For this purpose an interview guide was prepared and it outlined the basic points and issues regarding which information was to be gathered through informal conversation. These informal conversations proved significantly beneficial in knowing many important undercurrents in the community life, latent tensions and conflicts, feelings and attitudes towards mutawallis and management of waqf affairs and the antagonism persisting between the "Deobandi" and "Barailvi" sections of the community. The information, thus collected, threw sufficient light on the patterns of community relation and helped in understanding the sectarian organisations and their approaches.

The investigator also gathered valuable information through first hand observation. During stay in the field the author observed the celebration of Muslim festivals like Shab-e-Barat, Id-ul-Zoha, Id-ul-Fitr and Muharram, etc. The activities of the villagers, their participation and enthusiasm on these occasions and the patterns of organizations and institutions actively working in the village were observed by the investigator himself. Moreover, during stay in the village got opportunities to observe five marriages. These marriages were performed in different families varying in economic status caste, level of education and social position. The investigator got the opportunity of observing the performance of marriages with different social, economic and cultural backgrounds. The observation technique was also utilised for collecting information during Friday as well as in daily prayers. The activities during day hours of Ramazan, the time of breaking fast, night prayer (Tarawih) and sahar (pre-dawn meal) were also observed by the investigator. In this way observation technique was used for collectiong a good deal of valuable information about collective life which it would not have been possible to gather through interviews only.

In addition to the above techniques the secondary sources like Gazetteer, Census Reports and other such documents preserved by some of the villagers were also consulted by the investigator to collect information regarding the area of the village, the area of cultivable and other categories of land and such other details. Moreover, documents were also consulted to collect information about the establishment of waqfs, mosque, madrasas and the schools. Some of the waqf deeds were supplied by the villagers which helped in understanding the nature, purpose and assets of the waqf estates at the time of their execution and the amendments in the waqf assets. Thus documentary sources also provided valuable information regarding social, economic and religious aspects of community life in the village.

The information collected from all these sources have

been presented and analysed. The investigator had discussed different aspects of community life in the village on the basis of these findings and an attempt has been made to find out the nature, direction and magnitude of change in the village in respect of attitudes, values, religiosity, economic life, social relations, festival celebrations aed performance of marriage and such other socio-cultural rituals like Maktab, Aqiqa and Khatna, etc. In this way a systematic and methodical attempt has been made for achieving the objectives of the study and for analysing the social structure of the village.

For a systematic presentation of the above-stated study the thesis has been divided into nine chapters. The first chapter entitled, 'Introduction' deals with the concept of social structure, the concept of structure adopted in the present study and the methods and techniques used for collecting data from the village.

The second chapter 'Islam and the Indian Muslims' presents a theoretical account of the Muslims in India, their adherence to the ideal sanctions of Islam, the traditional social life and deviation from ideal sanctions and the gradual changes taking place in social, economic and political relations and institutions through the ages. This analysis is not a mere historical account, rather it has been presented in sociological perspective. As the study is concerned with a Bihar village, specific mention of Muslims in Bihar has been made in this chapter.

The third chapter 'Earlier Studies of Muslim Society' is concerned with the analysis of different studies conducted by sociologists and other social scientists to understand Muslim communities living in different parts of Indian sub-continent. All these earlier studies included in this chapter are micro-social studies analysing the Muslim communities in specific localities or regions. Care has been taken to include those studies which throw light on different types of Muslim communities living in the Indian sub-continent. Moreover, these studies are concerned with different relations, marriage and family and social stratification.

The fourth chapter, 'Village and the People' presents a brief account of the universe under study. The chapter gives a description of the locality and surroundings of the village, its past and present, as well as the people residing in this village. The association of the people with the village, their traditions and present state of affairs are also given in this chapter.

The next chapter, 'Social Relations' marks the beginning of data analysis. On the basis of the findings, social relations prevailing in the village have been analysed. For this purpose the patterns of social stratification, marriage, family and kinship, education and purdah institution found in the village have been analysed. These discussions are based on data analysis alongwith a brief theoretical description of these aspects of social relations.

'Economic Relations' have been analysed in the following chapter. The type of economic activities and economic relations in the past and the mode of economic life at present have been analysed on the basis of the findings during field survey.

The next chapter, 'Political Relations' throws light on the political orientation, political awareness and political participation of the people in the village. What changes in political relations are taking place at present under the parliamentary system of democracy and new trends of political developments, have also been analysed in this chapter on the basis of findings.

The next chapter entitled, "Cultural Relations" presents an account of the beliefs of the villagers in religion, superstitions and other related problems. Moreover, the customs and rituals prevailing in the village as well as the festivals observed by the people have also been analysed. An attempt has been made to find out to what extent these rituals and festivals are faith-oriented and to what extent customary or tradition-oriented.

The last chapter, 'The Winds of Change', presents a summarized and analytical account of the discussions in the preceding four chapters. On the basis of the findings it has been attempted to discover the changes taking place in social life, economic relations, political activities, customs, manners and rituals. Thus an attempt has been made to find out what changes are taking place in the social structure of the village. Whether the structure is still faith-oriented or tradition-oriented or whether the relations and institutions of different types are being rationalised.

In the last the appendices have been given containing glossary, selected bibliography, interview schedule and map.

2

Islam and the Indian Muslims

Islam is neither a new religion known only for the last fourteen centuries, nor it is named after its founder. Actually there is no particular founder of Islam. All prophets of God, appearing in various countries and at different times had worked for the same religion. The religion took a perfect shape through its last prophet, Hazrat Muhammad.

Islam is a religion not of faith or rituals only. It is a way of life by putting the faith into practice. For this purpose it has got complete and perpetual code of conduct for all times and for all the persons who profess or embrace Islam in any part of the world. The sources of this code of conduct are two, first the Qur'an and the second the Traditions, the latter also known as Hadith or Sunnah. Traditions have meant a complete and authentic account of the life, sayings and actions of the Holy Prophet uniquely recorded, preserved and compiled by his companions.

Islam is the universal, the cosmopolitan, the oldest and yet the latest of all religions. It emphasises the unity of mankind as Islam implies one God, one religion and one Humanity.

Islam, the monotheistic religion, pays stress on equality and brotherhood in faith. It gives importance to piety and devotion rather than birth or colour or any worldly ground as criterion for greatness and nearness to God. Nobility of descent and pride in the purity of blood were ingrained in the social consciousness of the Arabs. Islam is opposed to any distinction on any other worldly ground. Racial discrimination is not permissible in Islamic law.[1] Prophet Muhammad directed his attention towards the establishment of a new society of equals.

The life of Muslim community is to be regulated strictly according to the Islamic Sharia. The belief in religion is not confined only to the spiritual life rather Islam is a divine code of conduct for the human life whether concerned with the private life or group activities, social life or political activities.

Mujeeb says, "The Muslim community has been a political as well as a religious society. Both these a;pects have been regarded as inseparable, because Islamic teaching insists upon the integration of the worldly and the spiritual life. It ordains that the religious and the worldly life should be organised on the basis of the same values, that equality before God should be given a social and political expression in the form of legal and political equality, that the bait-al-mal (public treasury) should be regarded as a means of promoting public welfare."[2]

These facts clearly suggest that the entire activities of the Muslims are to be guided by the Islamic sanctions derived from Qur'an and Hadis. Since belief in Qur'an and Hadis is fundamental for every believer of Islam, the sanctions derived from them constitute supreme laws and cannot be challenged. Any judgment independent of this supreme law is not permitted and any act against it is a sinful act. A real believer is he who obeys these sanctions.

With Islam the doctrine of Divine Unity is not a religious dogma. It is a principle of action to be carried into practice, and is made the basis of the advancement of humanity to a higher goal. Man is described by Qur'an as "Khalifa" or

1. Hoda, Najmul, Universal Brotherhood and Islam, in Annals of Oriental Research of the University of Madras, V. 3¹, Part I, Madras, pp. 4-5.
2. Mujeeb, M., The Indian Muslims, George Allen & Unwin Ltd, London, 1967, p. 26.

the vicegerent of God, and is gifted by Him with the power of controlling the rest of creation for his benefit under Divine Laws.[3]

It appears from the afore-mentioned facts that the life of the Muslim community is to be regulated on the basis of the principles of Sharia. The Muslim community was also to be guided by ideal Islamic sanctions. But gradually a gap between the principles and the actual practice started taking place. A perusal of the history of Islam reveals that mainly till the life of Prophet Muhammad the Muslims followed the Shariat in true sense of the term. In the subsequent decades after the death of Prophet Muhammad and at the end of the period of the Orthodox Caliphate, the noble precepts and practices were twisted to suit the whims and moods of the followers. Aristocratic and militant tendencies developed in this community. By the time Islam came to India and Muslim rule was established in our country, those tendencies which went against the teachings of Prophet Muhammad had taken deep root, and the Indian atmosphere was conducive to their development. The Arabs conquered Sindh and laid the foundation of a new Indo-Arab race and culture. Then followed by Turks, Afghans, Mughals and Pathans, Islam entered into the Indian subcontinent and spread far and wide. Muslims arrived in India in three distinct movements: first as traders and missionaries to India's southern coasts; then in the expanding wave of the Umayyad conquests; and finally in a more organised conquest-cum-immigration movement of the Central Asian Turks and Afghans.[4]

By the time Muslims came to India the religious bonds had become more principle-oriented and less practice-oriented. After coming in contact with the Indian society and culture a fresh wave of change started, mainly because of tolerance for other cultures. Siddiqui argues, "The ruling Muslims did not deprive the subject Indians of their status. They continued

3. Mahajir, Ali Musa Raza, Tenets of Islam, Islamic Literature Publishing House, Bangalore, 1963, p. 14.

4. Ahmad, Aziz, Studies in Islamic Culture in the Indian Environment, Clarenden Press, Oxford, London, 1964, p. 77.

to follow their ancient customs and institutions. The Brahmins looked after the temples, directed religious ceremonies "[5] Further, the conversion of a large number of Indian inhabitants into the fold of Islam contributed to the complexity and heterogeneity of Muslim population, because only change in faith and belief occurred, while the age-old customs and the behaviour patterns remained almost the same. The existence of numerous occupational castes or caste-like groups of weavers, tailors, dyers and darners, mirasis, bhangis, green grocers, etc. in the Indian Muslim society is a glaring instance in this regard. The converted Indian Muslims shared something in common, but at the same time they differed widely in certain other aspects. Yasin observes that from the time of Sultan Mahmood Ghaznavi to the reign of Jehangir the Indian Muslims had developed into a heterogeneous Indianized community.[6]

Influences of Hindu culture on Muslim community came from different directions, in different forms and at different rates. A large number of Hindu rituals, for instance, those related to child birth, death and marriage, etc. were to a greater extent accepted by the Muslims as social usages. Mujeeb also observes, "There are no accepted traditions which justify and provide a legal basis for actual relationship between Muslims and Hindus, though many practices borrowed from the Hindus which became a part of the ceremonies of marriage, child birth and death were furnished ex-post-facto with a legal basis."[7]

Supporting the same viewpoint Yasin says, "In spite of the jarring elements of political dissensions and in spite of the corrosive influence of religious antagonism, centuries of constant association and the growth of a common language

5. Siddiqui, N.A., Population Geography of Muslims of India, S. Chand & Co. (Pvt) Ltd., New Delhi, 1976, pp. 7-8.
6. Yasin, Md., A Social History of Islamic India, Lucknow, 1958, p 131.
7. Mujeeb, M., The Indian Muslims, George Allen & Unwin Ltd., London, 1967, p. 38.

and culture had brought the two communities near . . . ."[8] Actually the transfusion and adoption of these socio-cultural traits brought the two communities closer to each other. Commenting on the influence of Hinduism, Mujeeb remarks, "We would find that while the Muslim proclaimed his mission and trumpeted his intentions, Hindu influences moving silently and unobtrusively like the water of flood, surrounded him from all sides having only small island where the flag of Islam flew high and defenceless."[9] These new customs became so deeply rooted that even on the religious and sacred occasions their performance became common. As Mujeeb observes, "These were also Naqshbandi sufis who thought it sinful to listen song or music. These sufis were not thrown aside by the current of life. The Prophet Day was celebrated regularly and the Arab in 'Arab Sarai' near Humayun tomb made it a charished occasion for those interested in the various styles of reciting the Qur'an. People who talked of spiritual things, also had their time and place in a world that accommodated every kind of virtue with every type of vice."[10] Mujeeb further says, "Id-ul-Fitr, Id-uz-Zoha and Muharram, Holi, Diwali and Dasehra were no doubt celebrated but the festival that finds most detailed mention in the Muraqqa' is the Hindu festival of Basant as observed by the Muslims."[11]

On the basis of above facts, it may be pointed out that from the day Muslims entered the Indian territory they led their life very leniently and liberally. They did not follow the Islamic code of conduct strictly and embraced the local customs and way of life as well. Due to this cultural contact various aspects of Hindu life-style were adopted by Muslim communtiy.

Muslims remained not only liberal in accepting and adopting most of the Hindu ways of life, but Muslim rulers were

8. Yasin, Md., A Social History of Islamic India, Lucknow, 1958, p. 132.
9. Ibid., p. 203.
10. Mujeeb, M., The Indian Muslims, George Allen & Unwin Ltd., London, 1967, p. 204.
11. Ibid., pp. 205-6.

also liberal and broad minded in the recruitment of personnel for administration. All those who possessed talent and ability—irrespective of religion and faith—were taken in the state services. Muslim rulers and administrators tried to make India a welfare state. They looked after the interest of their subjects—elites and commoners alike. In the words of Siddiqui, "Muslims made efforts to make their government a welfare state. Many measures such as price control and regulated distribution were undertaken from time to time. Hospitals, educational institutions, canals for irrigation and roads for travelling were constructed. By and large people were contended."[12]

Due to liberal and adaptive policies of the Muslim rulers and emergence of harmony and synthesis between the alien and native religions and cultures and favourable conditions for innovation, invention and discovery developed in different branches of learning.

As a result and the regular contacts and interactions between the two communities, a process of Hindu-Muslim synthesis started in the country. This process of synthesis resulted in the development of Urdu and Hindi as the languages of the commoners. Moreover, the synthesis is also evidenced from the buildings constructed and the art and music developed in this period. This process of synthesis was also found in everyday life as reflected from rituals, manners and customs.

At every stage of history the state of Bihar has hosted different religio-cultural groups and races and present Patna has been an important seat of Muslim culture and civilization. Hence, Muslims of this region have also been much influenced by the cultural diffusion. As a result of the impact of Hindu culture, caste-like hierarchy also developed among Indian Muslims. The community was broadly divided into the two categories of Ashraf and Atraf or Kamin or Peshawar and non-Peshawar Muslims. The Ashrafs or non-Peshawar Muslims claimed a foreign breed, whereas the Atraf (Kamin)

12. Siddiqui. N.A., Population Ceography of Muslims of India, S Chand & Co. (Pvt) Ltd., New Delhi, 1976. p. 9.

or Peshawar were the Muslims of indigenous population. Thus the ideal sanctions and practices of Islam were ignored and egalitarian nature of Muslim society turned into the stratified one. Writing about the life of the Muslims of Patna and Gaya Buchanan says, "I doubt much, whether such conversions, as have been made by Muhammedans among the Hindus, have been in either respect advantageous to the prosylytes. They call indeed upon Allah, and the Prophet; but still I doubt much if they have been weaned from any one of their former superstitions.[13] Thus the picture of the Muslims of Patna and Gaya presented by Buchanan shows that converted Muslims of those days did not follow their religious sanctions strictly and a process of Indianization of Indian Muslims had started.

Britishers, the last to come and rule India, also left a deep impression on the socio-cultural life of Indians. Western culture and English language influenced the Muslims most. Sir Syed Ahmed Khan and his associates, especially Hali took a lead in spreading English education and western life pattern. Sir Syed founded the Anglo-Arabic school and then a college which ultimately converted into Aligarh Muslim University. This institution created a renaissance in Muslim community of India and specially in the Muslims of U.P. and Bihar.

The partition of the country in 1947 resulted in the large-scale migration of Muslim youth to Pakistan leaving behind the Muslims here in a state of despair and frustration due to economic collapse, frequent communal riots and distrust among them expressed by the extremist non-Muslims. There was a major shake up and the Muslim community in Bihar not only in economic aspect or political life, but also in respect of family life, fixation of marriage and maintaining kinship ties. The second jolt to the Muslim community in Bihar was given by the formation of Bangla Desh and the exodus of Biharis from Bangla Desh. It produced far reaching impact on social, economic and cultural life and the Muslims in Bihar.

13. Buchanan, Francis Hamilton, An Introduction to the Districts of Behar and Patna in 1811-12, Vol. I, p. 30.

Till 1912, the state of Bihar had been the part of Bengal and in the same year separated by British Government. It is bounded on the north by Nepal, on the east by West Bengal, on the west by Uttar Pradesh and Madhya Pradesh and on the south by Orissa.

Geographically the state consists of two distinct physical units—the Gangetic plain and the Chhotanagpur plateau. The river Ganga divides the plain into two natural regions—North Bihar and South Bihar.[14]

As regards the advent of Muslims in Bihar, Ikhtiaruddin Mohammed bin-Bakhtiar Khilji (1192-1204) ruled here with the conquest of Bihar and Bengal. But there are also some indications which suggest the advent of Muslims to Bihar during the reign of Mohammed of Ghazni in early 11th century.[15] With the advent of Khilji in Bihar, the Muslims ruled for centuries and gradually a large number of Muslims settled in Patna, Gaya and various other parts of Bihar. In early eighteenth century (1704) Azimushan (the grandson of Aurangzeb) became the ruler of Patna and named this city as Azimabad after his own name. During this period huge number of Muslims belonging to different walks of life came from far and wide and settled here. Again in the British regime this city was renamed as Patna.

The history shows that Bihar, the sacred land of Bhagwan Buddh and Mahavira, Guru Govind Singh and Hazrat Makhdoom Sharfuddin Yahya Maneri, could not keep herself aloof from other cultures, races and groups.

The district of Gaya is bounded on the north by Patna district, on the south Hazaribagh and Palamau districts, on the east Nawada district and on the west Aurangabad district. The administrative headquarter of the district is located at Gaya which is the chief town of the district and is almost centrally located. The total population of the district according to 1981 census is 3,134,175 while only rural population is

14. Bihar, 1958-59, Facts and Figures, The Department of Public Relations, Patna.

15. Azimabadi, Maulvi Fasihuddin, Balkhi, Tarikhe Magadh (Urdu), Anjuman-e-Taraqqi-e-Urdu (India), Delhi, 1944, pp. 95-96.

2,794,171.[16] This shows that about 89% of the total population of Gaya district lives in the villages. According to Vayu Purana Gaya was the name of a demon.[17]

Gaya is one of the holiest spots for the Hindus. According to the religion of Puranas it is incumbent on every Hindu to visit Gaya and make offerings for the souls of his ancestors.[18] Situated seven miles south of Gaya town is Bodh Gaya, the most holy place for the Buddhists. It is at Bodh Gaya that Lord Buddha achieved 'nirvan' or enlightenment.

A large number of local people converted to Islam in Bihar, as it did happen in almost every part of the country. These neo-Muslims accepted Islamic theocracy but could not shirk off their age old customs and traditions. Thus the Muslims of Bihar, like that of other places in India, were divided into various caste-like sects and occupational groups. The concept of upper-lower, Ashraf-Kamin, occupational and non-occupational groups developed, resulting in the emergence of social differentiation and social stratification like that of the Hindu society. A large number of rituals and usages of Hindus were largely accepted and commonly practised by Muslims, especially in the rural settings.

In the light of above-given facts, it appears that changes have been taking place among Indian Muslims, including the Muslims of Bihar, under the influence of indigenous and western cultures they have also been exposed to the influence of modern forces. The modern forces like secular and democratic education, media of mass communication, advanced technology, industrialization, urbanization and mass participation, have produced significant impact on the Muslims of Bihar living in urban as well as rural areas. The impact is of varying degrees in urban and rural settings, but changes are found in the Muslim communities of both types. At present the Muslims are exposed to three different forces. On

16 Azimabadi, Shad, Tarikhe Bihar (Urdu), Subhe Sadiq, Patna, 1893, pp. 49-50.

17. Census of India, 1981, Series A, B.B. Lal.

18. Chaudhury, P.C. Roy, Gaya District Gazetteer, 1957.

the one hand they are immersed in the ocean of traditional Indian culture, on the other hand they are exposed to modernization. But at the same time they also cherish Islamic values. The Friday Prayers, the Id Prayers, the annual Haj, organization of 'Waz' or religious sermons by Mullas are instrumental in inculcating Islamic values. This indoctrination of Islamic values is further strengthened by the preachings of the organizations like Jamaat-e-Islami and Tabligi Jamaat. Hence at present the Muslim community stands at the tri-juncture of Indianization, Modernization and Islamization.

3

Earlier Studies of Muslim Society

The rise of Indian sociology owes its origin mainly to the interest in understanding Hindu social organisation and the typical caste institution. A large number of Indian as well as western sociologists interested in understanding Indian society have paid specific attention to the analysis of traditional caste system and the changes taking place therein. But along with this interest in Hindu social life, some attention is also now being paid to understand the socio-cultural life, organisation, patterns of social institutions and the changes taking place in these aspects among Indian Muslims who constitute the largest minority of the country. In this way the sociological study of Muslim community has also come to the forefront in the development of sociological literature in India today. A number of studies have been conducted on Indian Muslims in different parts of the country. In the beginning these studies were conducted by social historians and social anthropologists but later on the sociologists also joined in analysing and understanding different aspects of community life among Muslims. These studies were generally micro-sociological in nature concentrating mainly on the analysis of Muslim communities living in specific villages, towns or localities. These studies throw some light on various aspects like patterns of stratification and social hierarchy, family and marriage, economic organisation, religious attachment and degree of religiosity, ritual and festivities and patterns of interaction in Muslim community. Moreover, in course of such studies efforts have also been made to find out the impact of traditional Hindu culture, deviation from Islamic sanctions, acceptance of western values and exposure to the forces of modernity in Muslim community. A glance at these studies would also reveal that all of these are not concerned with the Muslim community in general In some cases, specific Muslim sect or groups like Bohras, Khojas, Meos, Moplas have been studied. In other cases, Muslim villages or Muslim communities living in rural areas and dominating the village life have not been taken into account in detail. In the same way some of the studies are concerned with the analysis of Muslim communities in urban areas. Thus such studies on Muslim communities, no doubt, provide materials on different aspects of social life in the context of the past tradition as well as the present phase of transition.

The important studies in this field are those by Ghaus Ansari, S.C. Misra, M.K. Siddiqui, Imtiaz Ahmad, Zeyauddin Ahmad, Saghir Ahmad, S.M. Raz, Ali Ashraf, S.M. Raza, P.C. Aggarwal, Victor V. D'souza. Zarina Bhatty, Hamza Alvi, T.N. Madan, etc.

The first empirical study on the Muslim community of India was conducted by Ghaus Ansari.[1] His study was aimed at analysing Muslim castes in Uttar Pradesh. His analysis of caste stratification among Muslims is a valuable sociological contribution because the sociological concepts have also been utilised by him in analysing caste structure and intercaste relations. This study is a pioneering work on Muslim Sociology in India.

A survey of the study conducted by Ghaus Ansari shows that his work is divided into two major sections: the first is based on theoretical discussions and the second is based on empirical enquiry. In the first section the author analyses the definition of caste and its origin and development. He

1. Ansari, Ghaus, Muslim Castes in Uttar Pradesh: A Study in Culture Contact, Eastern Anthropologist, Lucknow, 1959.

concludes that caste exists in different cultural strata of the Indian societies.

In the second part of the section, the author first traces a brief history of early Islam, discusses Islam in Central Asia and gradually comes to the analysis of Islam in India and Uttar Pradesh. This analysis is a historical account of the advent of Islam to this country. In the third part of the same section the author examines the concept of equality in Islam, the contradiction of caste hierarchy and gradually the development of inequality in Muslim society. In his opinion the concept of equality was a mere imagination or ideology but in actual practice inequality was quite obvious in the Muslim society. A number of considerations drew lines of demarcations among Muslims on the basis of birth, heritage, etc. Similarly ethnic factors also became significant in distinguishing one social category from the other and contributed to the development of a social hierarchy and stratification. He observed that when Islam came to stay in India in the 12th century A.D., its social organisation had already changed though the concept of equality and brotherhood remained as an ideal as it exists even today. In practice there have been social grades within Muslim society.

The author observed that after the Muslims settled in India, gradations and concept of superior and inferior gradually developed in Muslim society. The main line of demarcation was between the Muslims of foreign extraction and those of Indian origin. The indigenous population could not get the same status in Muslim society even after embracing Islam, as enjoyed by Muslims claiming foreign breed.

In part two of the book the author also analyses the existing caste system in Muslim society and discusses the factors responsible for changes in it.

In brief, Ghaus Ansari discovers the elements of caste among Muslims. The special features of caste-based society also developed in Muslim society under the influence of Hindu culture. He concluded that the Muslim caste system is a result of Hindu influence. The Indian Muslims have acquired this system from the Hindus through constant and continuous cultural contact; the system of caste grouping resulted in the concept of social distance between the two communities, the Hindus and the Muslims.

Further, S.C. Misra's[2] "Muslim Communities in Gujrat", is also an important contribution in this field. Misra has studied the various sects of Muslim communities living in Gujrat. Among them the Bohras, the Khoja and the Memon communities have typical social structure and social organisation. These communities primarily consist of businessmen and traders. Misra has studied the totality of life in these communities, specially analysing their customs, manners, social life and legal institution. He gives an account of the rise of Muslim population in Gujrat. He has mainly analysed the Bohra community and their 'Da'is' in the state and the 'Nizari' missionaries and their followers in the state of Gujrat.

After the Prophet's death and with the spread of Islam in different parts of the world inequality increased in the Muslim world and distinctions and differences in social status and prestige emerged. Thus a base was provided for the development of caste element in Muslim society. The Muslims who came to India were having Turkish social system in the background and it laid emphasis on birth which was a negation of Islamic sanction. Hence by the time the Muslims came to India, the elements of caste system were growing in Muslim society but still they lacked the sophistication and diversification of traditional Hindu caste system. But, gradually, under the impact of Hindu culture and with the conversion of indigenous population to Islam, the caste sanctions became more apparent in the Muslim society and the elements of caste system cropped and, consequently, a number of castes developed among the Muslims of Gujrat.

According to his observations the Saiyids occupy the highest position in the Muslim community of Gujrat. The Saiyids are generally reluctant to give their daughters in marriage outside their immediate kin groups. Next come Shaikhs who are closer to Saiyids due to their claim of descent

2. Misra, S.C., Muslim Communities in Gujrat, Asia Publishing House, Bombay, 1964.

to Arab breed. They have also tried to preserve the sanctity of their lineage through restrictive marriage within the caste. In some cases marriages between Saiyids and Shaikhs have taken place and hence hypergamous patterns of marriage alliances are found. The Pathans occupy the third place in social hierarchy. In addition to these main caste groups there are a number of craftsmen engaged in different ancestoral occupations. Moreover, there are service communities which occupy the lowest position.

The author has analysed the traditional hierarchy and the changes taking place in recent times. With the change in economic condition the lower castes are trying for a better position. This has resulted on the one hand in internal cohesion of each caste or jamaat and, on the other, in the tensions and conflicts among various castes or jamaats. The old and new values are clashing against each other.

Misra also examined the institutions of family and marriage. As regards the family structure, the author finds that like Hindus the Muslims have also patriarchal, patrilocal and patrilineal family organisation. But it is interesting to note that in certain Muslim communities like Memons and Khojas the customary laws of succession go against the Islamic laws and the women are exempted from the benefit of succession. The Muslims also have joint family system and they use the same phrase samjukta parivar for large households consisting of several married and unmarried brothers and other relatives. The purdah is strictly observed among orthodox Muslims and women appear only before 'mahram' and not before 'ghair-mahram' or namahram. After attaining the age of puberty a girl secludes herself from ghair-mahram individuals.

As regards the change taking place in the Muslim communities the author finds the Muslims exposed to the influence of various processes. On the one hand they are being influenced by the process of rationalisation and Islamisation and, on the other, they are influenced by westernisation. A clash of values has set in. Islamisation tends to favour strict purdah observance whereas westernisation is opposed to it. The author finds that the upper class families are more exposed to westernisation process while the middle class families are under the influence of Islamisation.

The author also finds that with the decay of traditional grip and with the replacement of customary law and practice with a more legal pattern the religious beliefs are also becoming unimportant. The religious sanctions appeared to be less effective in regulating people's behaviour. This trend is more obvious among the Ismaili Khojas. With the spread of education, improvement in economic condition and greater degree of mobility, their outlook has been rationalised and westernised to a greater extent. Only in the case of the poorer section of the Muslim community there is a greater attachment to religion and there is also a desire for social improvement and Islamisation. Changes are obvious in dress patterns, manners, rituals, life style, levels of social contact and patterns of social relationship.

P.C. Aggarwal's[3] study on Meos of Rajasthan and Haryana are in the form of the different research articles. One referring to the Meos of Rajasthan and Haryana and the other analysing caste hierarchy in a Meo village in Rajasthan. In both the articles the main concentration is on the analysis of social hierarchy and social stratification.

Describing the Meos of Rajasthan and Haryana he points out that the Meos living in the Mewat region located in the border areas of Rajasthan and Haryana, constitute a large Muslim caste. He describes their habits, geographical boundaries, the origin of name 'Mewat', historical background of the Meos' life and their spatial distribution. He comes to the conclusion that the Meos are indigenous converts and claim Rajput ancestry. Both economically and physically they occupy a dominant position in the region and their political ascendancy helped them in claiming higher place on the ladder of social status and they occupy a respectable place in the region.

3. Aggarwal, P.C., The Meos of Rajasthan and Haryana, and, Caste Hierarchy in a Meo Village in Rajasthan, in Imtiaz Ahmad (ed.), Caste and Social Stratification among the Muslims, Manohar Book Service, Delhi, 1973.

Aggarwal also analyses the hierarchical arrangement in the village. He finds that the entire village is divided into two broader categories of unchi caste (high caste) and the kamin (service caste). The third broader category is of Harijans (untouchables). Moreover, in each of the three categories there are different castes and they do not occupy the same status. But a complete agreement regarding the status of these castes does not exist. Hence an ambiguity exists about their relative position in society.

Another significant study of a predominantly Muslim village in eastern U.P. was conducted by Imtiaz Ahmad.[4] He conducted a study on caste and kinship in the village called Ramsarchighat in the sub-division of Barabanki district in eastern U.P., which is located at about 49 miles from Lucknow. Ahmad carried out his field work between 1960 and 1962 and revisited the village in 1967 and 1972.

Ahmad found evidences reflecting a trend of change in the traditional hierarchy and the conventional concepts of superiority and inferiority. In the past there was only one mosque in which all Muslims of the village offered prayer. But the front rows were reserved for the Khanzadas, while Julahas and other castes had to stand behind them. The Iman of the Masjid (one who leads the group) was also a Khanzada. When the Julahas of the village improved their economic condition and performed Haj pilgrimage, they reacted against this traditional practice. They wanted to do away with this discrimination, while the Khanzadas stressed on discrimination. Hence the Julahas raised funds and constructed another mosque in the village. In the beginning the first mosque was used by Khanzadas and the second by Julahas and others. But gradually this gulf narrowed and some Khanzadas also offered their prayers in the new mosque. It shows a changing trend in the intercaste relations.

Ahmad also finds out that there is a concept of superiority and inferiority among zāts in the village but a universally

4. Ahmad, Imtiaz, Caste and Social Stratification among the Muslims, Manohar Book Service, Delhi, 1973.

accepted gradation is not found. Each person places his own caste a little higher than the place accorded to it by men of other castes. Hence among lower castes there is race for achieving a higher place.

Ahmad also analyses the kinship system and kinship structure in the village. He points out that the basic unit of the kinship system is the household (ghar) in the village. A household is primarily a group of kith and all other kinship relations are derived from it. The size of the household is not uniform. In some cases one individual lives in a house and regards it as single household. In some other cases household comprises of parents, unmarried sons and daughters, married sons and their spouses and unmarried children. A large household is desirable in the village. Thus complex and joint family system is prevailing in a large number of cases. When tensions develop in a joint household, the breaking up of this unit takes place and two or more smaller households develop. The joint nature of the household is mainly due to joint ownership of landed property.

Another kinship group in the village exists in the form of Bhai-band or biradari. Biradari is distinct from a "zāt" in the local dialect. The term "biradari" is used by a person while he refers to the households of his own caste and the term zāt is used for the households belonging to the castes other than his own. Thus the term biradari expresses a higher degree of affinity and connotes group feeling, whereas the term zāt is associated without group feelings. Both biradari and zāt are collection of households belonging to one caste or social group.

In the light of above findings Ahmad draws the conclusion that the viewpoint that kinship is the salient basis of social organisations in Muslim communities in the South Asia is not justified, and caste is not relevant in the structuring of social organisation in this community. He rejects this viewpoint on the basis of his findings which suggest that both caste and kinship are significant in the structuring of social organisation in Muslim community. He also points out that caste and kinship co-exist and overlap in the village. It means that both caste and kinship may be regarded as bases of social organisation.

M.K.A. Siddiqui[5] also made an important study of the Muslims living in the city of Calcutta.

On the basis of his study Siddiqui has identified nearly sixty endogamous castes like ethnic groups in the Muslim community of this city. He has also discovered that segmentation of the Muslim population is mainly on the basis of national, regional consideration. On the basis of his findings he has tried to locate the elements of caste system in the Muslim community. He has come to the conclusion that hierarchy in Muslim community contains various features of Hindu caste systems. These are endogamy, caste council, occupational specialisation and notion of social gradation. But at the same time he points out that the ritualistic base of hierarchy prevailing in Hindu society is absent in the Muslim hierarchy. On the other hand the Muslim hierarchy is found to be rationalised in non-ritual terms. Hence he concludes that some elements of caste society have appeared in the Muslim community as a result of centuries of interaction between Muslims and Hindus. But the Muslim hierarchy cannot be described as a system identical with the caste system in Hindu society.

It is also highlighted by Siddiqui that the different occupational groups in the Muslim community are not confined to their own religious community rather functional co-existence and interdependence are found among various occupational groups of Hindus and Muslims. He is also of the opinion that hereditary lineage and traditional occupation and status occupy the basic place in determining the social framework and the bases of social, cultural and economic interactions.

One more study may also be quoted here which was

5. Siddiqui, M.K.A., Muslims of Calcutta: A study in Aspects of Their Social Organization, Anthropological Survey of India, Government of India, Calcutta, 1974.

undertaken by Zeyauddin Ahmad.[6] The paper entitled, "Caste Elements among the Muslims of Bihar" is an outcome of his deep and detailed study based on documentary sources. Taking help from historical evidences he has shown the changes taking place in the socio-cultural life of the Indian Muslims in general and of the Muslims of Bihar in particular. He argues that the egalitarian social order of Islam stands in sharp contrast with the ideology of caste. Yet along with this ideal, the Muslim society in Bihar, as Ahmad observes, is divided into numerous caste-like groups and has the various elements of the caste system such as endogamy, hereditary occupations, caste names and social hierarchy. Broadly speaking, there are two categories of Muslims, those who claim foreign ancestry and those who are progenies of converted Muslims. Present day Muslim society in Bihar, he asserts, presents a strange synthesis of Islamization, Hinduization and modernization.

S.M. Raz's[7] work is also worth mentioning while dealing with Muslim social life. His book entitled, "The Process of Socialization" delineates the process of growing up in three communities of Oraon (tribe), Tiwari (a Hindu upper caste) and Jolahas (a Muslim lower caste) living in the same village named Karkara in the district of Ranchi of Chhotanagpur Plateau of Bihar. The work is based on the data collected through field investigation, observation, analysis and detailed interview of the parents and children in the three diverse cultural communities of the tribals, the Hindus and the Muslims. The author feels that the socialization prepares the child in each community for its adult role. The attitude differs in every community with regard to toilet training, obedience, rituals, customs, purdah and the seclusion of women, and so on. The author brings out the essential features of the socialization process in the multicultural

6. Ahmad, Zeyauddin, Caste Elements among Muslims of Bihar, in Harjindar Singh (ed.), Caste among Non-Hindus in India, National Publishing House, New Delhi, 1977.

7. Raz, S.M., The Process of Socialization—A Multi-Ethnic Study, Chetna Publications, New Delhi, 1976.

society and explains why there are dlfferences. This is of course a pioneering study of great social significance.

An important study of Muslim community in Bihar has been done by S.M. Raza.[8] He deals with the changing patterns of Muslim community in Bihar in general and of the urban community of Patna in particular. The author has covered all aspects of Muslim life, i.e. purdah, social stratification, patterns of education, economic life, religious and cultural patterns, marriage and family and attitude and values. For analyzing changes in the community life the author has analysed the ideal sanctions of Islam, the traditional practices in Muslim community and the existing trends among urban Muslims. For analysing ideal sanctions the author has summarised the Qur'anic versions and the Tradition of Prophet Muhammad. For analysing traditional practices he has taken help from available literature on Indian Muslims in general and the Muslims of Bihar in particular. For the study of existing trends he conducted field work and collected facts. In this way he first analysed the deviation from ideal sanctions to the traditional set up and then change from traditional way of life to modern patterns of community life. In analysing the changes in the present age he has analysed the impact of Indian culture as well as western culture and the processes of modernization and Islamization.

Sarfaraz Uddin Ahmad's[9] article on "Social Stratification and Change among Muslims", a micro-study of Patna Town, also throws some light on the social life of the Muslims of Bihar. The writer, who happens to be the author of the present research work, used both primary as well as secondary sources of data, analysed and discussed it in detail. All status groups spread in different areas of Patna were contacted for this miniature study. The author discussed the changing

8. Raza, S.M., Changing Patterns of Muslim Community in Bihar, unpublished Ph.D. Thesis, Patna University, 1976.

9. Ahmad, Sarfaraz Uddin, Social Stratification and Changes among Muslims : A micro-study of Patna Town, in M.N. Karna (ed.), Bihar's Economy and Society, Concept Publishing Company, New Delhi, 1981.

patterns of stratification among Muslims and finds that the Muslim community is not insulated from its socio-cultural milieu and co-mingling of traits between the Hindus and the Muslims has brought almost a new system of stratification based on both the caste and class considerations. The author supports the caste-class continuum hypothesis.

It is also important to present here the contribution of Saghir Ahmad[10] who wrote a book entitled "Class and Power in a Punjabi Village" based on his field work conducted in the village of Sahiwal in the West Punjab in 1964-65. The author presents an analysis of changing class relationships through a study of the effects of land and electoral reform in the early 1960s.

Land reform, Ahmad found, did not significantly reduce the power and wealth of the landlords, instead, by favouring cash crop cultivation, it promoted a change from tenant farming to capitalist farming based on wage labour. Similarly he discovered that changes in the electoral system merely perpetuated existing power relations, based as they are in relations of production. By revealing how "old and new forms of exploitation" combine to squeeze the peasants and artisans for the landlords' profits, his study provides insight into the conditions that give rise to peasant revolts. He describes under economic structure the different economic roles in the village and analyses their relation to existing patterns of agricultural and craft production. He also analysed the social hierarchy which gives rise to the relationship between economic and political decision making and the changing forms and manifestation of political control.

Jean Ellickson[11] conducted a similar study in the village Shaheenpur (pseudonym) in Comilla district of Bangladesh (the erstwhile East Pakistan) in the years 1968-69. The author studied different aspects of the Muslims' socio-cultural life

10. Ahmad, Saghir, Class and Power in a Punjabi Village, Monthly Review Press, New York, 1977.

11. Ellickson, Jean, Islamic Institutions in Bangladesh, in T.N. Madan (ed.), Muslim Communities of South Asia, Vikas Publishing House Pvt. Ltd., New Delhi, 1976.

in the village, especially the enactment and effectiveness of the Pakistan Muslim Family Laws Ordinance 1961, regulating marriage, divorce and inheritance.

The author finds that the villagers were not in favour of the enactment of these national laws, because they thought it to be imposed by the outsiders and which was not in accordance with the Islamic Sharia as held by the village Imams or as per dictates of village customs. Thus the villagers had greater faith in local customs as well as in the sayings of Imams. Nevertheless, on the other hand, a few persons started using it for their own gains. Their aims were not to overturn the village social structure, but merely to gain a momentary advantage.

The author, while dealing with the observance of purdah system, found that the rural women maintained strict purdah whenever they went outside their homes. He found that a few rich Muslim ladies who own burqa always use it whenever they go outside. Majority of the rural Muslim women do not attend public places and if circumstances compel them they use rickshaw covered from all sides to avoid public gaze.

The author also found a dispute settlement or mediation council which acts as the primary organ of social control in the village. Villagers generally do not take their affairs and problems outside the local arena or to have outside agencies come in to interfere in the village matters.

The remarkable feature of all these studies is that the study of Muslim society has been carried out on a particular aspect of the community life. Some of them are studied by the scholars of different social settings and some of them give impressionistic account of their work. Hardly any one of them attempted to study Muslim community as a whole in a particular area or region. Moreover many of the studies are either partial or superficial in nature.

Moreover, no serious study of this kind has been made in Bihar, especially in rural setting. Much of the types of such work in Bihar comprise itself only to brief articles and a few short monographs and that also in urban setting.

Thus little has been done in this direction for getting detailed information about the Muslim community living in rural areas. Hence the necessity of the present study of a predominantly Muslim village in Bihar is absolutely essential in order to be able to form an integrated sociological picture of the Muslim community in Bihar. For this purpose a typical predominantly Muslim village has been selected. The chief characteristic of this village, located in the district of Gaya, is that it is solely a Muslim village of moderate size. The non-Muslim occupational castes live in the surrounding areas known as tola or bigha.

4

Village and the People

Pinjrawan, the village and mauza under study is also a Panchayat in Kurtha Police Station and Block Development Office under Jehanabad sub-division in the district of Gaya. This is a multi-caste Muslim village of moderate size.

Jehanabad is the northern sub-division of the district extending over 607 square miles and is situated at the confluence of the Morhar and Jamuna rivers. This sub-division has about 876 villages. It contains one town, i.e. Jehanabad itself, which is also a sub-divisional headquarter, and two revenue thanas, Jehanabad and Arwal. The surface is generally flat and well-irrigated and the soil supports large population than any other part of the district. The staple crop is rice which is grown on more than half of the cultivated area, and next in importance are gram and wheat. The sub-division comprises four police stations, Jehanabad, Kurtha, Ghosi and Makhdumpur and four fiscal Parganas, namely, Arwal, Bhatawar, Ekil and Okri.

For the convenience of the public there is a small wayside railway station called Jehanabad Court near the town and the main station of Jehanabad is at a short distance to the north. Jehanabad was once famous for its weaving industry, and in 1760 it formed one of the eight minor branches connected with the central cloth factory of the East India Company at Patna.

A large number of the Jolaha or Muslim weaver class still live in the neighbourhood and produce handloom cloth. The trade of Jehanabad now chiefly consists of foodgrains, oilseeds, etc. The situation of the place being on the railway midway Patna and Gaya is helpful for trade.

The district of Gaya has a total area of 6,545.0 kms. It is bounded on the north by the Patna district, on the east by Nawada, on the south by Hazaribagh and Palamau districts and on the west by Aurangabad district. The total population of the district, according to the 1981 Census is 3,134,175. 90 per cent of the total population of the district inhabits in the rural areas in the district of Gaya.[1]

Gaya formed parts of Bihar and Ramgarh districts till 1885. When the Bihar sub-division was transferred to the Patna district in that year a new district known as the district of Gaya as its headquarter was created.[2]

Gaya is an important town of the State of Bihar[3] from historical and cultural points of view. It presents the history of Pre-Aryans Indian as well. It has various marks and imprints of river valley civilization.[4] O'Malley writes, "Gaya was occupied in pre-historic times by aboriginal's races whose power is still attested by the remains attributed to them, the traditions of their rules and the names they gave to places where their descendents are still found in considerable numbers in the hilly tracts to the south of the district.[5]

In the religious history of India, Gaya occupies an important place. According to the religion of Puranas it is

1. Census Report, 1981.
2. Choudhry, P.C. Roy, Bihar District Gazetteers—Gaya Secretariat Press, Patna, 1959, p. 1.
3. The name Bihar was given by the Muslim rulers who were struck by the large number of monasteries (Viharas) which they saw near Biharsharif, Diwakar, R.R. (ed.), Bihar Through the Ages, p. 5.
4. The village Itawan lies in-between the branches of the river Joba near Akbarpore in the present Nawada district.
5. O'Malley, L.S.S., Gazetteer of the Patna District, 1906, p. 21.

incumbent on every Hindu to visit Gaya and make offerings for the souls of his ancestors. The name Gaya according to Bhagwat Purana owes its origin to a demon king Gayasur who dwelt in the town in the Treta Yuga.[6]

The village under study is solely a Muslim village surrounded by nine tolas of occupational Hindu castes, excluding one Muslim tola (a new settlement). These are named as Sablak Sarai, Jai Bigha, Math, Bhattu Bigha (also known as Ramzan Bigha), Maneh Pakar, Purwari Badh, Par Daru, Chulhan Bigha and Shahjiwan Dargah (now known as Makhdumabad—a new Muslim settlement). All the eight old tolas or Bighas of non-Muslims are inhabited by the backward and scheduled Hindu castes. Prominent among them are Gowalas (Yadavas), Koiri, Barahi, Mallah, Dusadh. The ninth one, i.e, the Muslim tola is inhabited by occupational as well as non-occupational Muslim castes like Churihara, Ansari, Faqir, Mulezada, Shaikh, etc.

Pinjrawan is also the headquarter of Pinjrawan Panchayat which guides and controls the activities of eight survey villages—Pinjrawan proper, Motipur, Musharhi, Dhondhra, Painathi, Gangapur, Gangia and Madarpur. Generally the sarpanch is elected from this village.

Pinjrawan is situated at a distance of about half-a-mile east from the Kurtha-Kinger road. A chaur (mud road) connects the village from the main road at three places—Motipur, Majgaha (Babban Rauza) and Shahjiwan Dargah. There are numerous buses, public as well as private, plying on the road which emanates from Kurtha and goes to Jehanabad and Arwal sides. The nearest railway station of this area is Jehanabad Court and Jehanabad proper. Jehanabad Court is at a distance of about ten miles and Jehanabad Junction is about fourteen miles. Compared to Jehanabad Court Rly. Station, Jehanabad Junction railway station is very old, where each train passing through this route stops. Most of the travellers of this area start and end their journey

6. Shashtri, Hara Prasad, Journal of the Bihar and Orissa Research Society, 1928, p. 330.

from Jehanabad railway station because of greater conveniences.

Kurtha is at a distance of four miles south, where its police station and block development office are located. Kurtha is an important daily market of this locality which is rapidly growing into a town. Apart from Kurtha, Ibrahimpur, Motipur and Mangla-hat are the nearest market centres for the day-to-day items of consumption. Mangla-hat is the weekly market, mainly of cattle and grains organised on every Tuesday. The nearest public medical centre is situated at Motipur, less than a mile from this village. But this medical centre is practically non-existent because of the absenteeism of its staff. People of this locality also do not have any faith and care in this medical centre. They go for their treatment or medical aid to any public or private clinic at Kurtha or Jehanabad, or Gaya, or Patna as per the seriousness of disease and their economic condition.

As regards the post office, a small postal service centre is located in the village itself.

Total land area for the village settlement is about forty acres, in which there are 150 houses. These houses are mainly of two types—pukka or kuchcha, or mixed. Pukka houses are those which are totally built by bricks with cement casted roofs. Such houses number only 10 in the whole village. Rest 140 houses are mainly of mixed type, i.e. made of brick, sand, mud with thatched roof. A small aangan (courtyard) is common feature for almost all the houses. Some of the villagers also build a second storey known as kotha or mud-kotha. The number of cemented brick-built houses, nowadays, is on the increase. The prosperous cultivators who own lands and cultivate themselves also build a bailghara (oxen house or cattle house) attached to the main house in which agricultural implements and straws, etc. are stored. This part of the house is planned generally on the baekside of the house. The cattle of the poorer classes are kept inside the residential portion, which makes the houses filthy and unhygienic. There is also a provision of baithka or dalan (verandah) in almost all the houses of upper caste/class families. Generally the upper class people have three apartments in the same holding—

baithka, main house and the bailghara. The baithka is the front portion of the house, the main house in the middle or in the centre and the bailghara is located on the backside of the house. The poorers do not have such clear-cut and distinct house plan. Their rooms are small and congested with few small holes below the roof. These holes, according to the house-holders, are for air and sun; but, actually, these are not sufficient for ventilation and sun-rays. The reason for not having windows in most of the cases is due to the fear of theft, and in some cases also due to the fear of enemy's attack while asleep because fractions and feuds are the common features of village life.

Likewise, there is no sewage system in the village and, consequently, dirty water usually accumulates inside and outside the houses making the atmosphere unhygienic and unhealthy. In such dirty conditions the villages easily fall victims of different types of diseases.

To serve the purpose of the latrine a deep pit, called sandas, is dug out in most of the houses which does not provide a thorough system of sanitation. In every upper-caste house, whether rich or poor, a sandas latrine is must. Because it is both a matter of purdah and prestige for the shorafas. In some ashraf families even the latrine for males and females are separate. While most of the lower caste people do not have a latrine in their houses partly because of their economic inability to build it and partly due to their being accustomed to the old mode of life. The open spaces in the outskirts and the fields are commonly used by the villagers where they go before the sunrise or after sunset to make up the lack of proper privations in their houses.

In the same way commonly no bath room system is found among the villagers. In very few cases a separate bathroom is built and utilised for this purpose. Generally a bath place near the well or in the corner of a secluded place is selected and utilised mainly by women folk. The men mostly take bath outside the house, in the river or tank or pond or well or the well of the mosque, whatever convenient they feel.

The Domestic Group

The domestic group or the ghar forms the basic unit of the village life. The domestic group may be defined as an aggregate of individuals who reside in the same house, maintain a common purse, eat food prepared in the same hearth and act according to the collective decision. In some cases the families of married sons, with or without their parents, live in the same house, cultivate land in common, own cattle jointly, but nevertheless divide their incomes, cook and eat food separately and follow their own decisions. Such families are here considered separate households. According to this definition there are a total 159 households, containing 1,033 people in the village. In case of tension and conflicts among the members of a family the larger domestic group breaks into separate domestic groups and if division of the old house or building do not occur and properties also not divided, purse and hearth is divided. If the head of the family or the father possesses enough land for "sakna" he gives his children equally or in the case otherwise the son purchases the land himself. Thus it becomes the duty of the departing persons to purchase new land and build new house on their own. In case of the agriculturist family the land is not formally divided to the sons and daughters in the life-time of the head of the household.

Head of the Domestic Group

In most cases the parents of the domestic group have died. In almost all the cases where only the mother was alive, she was living with either the eldest or the youngest son. If, however, there were unmarried sons and daughters the mother lived with them. It was rare to find a mother living with one of the middle sons. The father and the mother in almost all the cases belonged to the same caste.

It must be remembered that age distribution in Table 4.1 is almost an approximation. The villagers seldom remember their days of birth or even the year. When asked to give a child's age, a villager will make a statement like, "My son

Table 4.1
Age Distribution of the Respondents
N=58

Age Category	*Age Distribution*	
	Number	*Percentuge*
Up to 20 yrs	26	16.46
21 to 35 yrs.	28	17.73
36 to 50 yrs.	40	25.31
51+	64	40.50
Total	158	100.00

was born in the year the Idgah was built" (1945), or, "He was born just after few days of the earthquake" (1934), etc. In view of this, in most of the cases I had to estimate ages by relating stages of growth with significant events. Older men usually tend to exaggerate their ages, so it is not surprising that I found many men who are commonly believed to be eighty or ninety years old or so but who, on enquiry, were found to be 5 to 15 years less. The habit of exaggerating one's own age is understandable in a society where old age demands reverence and respect.

With regard to the marital status Table 4.2 shows the situation:

This is obvious from Table 4.2 that 77.22 per cent of the respondents are married, 13.29 per cent are unmarried and 9.49 per cent are widowers. This is further clear that only about 13 per cent of the respondents are unmarried, or in other words youths while the rest belong to middle and old age groups. During interview it was also found that the villagers prefer and try their best to marry their children in the nearby villages, especially in case of their daughters.

As regards the population composition of the village, the investigator applied the census method and found the data as in Table 4.3.

Table 4.2

Marital Status of the Respondants
N=158

Category	*Marital Status*	
	Number	*Percentage*
Married	122	77.22
Unmarried	21	13.29
Widower	15	9.49
Total	158	100.00

Table 4.3

Population Composition of the Village
N=159

Category	*Population Composition*	
	Number	*Percentage*
Adult male	299	28.94
Adult female	295	28.55
Total	594	57.49
Male child	233	22.55
Female child	206	19.44
Total	439	42.49
Grand Total	1033	99.98

Table 4.3 shows the population composition of the village. It reveals that out of the total 1033 persons in the village, there are about 299 adult males and 295 adult females. Thus the adult male and female population constitutes about 57.49

per cent of the total population of the village. Likewise, male and female children together constitute about 42.49 per cent of the total population. The male-female distribution is 51.49 per cent and 48 49 per cent respectively, which very much correspond to the general sex ratio of the country.

Table 4.4 presented below shows the number of members in the family. From the data shown we may form an idea about the sizes of the family found in the village.

Table 4.4

Number of Members in the Family of the Respondents
N=158

Category	*Family Members*	
	Number	*Percentage*
Up to 5	35	22.16
6 to 9	54	34.17
10 +	69	43.67
Total	158	100.00

It may be concluded from the data shown in the table that there are mainly three sizes of family in the village. They are smaller, medium and larger size of families. The smaller family is composed of altogether maximum five members. These are mainly the nucleus families, while on the other hand about 44 per cent of the families are composed of more than ten members. These are mainly the joint families of the village. It further shows that still in the village joint family is dominantly found and practised.

We find that Indian villages are characterised as agriculture and the main occupation of its inhabitants. The all-India data also shows that about 72% of the villagers depend on agriculture. But the following data show somewhat different picture of a Muslim village.

Table 4.5
Occupational Distribution of the Villagers
N=159

Occupational Category	*Occupational Distribution*	
	Number	*Percentage*
Cultivators	72	45.29
Businessmen	10	6.29
Labourers	16	10.07
Service-holders	13	8.17
Multiple occupation	12	7.54
Others	36	22.64
Total	159	100.00

The data provided in Table 4.5 above show that out of the total 159 respondents in the village 72, i.e., about 45.29% are engaged in cultivation, whereas the lower percentage (6.29%) belong to businessmen. On the other 8.17% of the respondents are those who are service-holders but reside in the village itself. These service-holders are engaged in the nearby areas of the village. Rest 10.07% are engaged as minerals, they are not settled in any one type of job for their livelihood rather they have to do different types of work in different seasons and situations. Likewise, 7.54% are those who are permanent multi-occupationals. If both the categories of labourers and multi-occupationals are combined, it reveals that 17.60% of the respondents in the village belong to lower class. Thus, still majority of the Muslims in the village belong to cultivating class who own landed property in greater or smaller quantity.

Food Habit, Dress and Nutrition

In general, the people of Pinjrawan eat three meals a day—the first in the morning, second in the noon and the hird after sunset. In between a villager has an occasional intake of light refreshment of some roasted corn or some seasonal item, or only a cup of tea. Early in the morning a peasant likes to have a cup of tea or some leftovers from the ptrevious night while going to the field. The first regular meal consists of bread with any seasonal vegetable, more often with potatoes. The lunch consists of rice, pulse and any vegetable and often with achar or chatni. Likewise in the dinner also most of the villagers prefer the same menu as that of the lunch. Bread is not a liked one item in the dinner excepting in the winter season or in times of crisis ghee or butter is used only by those who possess cow or buffalo or by those who can afford to purchase it. Likewise, meat is eaten occasionally both due to unavailability in the vicinity and financial inability. Thus there is a minimum use of fat and protein by the villagers in general. This is evident from their lean and thin physique. An elaborate meal, eaten only on special occasions, must include pulao and a meat, mattha and a sweet dish. The quality of the food is assessed by the villagers according to the number of items and amount of ghee used in cooking—the more the better.

There is no apparant difference in the everyday clothes of rich and the poor villagers. The men wear a shirt mostly with a banyan, a paijama or lungi. The youger generation, especially students and town-dwellers, wear mostly full-pant and shirt. The girls wear mainly shalwar or ghrara and jumper, and sometimes sari and blouse. But the married women wear mostly sari and blouse. The men wear shoes or sleepers, no matter how tattered they may be while the women use light sleepers.

There are, however, real distinctions between the ceremonial costumes of the rich and poor. Clothe for ceremonial dress is of finer and lighter quality. Silken and synthetic clothes are considered superior and prestigious.

While food and clothes account for a substantial portion of a villager's income, another major expense is for health. Given the food and environment, this is not surprising. Health care is curative rather than preventive and doctors and hakeems are consulted only after a person is visibly affected by some physical malady. Not a single household in the village may be found where every one is medically fit and sound.

In the village itself there are few but only two homoeopath doctors who are recognised and more often consulted by the village folks. The villagers prefer to go to these homoeopaths because of their availability in the village and because the medicine is cheap and is available even on credit. Other medical practitioners like allopath or hakeem is not available in the village. For this the villagers have to move out of the village, which is troublesome and costly. The superstitious villagers sometimes also consult the 'moulvis' or go to the mazars for their cure, generally when they feel that the worldly medicines may not bring them in normal health. This is done mostly by the weaker section because of their ill economic conditions and ignorance.

Everyday Life

Different groups of people have somewhat different types of daily life. The labourer wakes up in the dawn and, if available, takes early in the morning some food cooked overnight which is called basia and leaves for his work. He works in the field the whole day and comes to the home for the midday meal when there is no one to carry his food in the field where he is engaged. He comes back generally in the evening and after a wash he has some refreshment. The meal at the night is usually taken quite early and the activities of the labourer's household comes to a close and the family retires.

The women folk of a labourer's family, generally of the lower caste or class, add to the family income by working in the house of some rich neighbour and they keep themselves busy in doing household work, such as, cooking food, washing clothes, looking after the children or doing a little marketing. Such women also scrap grass or pluck leaves or twigs for their cattle which is to be done in the day.

The leisure hours in the evening are spent in visiting friends, gossiping with them or doing some household works.

The middle class people waste a lot of their leisure time in sleep and talks on village politics, local events, bureaucrats of the different departments of the block office, or about the season and crops or town gossips.

For a section of middle class people of the village attending the block office, police station or court appears to be both a necessity and a form of entertainment. Usually the visitors of such places develop a sort of informal relations with the officials concerned. Such people are taken to these offices as pairvikars for their works done, because they are the usual link between the officials and the clients.

The daily life of the people belonging to the more affluent class in the village revolves in an idle groove, such as taking a heavy and delicious meal, long siesta, visiting friends, indulging in idle gossips or going for the shikar. Ladies of a middle class family in the village have got to do a lot of household works. They have to look after their children, do the cooking, clean the house, and wash and mend the clothes of the family and at their leisure time they would probably do a little needle work or some embroidery work. Certain handicrafts, such as, making baskets from a particular kind of reed, toys and dolls from waste papers and waste clothes. It is quite common for ladies to knot sweaters, mufflers, etc. and knitting of pillow covers, bed covers, and dopatta, cap, etc. are widely prevalent.

Washing is the common habit among all classes in the village. The mouth is usually cleansed with twigs of neem, karanj, etc. In some families tooth powder of cheap quality is also used. While tooth brush and tooth paste is more confined to the richer section or who have regular contact with towns. Bathing daily in the morning is a general habit of males, while females are slack, but they usually take bath on Fridays. For this, soap of any quality is widely used. But in few families clay is also used for this purpose.

Oil is usually used for head or body. The oils that are used are mustard, cocoanut, til or some other scented oil. Almost every well-to-do family uses to keep some atra or musk for the use on Friday or on ceremonial occasions.

Ornaments

The women use various types of ornaments made of gold and silver. The metal and quantity of ornaments differs with class differences. However, use of ornament in any part of the body is liked and appreciated culturally. These ornaments are mainly used by the suhagin (whose husband is alive). The widow leads a very simple and austere life. She would not wear ornaments (excepting any one item in the ear) of different qualities neither coloured and printed saris. The widow wears white dress from the day her husband dies in a simple and traditional style. The unmarried girls also live simply and wear one or two ornaments of simple design.

Patterns of Entertainment

Tea and sharbat are the usual drinks of the villagers. The toddy or tari is occasionally used by the people which was common in past, especially in the lower class Along with the toddy, fried or boiled gram with chillies and/or roasted meat are also used. Villagers usually avoid going to the toddy shops rather use it wherever feel convenient, but not in their living houses. Particularly in the months of April to July its demand increases.

Food is ordinarily cooked on an open oven which has one or two mouths. They are mostly made of clay or by bricks or by both and there is an opening below, and through the opening the fuel feeds the fire.

Cold drinks prepared with various kinds of seeds of flowers, curd, lemon, khira, saunf and sugar are in vogue. Smoking of biri, cigarette or hookah is also common there. Ladies of lower castes and class, especially labour, also smoke biri. The chewing of pan is very common among Muslim men and women folks of the middle and upper classes.

Reading habit is not found among the villagers of any educational category. Reading of newspapers, magazines and books after purchasing them has not yet become the regular feature. Thus economic hardship cannot be said to be the reason of non-subscribing the reading items. But it is due to the lack of such habit. On the other hand most of the middle and old age people recite Qur'an regularly and attend prayers in the mosque.

There is one library in the village known as 'Gulistan Library', which contains only novels, magazines and religious books. Fresh arrivals are very few. Regular subscription of any item is seldom found. This is because it has gone under one man's control for the last 8-10 years. Others do not have interest in its management or in its progress. Thus it has become the prey of apathy, lack of general attraction and good patronage.

Radio is a common source of entertainment now-a-days in the village. It is an item of luxury also for most of the villagers, while, for the lower class, a symbol of status. Regular listeners of certain programmes are few in the village. The number of radio sets are far more than the radios in order and used by the people. It is because most of these radios are a marriage gift which are not regularly repaired and properly kept in order due to the recurring expenditure on it and the economic inability of most of the holders to meet the expenses.

Outdoor amusement and entertainment do not form a regular feature in the life of the average villager. The monotony is broken when the villagers visit the melas, rouza or dargah and participate in Urs, etc., or go to the town to meet any necessity. Female's best entertainment is to attend marriage ceremonies of their relatives, especially in the other villages.

Beliefs and Superstitions

Muslims of this village and of the surrounding areas freely indulge in superstitious observances and copy Hindu rites. There are certain forms of worship common among Muslims which are neither based on Qur'an, nor apparently adopted from the Hindus. The most common of these is the adoration of departed peers or buzurgs. When a holy peer leaves this life he is supposed to be still present in spirit and his tomb becomes a place of pilgrimage to which persons resort for the cure of disease or the exorcism of evil spirits, or obtain the fulfilment of some cherished wish, such as, the birth of a child, cure of any family member or success in litigation, etc. In the village the adoration of five Peers (Panch Peer) is common to which some Hindus also regard and worship.

Closely allied to the adoration of Peers homage is paid to certain mythical persons, of them the principal are Kamalo Bibi, Shaikh Sadhu and Shah Jeevan. The spirit of Shaikh Sadhu is worshiped to get rid of disease or any such other troubles.

Kamalo Bibi lived in Kako, a village about 15 miles away from Pinjrawan. Her tomb is resorted to by both Muslims and Hindus and regarded as a great place for the cure of any illness or for getting an offspring or for the physical or mental cure.

The celebrated saint scholar of Biharsharif, Hazrat Makhdoom Sharfuddin Yehya Muneri is also a great source of spiritual solace for the Muslims of this area in particular and for others in general. A rouza of this saint attached with a kund, named after him is at Rajgir. Every year urs at this rouza is held, in which lakhs of men and women both Muslim and Hindu attend, worship and pray for their well-being.

Along with the belief in peers and legends, the villagers also have faith in evil spirits. The personification of the evil spirit carries out this idea, as it is described as being fearful of shape and black of hue, tall as palm tree with long projecting teeth and streaming dishevelled hair. They generally drop down on the unwary traveller from trees and one Panduba by name comes out of the rivers and tanks and drags in and drowns the belated wayfarer. If the bhoot is obstinate and will not spare his victim, physical compulsion is resorted to. The man is soundly beaten and red pepper and turmeric smoke are put to his nose. All those are performed by Ojha or wizard, who is believed to command a spirit of greater power.

The villagers are also superstitious about the dain or witch. The witches are known to be a middle age woman, generally of low caste who works secretly. They are charged with cutting open children and taking out their liver and also with the practice of making images of flour to represent their enemies and piercing them with knives and needles.

Likewise, the villagers also fear of the kichin or churail and believe in their existence. Kichin or churail is believed to be the spirit of woman who dies in child-birth who may be known by the fact that her feet are turned backward and that she has no mouth.

5

Social Relations

A. SOCIAL STRATIFICATION

Social stratification is a universal reality. Every society, whether it is rural or urban, tribal or advanced, industrial or agricultural, is stratified. Virtually all societies develop a system of hierarchical division on the basis of some characteristics and hence persons of one or different groups differ from one another on the basis of power and privileges. If no stratification existed in a society it would necessarily have a small homogeneous population. Its occupation would be of such a nature that no significant division of labour would exist and hence the phenomenon of social change and social development will be absent. Virtually it is difficult to find and conceive of unstratified society except under unusual and very primitive circumstances.

Sorokin observes, "Any organised social group is always stratified social body. There has not been and does not exist any permanent social group in which all members are equal. Unstratified society with a real equality of its members is a myth which has never been realised in the history of mankind."[1] Andre Beteille also argues and supports the viewpoint that social inequality is a social reality. He says, "While many have talked about classless society, these ideas have found very little support in historical experience."[2] Marx also discussed the problem of social stratification. He through his materialistic interpretation of society, explained the existence of two different classes in different ages of human history. He pointed out that due to difference in mode of production and other related forces economic inequality develops in social life. Consequently two classes of haves and have-nots or upper and lower classes develop. These two classes have opposed vested interests. Haves exploit the have-nots and, due to their position, control government and rule over the masses."[3]

Max Weber also talked of social stratification. While agreeing to the viewpoint of Marx on the role of economic factor he added two more criteria, i.e., power and prestige, responsible in the formation of classes. He argues that though there are three different factors, they function in collaboration with each other and create hierarchy in social order. These three factors play three different parts in society. Property helps in formation of classes, power creates political party, and prestige breeds groups."[4]

Ideally, Islam stands for equality and universal brotherhood. The Qur'an and Tradition explicitly claim for equality and hence the concept of social stratification is not accepted in Islam. Referring to this fact Hasan-ul-Ameene writes, "The teaching of Islam contained in Koran and Sunnah are definitely hostile to the establishment of a class system in people's social relation. They preach equality among men as

1. Sorokin, P.A., Social and Cultural Mobility, Harper & Brothers, London, 1927, p 57.
2. Beteille, Andre (ed.), Social Inequality, Richard Clay (The Chancer Press) Ltd., Great Britain, 1972, p. 13.
3. Marx, K , Capital, 3 Vol., Kerr, Chicago, 1909.
4. Weber, Max, Class, Status and Party, in Essays in Sociology, (ed.) H.H. Gerth & C.W. Mills, Oxford University Press, New York, 1946, p. 69.

human beings, and consider such equality an essential foundation of Islam in so far as the aopraisal of man is concerned."[5]

Aggarwal, while referring to the verse 13 of Sura 49 of the Qur'an, supports the same point that Muslims deny caste or caste-like divisions in their society. He says, "There are a number of references in the Koran which emphasize the brotherhood of Muslims. It is quite clear that Islam upholds the egalitarian idea and instructs the believers that in judging an individual they should not give too much attention to such factors as race, national origin, or ancestry. What matters is the degree to which a Muslim practises the teachings of the Koran."[6] But we should not infer from these sayings that there is completely no stratum in Muslim society. Egalitarianism does not strictly mean the non-existence of any group. Siddiqui rightly remarks, "The acceptance of egalitarian concept as the basis of Islamic society does not, therefore, rule out the existence of certain kinds of groups of national, tribal, regional and linguistic nature. These groups are supposed to maintain distinction from each other by compelling for a virtuous life in the service of the Supreme being."[7] But the teachings of Islam concerning equality and universal brotherhood could not be practised by its followers for long. After the death of the Prophet, the Arabs in general and Quraish in particular started boasting of their hereditary and social superiority which resulted in the development of social ranking and social discrimination among the Muslims of Arab and outside. The Muslims after entering into the Indian subcontinent and having come into contact with the Hindus also stratified into caste-like status groups.

Referring to the emergence and growth of social stratification among Muslims in India, Mujeeb writes, "The institution of guild is found almost everywhere in the civilized

5. Ameer-ul-Hasan, Islamic Shi'ite Encyclopaedia, Vol. II, p. 15.
6. Aggarwal, P.C., The Meos of Rajasthan and Haryana, in Imtiaz Ahmad (ed.), Caste and Social Stratification among the Muslims, Manohar Book Service, Delhi, 1973, p. 21.
7. Siddiqui, M.K.A., Muslims of Calcutta, Anthropological Survey of India, Government of India, Calcutta, 1974, p. 6.

world in the middle ages. Among the Muslims of West Asia, it was known as the 'Siuf', in India it took the form of professional caste."[8] This fact is also supported by Ghaus Ansari, who says, "The ideal of equality among Muslims was practicable only in the then prevailing conditions of Arabia. In the course of expansion of Islam and its contacts with other complex cultures the democratic form of political organization and social equality within community gradually disappeared. The very structure of Islam itself in this process became the victim of social discrimination."[9]

Commenting on this, Zeyauddin Ahmad observed, "The Muslims of this sub-continent in general and Bihar in particular have become a heterogeneous population, stratified into several status groups. These status groups are hereditary, endogamous, and in most of the cases occupatiomal and followers of tradition. But an important characteristic of the system of stratification of Muslim society is that it is not as rigid as that of the Hindus. It has some flexibility and openness which helps in the movement of its members from one status group to another."[10]

Imtiaz Ahmad also presents an analytical discussion to arrive at a conclusion regarding caste and social stratification among the Muslims. On the basis of four characteristics of caste, i.e., (1) endogamy, (2) occupational specialisation, (3) hierarchy, and (4) an ideological-religious basis involved in restriction on social intercourse and commensality. He wanted to analyze whether these features are present among Muslims. He, on the basis of facts presented by different contributors, held that Muslim groups are endogamous, "Occasionally marriages between two or more divisions are allowed." He writes, "A close link between caste and hereditary occupation exists which functions as the basis of economic

8. Mujeeb, M., Indian Muslim.
9. Ansari, Ghaus, Muslim Castes in Uttar Pradesh, Ethnographic and Folk Culture Society, Lucknow, 1959, p. 28.
10. Ahmad, Zeyauddin, Caste Elements among the Muslims of Bihar, in Harjinder Singh (ed.), Caste among Non-Hindus in India, National Publishing House, New Delhi, 1977.

interdependence of castes. He has found that there is a notion of hierarchy among Muslims. Lastly, he observes that the Hindu's ideological justification of the caste system does not exist in the case of Muslims."[11]

In the light of the above discussion it may be concluded that though the system of social stratification is present in the case of Muslims also but it is not completely identified with the pattern of stratification found in the Hindu society. Caste system is a divine product among Hindus while in the case of Muslims it is just a social product. A Hindu is religiously bound to follow the caste sanctions in his behaviour pattern throughout his life, while Muslims are not the slaves of caste system. It is true that Muslim society is also divided broadly in two groups of upper and lower, i.e., Ashraf and Ajlaf, like dwij and kamin in Hindu society. But one can move from one stratum to the other in Muslim caste hierarchy. As envisaged by Ghaus Ansari, "Here the members of low ranking castes, in order to raise their status, claim descent from any Ashraf caste. There are numerous instances in Uttar Pradesh where converted Rajputs have added the title of "Khan" to their names and have claimed Pathan descent." Though change in nomenclature and social mobility is found among the Muslims, it is not quite easy for one to change his caste."[12]

Present day Muslim community of Bihar and elsewhere is confronted with numerous challenges—economic, educational, political, social and psychological. This has also influenced the pattern of social stratification. The so-called Muslim castes who were following their occupations traditionally are now switching over to the new occupations which appear to them more profitable. Thus a process of occupational mobility is fast seen. Every one is trying to adopt the occupation which gives him more earning, as well

11. Ahmad, Imtiaz, Introduction, in Caste and Social Stratification among Muslims (ed.), Manohar Book Service, Delhi, 1973, p. XXI.

12. Ansari, Ghaus, Muslim Castes in Uttar Pradesh, Ethnographic Folk Culture Society, Lucknow, 1959, p. 30.

as prestige. Zamindari abolition has adversely affected the Muslim's socio-economic life. Now consciousness for general or technical education, specially job-oriented education, has developed among them—whether Ashraf or Ajlaf. The Muslims in the villages are gradually losing their interest in traditional occupation of agriculture. Mostly the land is being sold to the non-Muslims because the new generation does not like to live in villages and depend on agriculture. Whether educated or not, skilled or unskilled, every young villager wishes to remain and do business or service into town. This fact also becomes clear from the findings in the present study.

Social stratification is a universal phenomenon. It exists in every society, irrespective of the nature and structure of social life. The concept of high and low, superior and inferior exists among the members of every society. Even in the societies where religious or social sanctions are opposed to stratification, social hierarchy persists. Islam believes in equality and the Islamic sanctions do not permit any distinction and discrimination on the basis of birth, wealth or ethnic affinity. But the Muslims believing in Islam are also not an exception to it. Social hierarchy and gradations are also found in Muslim community. The factor of heredity is also regarded as a determinant of status in social life along with economic position and political power. Ideologically the Islamic society should be free from social stratification but in actual practice the Muslim communities are also stratified. It is true not only for the Indian Muslims but also for the Muslim societies in different parts of the world including Arabia, the birth place of Islam. Thus there exists a gap between ideology and practice.

Keeping the above facts in view, a question was put to the respondants regarding the inevitability of social hierarchy for the existence of society. The responses obtained from the respondents are presented in Table 5.1.

It is evident from the table that 46.84% of the respondents regard social hierarchy inevitable for the existence of society. But 37.08% have replied in negative; whereas 17.08% have not expressed any definite opinion. It suggests

Table 5.1

Attitude regarding Social Hierarchy

N=158

Category	*Number*	*Percentage*
Favourable	74	46.84
Unfavourable	57	36.08
Undecided	27	17.08
Total	158	100.00

that the dominant opinion favours the persistence of social hierarchy and social stratification. In other words, the highest percentage of the respondents is not opposed to the practical stratification and persistence of the concept of superior and inferior in social life. It definitely shows the greater influence of socio-cultural factors than of religious sanctions on the attitudes and outlook of the people. It may be interpreted that social hierarchy is favoured not only in actual practice rather it is also supported at ideological level. It is just possible that the respondents enjoying higher status are in favour of social inequality, whereas those at the lower level of social hierarchy in the village are opposed to it.

The data collected to know the attitudes of the respondents regarding the phenomenon of inequality in society, arranged in Table 5.1 above have further been classified and arranged on the basis of caste groupings. All the castes found in the village under study have been broadly divided into two groups—upper caste and lower caste. Table 5.2 shows the caste-wise attitude of the respondents.

An analysis of the data shows that the attitudes of the upper and lower castes differ widely. 53.84% of the upper caste respondents favour the idea of the existence of inequality and differences in the distribution of rights and privileges in the society, while only 14.28% of the lower caste keeps favourable idea regarding the necessity of inequality in society.

Table 5.2

Caste and Attitude regarding Social Hierarchy
N=158

Caste Group		*Favourable*		*Unfavourable*		*Undecided*	
		No.	%	*No.*	%	*No.*	%
Upper Caste	(130)	70	53.84	37	28.46	23	17.69
Lower Caste	(28)	4	14.28	20	71.42	4	14.28
Total	158	74	46.83	57	36.07	27	17.08

On the other hand, only 28.46% of the upper caste do not favour its existence in society, whereas 71.42% of the lower caste disfavours its existence. The number of undecided respondents is greater among upper caste respondents (17.69%) than the lower caste (14.28%) respondents.

It is obvious from this analysis that the upper caste people of the village want their age old pride, power and privilege to exist. They are in favour of the continuance of the inequal distribution of status and role. They want to remain superior and privileged class whereas the lower caste people are quite against to this ideology. They believe in equal treatment and proper distribution of rights and privileges, prestige and facilities. Actually the upper caste ideology in favour of the existence of inequality in society is against the Islamic Sharia. Because Islam believes in equality and brotherhood among its followers.

In the next question the respondents were asked, "Do you think that there should be no discrimination of high and low with wealthy and educated persons even if they are from lower castes?" The responses collected from the respondents in respect of this question are presented in Table 5.3.

Table 5.3

Response regarding Social Discrimination
N=158

Response Category	*Number*	*Percentage*
Yes	96	60.76
No	41	25.95
Can't say	21	13.29
Total	158	100.00

It appears from the above table that 60.76% of the respondents have favoured the view; whereas 25.95% have replied in negative and 13.29% have remained undecided. It means majority of the respondents hold the view that the discriminatory behaviour should not be shown to wealthy and educated persons of lower caste or inferior breed. This majority opinion leads to draw this inference that for the respondents the breed or family is not much relevant in determining the social prestige and status. On the other hand, the factor of wealth and education should be more important consideration. In case an individual improves his economic position and educational qualification, he should be given a respectable place in the society. It suggests that a rigid stratification leading to social immobility is not favoured rather flexible stratification characterized by social mobility is supported.

After collecting information regarding the views on social stratification, another question put to the respondents was, "Should everybody get the same rights and privileges in the society?" The responses given by the villager respondents are presented in Table 5.4.

Table 5.4

Response regarding Rights and Privileges in the Society
N=158

Response Category	*Number*	*Percentage*
Yes	139	87 98
No	19	12.02
Can't say	—	—
Total	158	100.00

It is evident from this table that overwhelming majority of 87.98% of the respondents holds the view that equal rights and privileges should be enjoyed by all. Only a smaller section of 12.02% has replied in negative. It means that in spite of supporting the concept of high and low and favouring the persistence of social hierarchy, the majority feels that there should be no discrimination in the rights and privileges. Statuses may be different but in all the status groups the rights and privileges should be equally distributed. In other words, the socially inferior groups and individuals should not be deprived of the rights and privileges enjoyed by the persons of higher status.

Another question put to the respondents was concerned with knowing the most important factor determining in individual status. A number of factors or attributes were presented before the respondents and they were asked to express who is more respected in society according to their views. Table 5.5 given below presents the responses obtained from the villagers under study.

Table 5.5

Response regarding who should be respected in the Society

N=158

Category	*Number*	*Percentage*
Wealthy	3	1.89
Persons of high caste	7	4.43
Educated	73	46.20
Religious	43	27.21
Politicians	3	1.89
Anyone possessing good qualities	29	18.35
Total	158	100.00

It is evident from the above table that five specific categories of people associated with five different attributes were presented before the respondents. These categories were wealthy persons, persons of high caste, educated persons, religious persons and politicians. The responses shown in the table suggest that the highest percentage of response has gone in favour of education (46.20%). It means that according to 46.20% of the respondents educated people are more respected in the society. The second highest percentage is in favour of religious persons and according to 27.21% of the respondents religious persons enjoy greater respect in the society. It is also interesting to note that the lowest score of 1.89% has gone in favour of politicians and wealthy persons. The attribute of caste has been mentioned by 4.43% of the respondents. Thus it appears that factor of education and religion are more respected in the society. On this basis it may be interpreted that the social hierarchy supported by the people and practised in social life is not birth-oriented rather worth-oriented, and, in determining the status and practice of a person, his personal qualities are considered.

On the basis of birth the Muslim community is also divided into several caste-like groups. This caste-like division persists not only on the basis of the distinction in form of foreign breed and indigenous population, rather in each of the two categories itself there exists a status hierarchy. In the foreign breed there are caste-like groups of Syed, Shaikh, Pathan and Mallick, whereas in the indigenous population there are occupation-oriented caste-like groups of Ansari, Kalal, Mulezada and Rangrez. These castes are graded not only in term of foreign and indigenous breed but also as the basis of heredity, family, breed and occupation. Each caste is ranked according to the values prevalent in the society. The central values of the society serve as the basis in determining the hierarchy of Muslim castes.

Keeping the above facts in view, a list of different castes was presented to each of the respondents. Every respondent was asked to give the social ranking of these castes. In all eight castes of Ansari, Kalal, Mallick, Mulezada, Pathan, Rangrez, Shaikh and Syed were presented in alphabetical order and the respondents were asked to rank them from the first to eight ranking. Thus every respondent was required to give one ranking to one caste and thus eight different rankings to all the eight castes. The responses obtained from them are presented in Table 5.6.

Table 5.6

Social Ranking of Different Castes in the Society

N=158

Caste Category	*Rank Order* 1	2	3	4	5	6	7	8	*Total* No.	Percentage
Ansari	4 2.53	20 12.65	28 17.72	36 22.78	56 35.44	14 8.86	—	—	158	100.00
Kalal	—	—	—	—	—	12 7.59	28 17.72	118 74.68	158	100.00
Mallick	23 14.55	93 58.86	33 20.88	9 5.69	—	—	—	—	158	100.00
Mulezada	—	—	-	—	4 2.53	14 8.86	68 43.03	72 45.56	158	100.00
Pathan	7 4.43	61 38.60	68 43.03	22 13.92	—	—	—	—	158	100.00
Rangrez	—	—	—	—	8 5.06	20 12.65	77 48.73	53 33.54	158	100.00
Shaikh	8 5.06	78 49.36	60 37.97	12 7.59	—	—	—	—	158	100.00
Syed	119 75.31	39 24.68	—	—	—	—	—	—	158	100.00

It appears from the above table that different rankings have been given by different respondents to the same caste. It means that a uniform social ranking is not round. The table shows that first, second, third or fourth ranking have not been given by any respondent to any of the three castes of Kalal, Mulezada and Rangrez. In case of Kalal even fifth ranking is not given. On the other hand the Ansari, an indigenous caste, have been given first to sixth ranking but not the seventh and eighth ranking. In case of Syed nobody has given third or any other inferior ranking. In case of Mallick, Pathan and Shaikh the lowest ranking given by a few respondents is the fourth. These patterns of response suggest that Syed caste is given the highest ranking. Then come the castes of Mallick, Shaikh and Pathan. In the indigenous population the Ansari caste has the highest ranking.

In a more precise and specific analysis of caste ranking a statistical procedure was adopted. The first rank was given the weight of 8 units whereas the last rank was allotted the weight of 1 unit. The other ranks were allotted the weights ranging from 7 units to 2 units respectively. On the basis of this allotment of weight the score of each caste in each ranking category was calculated by multiplying the frequency of the category with the unit weight. The total score of each caste was calculated through adding all the scores of the castes in different ranking categories. The total score in each caste was divided by 158, the total number of respondents to calculate the average ranking of the caste. In this way the average ranking of all the eight castes were calculated, which are shown in the table.

It is evident from the table that the average scores of Ansaris, Kalal, Mallick, Mulezada, Pathan, Rangrez, Shaikh and Syed are respectively 4.99, 1.33, 6.82, 1.69, 6.34, 1.83, 6.52 and 7.75. It means that the highest average score has gone in favour of Syed caste, the next higher to the Mallick caste, the next one to the Shaikhs and then to Pathans. The fifth ranking has gone to Ansari caste, whereas the Rangrez caste has been ranked sixth, the Mulezada seventh and the lowest rank is for Kalal. It is also interesting to point out that there is a wider difference in the average score of Ansari caste and the remaining three indigenous castes of Rangrez, Mulezada and Kalal.

On the basis of foreign breed and indigenous population the traditional Muslim society is divided into two broader categories of Ashraf and Atraf. The Muslims claiming foreign breed and constituting the castes of Syed, Shaikh, Mallick, Pathan and Mirza, etc. belong to the category of Ashraf and are commonly placed among upper caste Muslim. The remaining Muslim population of indigenous breed is placed in the category of Atraf and constitutes the lower castes or backward classes of Muslim society. A distance between two categories has been existing in the traditional society and reservations in social mixing have been observed. This distance between the two categories has resulted in the development of certain stereotype concepts in respect of each other.

The respondents were also asked to assign some of the important characteristics of the different caste groups. These characteristics must be either positive or negative. For this purpose the respondents were provided with a chart containing the positive and negative characteristics generally found among different social groups. This was done in order to facilitate the respondents in expressing their views clearly. Under the positive characteristics there were several adjectives like, sociability, honesty, good moral character, docile, helping nature, high thinking intelligent, secular, sympathetic, cultural, co-operative, faithful, dutiful, hardy, sincere, while the negative characteristics adjective like, quarrelsome, ill-behaved, non-cooperative, selfish, discourteous, dishonest, cunning, aggressive, unmannered and uncultured, foolish, coward, characterless, communal, lazy, illiterate, exploiter, corrupt, etc. kept. To every respondent it was being shown and detailed so that they could not be confused in expressing their views. Every respondent was asked to see, select and express two characteristics, positive or negative, or both, for both the groups of upper and lower castes. The data so collected have been shown in Table 5.7.

It is found from the data presented in the table that 78.48% of the respondents have given positive characteristics in favour of upper caste men, whereas only 38.29% of

Table 5.7

Characteristics of Upper and Lower Castes

N=158

Caste Categories	*Positive Characteristics*		*Negative Characteristics*		*Total*	*%*
	No.	*%*	*No.*	*%*		
Upper Caste	248	78.48	68	21.51	316	100
Lower Caste	121	38.29	195	61.70	316	100

the respondents have attributed positive characteristics for the lower caste men. On the other hand, only 21.51% of the respondents have chosen negative characteristics for the upper caste people, while 61.70% of the villagers (respondents) have presented negative characteristics to the lower caste people. Thus upper caste have exceeded in the number of its positive remarks given by the respondents and the lower caste have got far more negative characters than its positive one. This picture may have appeared because of the overwhelming majority of the upper caste respondents (130 out of 158) and a smaller number (28 out of 158) of the lower caste people in the group of respondents. The picture may be viewed otherwise if it is arranged on the basis of caste background. It is mainly the pride and prejudice of the upper caste people who feel the lower caste people lower in all senses. They possess superiority complex and hate their inferior caste men and regard them socially backward.

B. MARRIAGE, FAMILY AND KINSHIP

Family is both a social institution and a religious sanction in Islam. Due to its multifarious roles in human life it has been existing ever since the appearance of man on this earth. Islam, contrary to the opinion of Morgan, Henry Main, etc., does not believe in the evolution of man and family and existence of the state of sex communism. Adam and Eve, according to the revealed religions, were the first human beings forming the monogamous family. Among the Indian Muslims, family largely exists in the framework of patrilineal descent, but differs in its forms and function. A patrilineal family is a tri-generational, commensal and co-residential group formed by close male patrikin with their wives and unmarried daughters. This group has a common budget, common residence and common hearth. Joint landed property, a family business or family craft are conducive to this type of family as they require pooling of their skill, labour and resources. In common parlance, such a family has been described as 'Joint family'. Such family is found among rural Muslims and other communities.

A family develops into a joint family after the marriage of a son and coming of a daughter-in-law. After the death of the father, brothers generally separate. Sons are expected to stay together along with the parents till all of them are married, after which they tend to separate, the parents generally choosing to live with one of the sons. Thus, joint family is broken into one relatively smaller joint family household and perhaps a few simple households. It is common to find an aged parent and dependent siblings living with a man and his wife and children.

Another feature of Indian family organisation is the recognition of a kind of oneness between the father's and son's households, or between the brothers' households.

Marriage is a universal institution found in known human societies of the world. Since the pre-historic period up to the present time, the institution of marriage has remained the backbone and carrier of human society and culture. Through this a man sustains the continuity of his race, culture, and attains sexual satisfaction in a socially accepted way.

Marriage is an important aspect of Muslim society. Every normal being is encouraged to marry for the continuation of society. Illustrating this point Zeyauddin Ahmad says,

"Muslims have been ordained to marry without fail. Islam does not permit celibacy. Marriage is considered to be one of the sacred duties of Muslim."[1] Prophet Mohammad discouraged Rohbaniyat (celibacy) and asked his followers to marry and multiply. The Prophet preaches:

> "Marriage is my custom; he who dislikes it does not belong to me. Marry and multiply, so that I may be glorified in my community over other communities."[2]

Nikah

In Muslim society, the marital union is denoted by the Arabic word "Nikah" (marriage). According to the Muslim Law 'Nikah' is the contract of husband and wife which legalises their sexual intercourse and imposes certain duties and rights on them. The performance of marriage ceremony in Islam is a simple affair. The actual ritual starts with the religious ceremony of Nikah. Nikah is a formal declaration of the contract between a male and a female to enter into the wedlock in the presence of few witnesses. Thus Islam does not allow a luxurious performance of marriage. Shushtery observes, "The chief function of marriage, according to Muslim law, is the ceremony of Nikah, an Arabic word which means conjunction and understanding in the sense of contract. It is a simple ceremony, for which the consent of the man and the woman to marry each other is necessary."[3]

Among Muslims there are either certain socio-economic categories or groups and sections within which marriage is restricted. Where intergroup marriages are approved, they are mostly on hypergamous basis. The concept of purity of blood among Muslims seems to be more responsible for preference

1. Ahmad, Zeyauddin, Marriage and Family among the Muslims of Bihar, in Family in India—A Regional View, (ed.) George Kurian, Mouton, Paris, 1974, p. 319.
2. Ibid., p. 319.
3. Shushtery, A.M.A., Outlines of Islamic Culture, Bangalore Publishing Company Pvt. Ltd., Bangalore, 1937, p. 717.

for marriage between close relatives, particularly between children of siblings and for exchange marriages. Besides, a common explanation for this preference is offered in terms of the desire to keep the property within the family since, according to Islamic law, a girl is also entitled to a share in her parental property.

Polygamy

Islam sanctions the system of polygamy. A man can have up to four wives at a time. But this sanction is based on some pre-conditions. According to Islamic sanction, Shushtery says, "A man, who has more than one wife, has to provide for each. The convenience of each wife has to be provided for according to his wealth and position in life. In his sexual relation, he is expected to be strictly just and treat all wives alike. If he cannot do this, he must be content to choose only one wife."[4] Thus it is clear that a Muslim male is allowed to have more than one wife only if he is sure that he can do justice to all of them according to his position. The basic idea behind this is not the sexual gratification only but to protect the modesty of women. A man can marry the second woman or more only after the consent and mutual agreement of the first or other previous wives and a 'mehr' should be fixed for each.

Mehr

According to the Islamic Law (Fiqah), 'Mehr' and 'Nafqa' constitute two vital conditions of the conjugal contract. Mehr being the consideration money, is payable just at the time of Nikah while 'Nafqa' is a regular right of wife till she remains tied in a loyal wedlock. In Indian Muslim society 'mehr' is generally regarded as a precaution against or penalty for divorce, giving a notion as if 'mehr' is payable only in case of divorce or separation; while, as a matter of fact, its payment can be deferred till a convenient time only

4. Shushtery, A.M.A., Outlines of Islamic Culture, Bangalore Publishing Co. Pvt. Ltd., Bangalore, 1937, p. 718.

with the concurrence of the bride. It is a debt which comes on the property of the husband in case of his defiance on demand or death. 'Nafqa' (subsistence) is a bit different from 'Mehr' inasmuch as it is conditioned with the loyalty of wife. In other words, a disloyal or defiant wife cannot claim 'Nafqa' as a matter of right, whereas she can claim 'Mehr' in full at any time. Besides, a loyal wife is also entitled to 1/8th of the husband's properties after his death. These are the social protections granted by Islam to a worthy wife. Mulla has also accepted 'Mehr' as the "consideration money for marriages".[5] It may be noted, as Mahmood remarks, "In India no uniform rates of mehr prevail in any part of the country".[6]

Talaq and Khula

Since marriage is a contract in Islam, the contract may be maintained life long or may be broken when desired. Thus marital relation between male and female among the Muslims is flexible in nature. When the agreement of contract is breached, either of the partners may initiate for breaking the marital tie. In case the husband divorces his wife it is called 'Talaq' and in case the wife divorces her husband it is known as 'Khula'. In case of Talaq it is obligatory on the part of husband to pay the amount of mehr, while in case of Khula the husband is not required to pay mehr to his wife.

Thus Islam has allowed the delinking of marital relations if it is not possible to continue it smoothly. But either of this is not appreciated. The Prophet himself declared that the sanctions have been given for divorce but it is the most disliked of all the sanctions concerning marriage and family. In the words of Shushtery, "Divorce was very common among pre-Islamic Arabs and, though a lawful act, was condemned

5. Mulla, D.F, Principles of Mohammadan Law, Bombay, 1968, S/265-66.

6. Mahmood, Tahir, Muslim Personal Law, Vikas Publishing House P. Ltd., New Delhi, 1977, p. 72.

by the Prophet who has said, "The thing most disliked by God is divorce."[7]

Right to divorce, if used wisely in an indispensable situation, it would be of immense value for both a male and a female. The concept of union for life or the sacramental nature of the marriage has gradually been eroded and through legislation the right of divorce has been introduced in all legal systems in India.

Muslim law had always recognised that in some cases the wife may be able to get a divorce. But the power of the husband to pronounce talaq unilaterally remains there and it has, in no way, been curtailed either judicially or through legislation.

Widowhood

Islam also sanctions the marriage of the widows. Any Muslim widow can remarry after completing the specified period of Iddat, i.e., four months and 10 days. The main object of this specified period is to determine whether the woman is pregnant from her deceased husband, so that the dispute of parenthood may be avoided. Islam does not only allow the widow marriage, but also encourages it and declared it to be a virtuous deed. But even among those who allow widow remarriage, many groups do not look upon it favourably. Among some sections of Muslims also widow remarriage is frowned upon.

Association of inauspiciousness with widowhood is found among every community in India. Widows themselves avoid taking an active part in ceremonial occasions. For instance, among the Bohras a widowed mother would not break the cocoanut for her son's birth-day. But Lambat says, "No stigma is attached among the Surati Vohras to the marriage of widows."[8]

7. Shushtery, A.M.A., Outlines of Islamic Culture, Bangalore Publishing Co. Pvt. Ltd., Bangalore, 1937, p. 718.
8. Lambat, Ismail A., Marriage among the Surati Vohras of South Gujrat, in Imtiaz Ahmad (ed.), Kinship and Marriage among Muslims in India, Manohar Book Service, New Delhi, 1976, p. 55.

Dowry

Technically, dowry is what is given to the son-in-law or to his parents on demand either in cash or in kind. According to the Hindu Shastras the meritorious act of 'Dan' or ritual gift remains incomplete till the receiver is given Dakshina. So when a bride is given over to the bridegroom, he has to be given something in cash or in kind, or in both. Since the bridegroom and his kins are believed to have done a favour by accepting the girl in their fold, they are honoured with gifts. Thus the concept of dowry is in contrast with the dower."[9]

Among Muslims of many regions also the custom of giving cash to the bridegroom is prevalent. The settlement of dowry has all the characteristics of a market transaction. Its rate is always on the increase. Its extent depends on the socio-economic status of the bridgroom and differs in different regions and in different caste groups. There are more or less well-defined grades of dowry in different professions.

Both in villages as well as in towns parents offer certain justification for demanding and accepting dowry. First, since they have to give dowry for the daughters, they are in a way forced to ask for dowry for their sons. Second, the fathers of educated boys like to get back the amount they spend on the son's education. Some also argue that because of changed circumstances in which a son generally has a separate establishment and has a job somewhere away from home, the parents cannot expect much help from him, and so they consider his marriage as the major occasion on which their investment in his education can be recovered. This shows that education has hardly any liberalising influence on the minds of the people in respect of dowry. On the contrary, education has increased dowry. A highly educated man expects a higher amount of dowry. The girl's parents want to buy a good future for their daughters.

9. Mahmood, Tahir, Muslim Personal Law, Vikas Publishing House, Pvt. Ltd., New Delhi, 1977, p. 72.

Finding

For analysing the institution of family and marriage in the village under study it was decided to collect information regarding the patterns of family life and marriage institution in the past, the practices found at the present and the attitudes and values of the people in respect of these institutions. With this objective in view, certain questions were put to the respondents for collecting relevant information.

One of the questions put to the respondents was concerned with the age of the respondents and of their partners at the time of marriage. This question was put only to the married respondants, 137 in number. The responses obtained from them are presented in Table 5.8.

Table 5.8

Age at Marriage of the Respondents and their Partners (in the past)

N=137

Age group	*Male*		*Female*	
	Number	*Percentage*	*Number*	*Percentage*
Up to 14 yrs.	—	—	22	16.06
15 to 20 yrs.	50	36.49	97	70.80
21 to 25 yrs.	65	47.45	18	13.14
26 to 30 yrs.	19	13.87	—	—
31 +	3	2.19	—	—
Total	137	100.00	137	100.00

It appears from the above table that the age of male's marriage has been higher than the age of tha female. As evident from the table, no male member was married before the age of 15 years. It suggests that child marriage was not in practice. But in the case of women, it is found that 16.06% of the respondents married before attaining the age of 15 years. It means that they were married at the age of 14 years or even less than that. The table further shows that the majority of the women (wives of the respondents), i.e., 70.80% were married in the age group of 15 to 20 years, whereas the highest percentage of men (47.45%) were married in the age group of 21 to 25 years. It means that the most favoured age group for the marriage of males is 21 to 25 years and for females it is 15 to 20 years. It is also important to point out that a considerable percentage of male respondents (36.49%) were married in the age group of 15 to 20 years. Hence it may be interpreted that though child marriage was not in practice, yet early marriage was prevalent. It is also found from the table that a very small percentage of women (13.14%) was married in the age group of 21 to 25 years. It means that 86.86% of women were married before completing 20 years of age, whereas 63.50% of male respondents were married after attaining the age of 21 years. It means that the majority of women was married within 20 years, whereas the majority of male after 20 years of age. It is also important to point out that no woman was married after attaining the age of more than 25 years, whereas 13.87% of men were married in the age groups of 26 to 30 years and 2.19% were married after attaining the age of 31 years or more. Hence it may be interpreted that early marriage of women was more favoured in the past and it was also found in the case of considerable percentage of men.

In the next respondents were asked to give the prevailing age at marriage in their family. This question was not put to all the 158 respondents. They were asked to give the age at marriage of male and female members of their families being married in the present age. The respondents' answers are presented in Table 5.9

It is also evident from the table that the majority of men (51.26%) are being married in the age group of 21 to 25 years; whereas the highest percentage of response in respect of prevailing age of marriage for women has gone to the age group of 15 to 20 years (49.37%). It is also evident from the

Table 5.9

Prevailing Age of Marriage in the Family (present days)

N=158

Age group	*Male*		*Female*	
	Number	*Percentage*	*Number*	*Percentage*
Up to 14 yrs.	—		12	7.60
15 to 20 yrs.	16	10.13	78	49.37
21 to 25 yrs.	81	51.27	57	36.07
26 to 30 yrs.	53	33.54	11	6.96
31 +	8	5.06	—	—
Total	158	100.00	158	100.00

table that a considerably higher percentage of response showing the prevailing age of marriage for men has gone in favour of the age group of 26 to 30 years (33.54%). In the same way, 36.07% of the response shows the prevailing age of women at marriage in the age group of 21 to 25 years.

When the responses given in Tables 5.8 and 5.9 are comparatively analysed, a significant change is noticed in the age at marriage. It is evident from this table that in the past 16.05% of women were married up to 14 years of age, but at present the percentage of response in the same age group has receded to only 7.60%, which suggests a less prevalent practice of early marriage. In the past 17.80% of women were married in the age group of 15 to 20 years and 13.13% in the age group of 21 to 25 years; whereas at present only 49.37% of response was in the age group of 15 to 20 years and 36.07% in the age group of 21 to 25 years. It means that the percentage of response showing early marriage has declined at present and percentage of response showing marriage after 20 years of age has considerably increased. It clearly suggests that the age of women at marriage has risen in the present age. Moreover, no woman in the past was married after 25 years of age, whereas 6.96% of response has gone in favour of this age group showing the prevailing age at marriage. Hence it may be interpreted that the traditional practice of early marriage has become less prevalent and the age at marriage is being rationalised. Thus a tradition-rationality continuum may be discovered in the age at marriage for the women in the village.

When the age at marriage of men in the above two tables are comparatively analysed, the same trend is noted. In the past 36.49% of men were married in the age group of 15 to 20 years, whereas in the present age the score for this age group is 10.13% only. Thus the early marriage in the present age has become much less prevalent. The tables further show that the age at marriage of men in the three higher age groups has increased in percentage in comparison to the past. In the past 47.44%, 13.86% and 21.18% of men were married respectively in the age groups of 21 to 25 years, 26 to 30 years and 31 years and above whereas the corresponding percentages in the three age groups are respectively 51.27%, 33.54% and 5.06%. It shows a rising trend in the age of men at marriage in the present age. Thus a rational outlook is developing and the traditional practice is becoming less operative. Thus the same tradition-rationality continuum persists in respect of age of men at marriage in the past and at present.

In the next question the respondents were asked to explain the reasons for change in marriage age in the present age. The responses obtained from all the 158 respondents are given in Table 5.10.

It is evident from the table that the most important reason behind the rise in marriage age is economic hardships mentioned by 57.58% of the respondents. The next higher percentage of response has gone in favour of non-availability of suitable match (24.06%). Only 12.66% mentioned the socio-cultural effect as the reason for rise in marriage age, whereas only 5.70% mentioned education as the factor for higher age in marriage. It is important to point out that if poverty stands in the way of early marriage of girls, it may be due to the difficulty in giving dowry. But in case of the

Table 5.10

Reasons for Change in Marriage Age in the Present Age

N=158

Reasons	*Number*	*Percentage*
Economic hardship	91	57.58
Socio-cultural effects	20	12.66
Educational	9	5.70
Non-availability of suitable match	38	24.06
Total	158	100 00

marriage of the boys there is no dowry problem. In this case economic hardship means the unemployment or absence of the source of earning livelihood of the male youths. It means that the parents prefer to marry their sons, or the boys themselves like to marry, only when they start earning. It is itself a rational outlook. Moreover, in the past no much attention was paid towards the suitability of match, whereas at present suitability is being stressed in a considerable percentage. It is also an index of rational outlook. Hence it may be interpreted that rationality has developed and rational outlook is playing a decisive role in raising the age at marriage.

After collecting information regarding marriage age in the past and present and the reasons for the change in marriage age, the respondents were also asked to give their views regarding ideal age of marriage for males and females. The earlier questions were concerned with the actual practice, whereas the present one was concerned with attitudes. The responses obtained from all the 158 respondants are presented in Table 5.11.

Table 5.11
Ideal Age for Marriage
N=158

Age group	*Male*		*Female*	
	Number	*Percentage*	*Number*	*Percentage*
Up to 14 yrs.	—	—	—	—
15 to 20 yrs.	—	—	85	53.79
21 to 25 yrs.	119	75.32	73	46.21
26 to 30 yrs.	39	24.68	—	—
31 +	—	—	—	—
Total	158	100.00	158	100.00

It is evident from the table that no respondent favours the marriage of a girl before attaining the age of 15 years. It is definitely a change in the outlook and attitude of the people in relation to the practice of the past and the present. It means that even in the present age the marriages of girls taking place before 15 years of age are not liked. It shows a gap between the attitude and practice. The table shows that majority of the respondents (53.79%) have favoured the ideal age for marriage of girls in the age group of 15 to 20 years. In the past more than 70% of the respondents while in the present only about 50% of the respondents married their girls in this age group. This shows a declining trend in the age of marriage of a girl. This is of course a rational trend with regard to marriage age of girls.

The table further shows that no respondent favoured the ideal age of marriage for men before 21 years. In the past 36.49% and at present 10.12% responses have been in favour of 15 to 20 years. It suggests a change not only in the present practices in relation to past but also a difference in the present practice and attitude. It is also found that 24.68% of the respondents have favoured the age of marriage for men in the age group of 30 years.

The facts further show that neither the respondents favoured the marriage age of a male before 21 nor after 31 years of age. Thus in this respect also there is a difference between the actual practice and the ideals before the respondents. In the light of these findings it may be interpreted that the attitude of the people in the village are changing from tradition-oriented. There is a gap between the ideals and the practices. Thus the practice is lagging behind the ideology.

In the next, respondents were also asked to give their opinion about marrying within kin group. This was done in order to know whether this sanction of Islam is being followed these days or not, people prefer it or have a dislike for such type of marital ties. Table 5.12 presented below shows the frequency of attitude regarding marriage with kins.

Table 5.12

Attitude of Marriage with Kins

N=158

Attitude	*Number*	*Percentage*
Favourable	93	58.87
Unfavourable	31	19.62
Undecided	34	21.51
Total	158	100.00

An analysis of the data distributed in three attitude categories depicts that highest number of the respondents (58.87%) favoured the idea of marriage within kin group, whereas only about 20% (19.62%) have disfavoured it. On the other hand about 22 per cent (21.51%) of the respondents have been found of the undecided category. It may be inferred from this gesture that some among them may also favour this idea. On the whole it may be concluded from the situation that still majority of the rural Muslims like such marital ties.

Table 5.13 shows the attitude of the respondents on the basis of their caste background.

Table 5.13

Caste Categories and Marriage Attitude with the Kins

N=158

Caste Categories	*Favourable*		*Unfavourable*		*Undecided*	
	No.	%	*No.*	%	*No.*	%
Upper Caste (130)	70	53.84	31	23.84	29	22.30
Lower Caste (28)	23	82.14	—	—	5	17.85
Total (158)	93		31		34	

The same data in Table 5.12 have been analysed in Table 5.14 on the caste basis. Response regarding this has been based on two caste categories, i.e., upper Muslim caste and lower Muslim castes. It is found that overwhelming majority of the lower castes (82.14%) has favoured the idea of marriage with the kins group, while in the upper caste only 53.84% have favoured this type of marital ties. This shows that though in both the caste groups this system is appreciated but among the lower castes it is much favoured. Another important feature of the distribution of data is that none from the lower castes disfavoured the idea of such type of marital ties, whereas 23.84% of the upper caste people disliked and disfavoured it. Likewise in the third response category of undecided respondents, 22.30% belong to upper caste group while less than this, i.e., 17.85% belong to lower caste group. It means that the number of indecisive respondents is greater in the upper caste group than the lower caste one. It may be concluded from the response patterns that the lower caste people are more conscious and serious in maintaining kinship relations.

The respondents were further asked to express the reasons behind maintaining the marital relation within kin group. It was important to explore here the causes underlying this idea. The data collected in this regard is presented in Table 5.14.

Table 5.14

Reasons for favouring Marriage within Kins

N=93

Reason	*No.*	*Percentage*
Purity is maintained	19	20.44
Religiously favoured	15	16 13
Economic gain	34	36.56
Relation strengthens	15	16.12
Selection of spouse easy	10	10.75
Total	93	100.00

The data showing the reasons behind the preference of this system is distributed among five reason-categories. The most favoured category here is economic gain. It shows that majority of the respondents, i.e., 36.56% have favoured this system due to economic gain. The respondents feel that marrying within one's own kin group helps economising the unnecessary expenses incurred in marriage. This implicitly shows that the greatest economic problem in marriage, the dowry, is in most of the cases solved. It means that in such marriages dowry is mostly neither demanded nor given. On the other hand 20.44% expressed that they like this system because it helps maintain the purity of blood and bone. The feeling regarding the maintenance of purity is found profoundly among the rural Muslims at large.

In the next two reasons have been accorded an equal importance in favour of maintaining kinship ties. The two reasons—religious and social (relation strengthens)—have got respectively 16.13% and 16.12% favour for marrying with kins. Only 10.75% of the respondents have expressed that such marital ties would facilitate in the selection of spouse. It is true because both the parties (parents and partners) know or could know each other very closely. In the Muslim community it is important to have prior information and satisfaction before marrying one's son or daughter. It is because marriage is a contract in the Muslim society which may be broken if anything intolerable comes in the way of smooth conjugal life. This is why both the parties try their best to be satisfied about each other before marrying their son or daughter. Getting information about one's own kins is a simple matter.

The respondents were also enquired about their attitude regarding inter-caste marriage. Table 5.15 presented blow gives an idea about their attitude towards inter-caste marriage.

Table 5.15
Attitude towards Inter-Caste Marriage
N=158

Attitude	*Number*	*Percentage*
Favourable	28	17.73
Unfavourable	121	76.58
Undecided	9	5.69
Total	158	100.00

It appears from the frequency distribution in Table 5.15 that out of the total number of respondents (158) 121, i.e., 76.58% have unfavourable attitude towards inter-caste marriage. Only 17.73% of the respondents have favoured inter-caste marriage, while 5.69% of the respondents are found in the indecisive stage. Thus it may be concluded that the overwhelming majority of the rural respondents do not like to break their age-old social custom of marrying within their own caste group. Though this type of attitude is in negation to Islamic sanctions, it exists in Indian Muslim society. Since Islam believes in equality and brotherhood among its followers, so the presence of caste hierarchy and maintaining caste distance is in negation to Islamic Sharia. Nevertheless the Indian Muslims, especially living in rural areas, have adopted various non-Islamic practices.

The same data regarding the attitude towards inter-caste marriage have been analysed on the basis of level of education of the respondents in Table 5.16 presented here.

Table 5.16

Educatiou and Attitude towards Inter-Caste Marriage

N=158

Education Category	*Favourable*		*Unfavourable*		*Undecided*	
	No.	*%*	*No.*	*%*	*No.*	*%*
Illiterate (42)	4	9.52	36	85 71	2	4.76
Below High School (79)	9	11.39	67	84.81	3	3 79
Below Graduation (25)	8	32.00	15	60.00	2	8.00
Graduation + (12)	7	58.33	3	25.00	2	16 66
Total (158)	28		121		9	

The table shows that the highest score in favour of inter-caste marriage has gone to highly educated respondents. Out of the total 12 highly educated respondents (about graduation) 7, i.e., 58.33% supported the idea of inter-caste marriage, whereas 32% belonging to education below graduation, 11.39% respondents having education below high school and only 9.52% of respondents having no education at all supported in respect of inter-caste marriage. An analysis of the data shows that with the rise in education preference for inter-caste marriage increases, and with the fall in education favour for inter-caste marriage decreases. This is of course a rational and Islamic bent of mind.

On the other hand, the data disfavouring inter-caste marriage shows the trend of lesser the level of literacy greater the dislike in respect of inter-caste marriage and vice versa. As much as 85.71% of the rural people belonging to illiterate category of respondents show an unfavourable attitude towards inter-caste marriage. Likewise 84.81% literate respondents having education below matriculation also disfavoured the idea of inter-caste marriage. In the same way, 60% of the respondents having below graduate education disliked this idea, while only 25% highly educated respondents gave their response against inter-caste marriage. Thus it may be interpreted that there is a positive correlatism between the level of education and attitude towards inter-caste marriage.

It is also important to observe here that only a meagre number of respondents from each group have remained indecisive in terms of their attitude towards inter-caste marriage. The highest percentage (16.66%) in this column is of highly educated respondents who were undecided at the time of interview. Likewise 8%, 3.79% and 4.76 respectively are below graduates, below high school and illiterate who are undecided to respond in favour of or against inter-caste marriage. Thus, on the basis of this table, the conclusion may be drawn that the rise in the level of education and general experience will facilitate the swing in favour of inter-caste marriages in the Muslim society in general.

A question was also put to the respondents to know their attitude regarding the marriage with mixed breed. Table 5.17 shows the frequency distribution of the respondents with regard to it.

Table 5 17

Response regarding Marriage with Mixed Breed

N=158

Response Category	*Number*	*Percentage*
Favourable	40	25.32
Unfavourable	105	66.46
Undecided	13	8.22
Total	158	100 00

The frequency distribution in the table shows that only 40, i.e., 25.32% of the respondents have favourable attitude towards marriage with a boy/girl mixed breed On the other hand 105 respondents, i.e., 66.46% possess unfavourable attitude towards such life partners, whereas 8.22% of the respondents remained undecided.

An analysis of the data reveals that majority of the village respondents do not prefer to marry their son or daughter to any one who do not belong to a pure blood and bone. It is because purity of blood and bone is given greater emphasis in selecting a bride or groom. This is a traditional approach, though not Islamic in nature. Such practices are not liked and encouraged by the villagers belonging to upper caste as well as of lower caste. Though there are a few cases in the village in which marriages with the mixed breed have been performed. But these have been done against the will of the parents and other kins. Two girls who married to such boys have been boycotted by the family and kins as well as by the villagers as a whole. For a long time they were not accepted by the family members but gradually they have been adopted into the fold and the matter has been normalised. But even after the development of a positive situation in the village the whole social atmosphere has not been normalised for such couples. Generally such marriages are performed in case of love or choice of the partners themselves.

The same data of Table 5.17 have further been classified and arranged in Table 5.18. This has been done in order to gain information from the different caste groups, more precisely to know the reactions of the upper and lower caste respondents separately.

Table 5.18

Caste and Attitude towards Mixed Breed Marriage
N=158

Caste Group	*Favourable*		*Unfavourable*		*Undecided*	
	No.	*%*	*No.*	*%*	*No.*	*%*
Upper Caste (130)	30	23.07	91	70.00	9	6.92
Lower Caste (28)	10	30.71	14	50.00	4	14.28
Total	40		105		13	

The response trend found in this table shows that the greater percentage of response in favour of marriage with mixed breed comes from lower caste respondents (35.71%) while only 23.07% of the upper caste respondents favour such marital ties. Likewise 50% of the lower caste respondents replied against this practice, whereas overwhelming majority of upper caste respondents (70%) have shown unfavourable attitude towards such marital relations. In the third option of response, i.e., undecided, only 6.92% of the upper caste respondents remained in indecisive situation while 14.28% of the lower caste respondents are found remaining undecided on this problem.

The analysis of the whole table shows that it is the upper caste which dislikes this practice more than the lower caste people. Though lower caste men are also against such marital ties but their number are less than the upper caste

Muslims. In other cases a higher percentage of lower caste people favour this practice than those of the upper caste people.

Similarly, the respondents were also asked to expose their reaction and feeling in case their son/daughter marries to anyone above or below his/her own caste hierarchy. Data pertaining to this is arranged in Table 5.19.

Table 5.19

Attitude towards Marriage with Upper or Lower Caste Person

N=158

Educational Category	*Favourable*		*Unfavourable*		*Undecided*	
	No.	*%*	*No.*	*%*	*No.*	*%*
Illiterate (42)	9	21.12	29	69.04	4	9.52
Below High School (79)	18	22.78	56	77.88	5	6.32
Below Graduate (25)	6	24.00	16	64.00	3	12.00
Graduate +	7	58.33	4	33.33	1	8.33
Total (158)	40		105		13	

In this table altogether four distinct questions were put and the responses were distributed in three attitude categories. Through the first question reaction of the respondents was tried to know in case of any of his family male marries to a girl above his caste rank. It was found that out of 158 respondents 81 (51.27%) gave a favourable response, 39.87% did not favour this action and the rest 8.86% remained undecided. Thus marrying one's male with that of a female of high caste is favoured and liked by the rural Muslims.

But, on the reverse, in case any female member of the respondent's family marries to a boy above her own caste, it was disliked by majority of the respondents. 60.13% of the respondents did not like and favour any female member of their families marrying with a boy of superior caste. Only 30.38% showed favourable attitude with regard to such action, while 9.49% made no clear-cut comment.

Likewise, reaction of the respondents was also tried to be known in case a boy of their family marries to a girl inferior to his caste rank. It was observed that majority of the respondents (57%) did not favour and like it. Only about 32% of the respondents gave their response in favour of this action, whereas about 11% remained undecisive. It is evident that inter-caste marriage may be favoured by the respondents but not with the caste member lower than theirs.

In the same way, responses were also gathered to know the reaction of the respondents in case any female member of their family marries to a boy below her own caste, in other words inferior to her own social status. It was found that the overwhelming majority of the respondents, i.e., 77.85% disfavoured it whereas only 12.03% favoured and 10.13% remained undecided.

On the basis of above facts it may be concluded that the rural Muslims favour the idea of marriage with the persons superior to one's own caste. Thus it shows likeness to inter-caste marriage but only with those who belong to superior caste. Thus a vertical or in some cases horizontal caste mobility is favoured and permitted in the Muslim society. On the other hand marriage with persons inferior to one's own caste is disfavoured and disliked.

During visits to the village for data collection the author learned about two cases of inter-caste marriages held a few years ago. Out of the curiosity to know about their conjugal familial and social life, many questions were asked from them. It was expressed by them that their conjugal life was quite normal and healthy. Both the couples were satisfied with their life partners. They had selected their life partners with their own choice and likeness to each other. They decided to marry each other and conveyed their decision to their respective parents. But the guardians did not accept their proposals and refused to oblige. This they had anticipated so it did not give them shock or frustration from future. The

Nikah ceremony was done in presence of few friends in the city of Patna. This gave shock to the parents and frustrated them severely. Correspondingly, they cut off their relations with the bride and groom. It was known that the shock and reaction of this incidence was felt and practised more by the fathers or male members of the family than the mothers and other female members. The mothers of both the boys gradually started the paving of ways and minimising the tension and reaction. In one case after about 2 years and in another case after about 5 years the problem was subsided and minimised. Thus the couples were accepted sooner or later in both the cases. Hence excepting the beginning of two and five years, respectively in both the two cases, the family life (i.e., joint family) continues to be normal and healthy.

So far as the social life of both the males and females is concerned it is found that some of the villagers still hate them and do not maintain happy and normal relations. It may be due to, as revealed by the two concerned males, the bitterly criticised marriage and propagated dirt against them and their life-partners. Nevertheless they are leading normal conjugal, familial and social life.

A question regarding the decision making process in important family affairs was also asked by the respondents. The data concerning this have been shown in Table 5.20.

Table 5.20

Response regarding Decision making Process in the Family

N=158

Response	*Grand-father/ Father*	*Parents*	*All family members*	*Family members & close kins*	*Only male members of the family*	*Depends on situation*	*Total*
No.	27	26	26	49	19	11	158
%	17.08	16.45	16.45	31.01	12.02	6.96	99.97

The responses tabulated show that decisions on important family matters are taken by different sources. In majority (31.01%) of the cases decisions were taken by family members in consultation with other close kins. In 17.08% of the cases such decisions are taken only by the male head of family, whereas in 16.45% of the cases decisions are taken by parents only, while another 16.45% replied that decisions in their families were taken in consultation with all family members. In 12.02% of the cases the response shows that decision were taken by only male members of the family. Only 6.96% of the respondents replied that it is difficult to express exactly as to who takes and who participates in the process of important family decisions. According to them it depends on the gravity of the situation and availability of good advisers. Thus some of the respondents did not say exactly about the persons responsible for any family decision about an important issue.

On the basis of the aforementioned facts it may be stated that no uniform system of decision making process is present among the villagers. There have been a decentralisation of power of decision in the family. Because in majority of the cases the decision maker is not only the father or male head of the family, though, traditionally in a patriarchal society, the male head of the family used to take every petty or major decision concerning with family affairs. In the present day village life decision on an issue is taken by various means.

C. EDUCATION

Education has been defined in various ways. Plato thought that a good education consists in giving to the body and to the soul all the beauty and all the perfection of which they are capable. Herbert Spencer believed that education has for its object the formation of character. Horace Mann felt that education alone can conduct us to that enjoyment which is, at once, best in quality and infinite in quantity. Thomas Henry Husley thought that education is the instruction of the intellect in the laws of nature under which I include not merely things and their forces, but men and their ways, and the fashioning of the affections and of the will into an earnest and loving desire to move in harmony with these laws.

One of the most famous contemporary views on education is that of John Dewey. He regards education as a reconstruction of experience which gives meaning to our existence and which aids us in the direction of subsequent experience. But Dewey himself realised the inadequacy of his definition because experience is a very broad term of many inferences, almost as broad as the (term) life itself. Experience may be directed, as the experiments of Hitler and Mussolini indicate, through indoctrination as well as through rational training.

This definition implies not merely intellectual growth as a criterion for education, but also emotional maturity and ethical awareness. Thus, education is incomplete without the formation of critical habits. John Dewey is of opinion that the purpose of education is not merely to contribute to the continuity of culture but also to change peacefully and rationally the material foundations of civilization. He further pointed out that education is not the preparation for life, but represents the continuous change of life. To identify education with knowledge derived from books is a rather narrow view, for education often arises in the matrix of practical activity. It implies not merely discipline of thinking, but also a passion for creativity.

The goals of education have differed in various historical periods. In primitive society, education enforced the status quo and became the bastion of tradition, while primitive education was conservative, modern education tends to be progressive and looks to the future rather than to the past.

In modern times there is a great emphasis on the scientific goals of education. Bacon points out that modern education or knowledge means power over nature. It aims at revolutionising the physical world and industrialising the nation. Thorndike tells about modern education that it is based upon psychology and biology, rather than theology.

In general, the Muslim education shows the relationship of freedom and creativity in life. When Muslim rulers like Haroon Rasheed encouraged freedom of expression, the arts and science flourished.

Education and Islam

Islam has greatly emphasized the acquisition of learning and education. It inaugurated the era of intellectual liberty, for the strong injunction of the Prophet that "the acquisition of knowledge is incumbent on every Muslim, created a universal desire among his followers for the same and within his lifetime was formed the nucleus of an educational institution."[1]

One Tradition declares, "Men of letters cannot be equated with those without learning and education. Likewise in another tradition distinction between 'Ilm' (knowledge) and 'jehl' (ignorance) has been presented which says, "Ilm is life and jehl is death."[2]

The Prophet is reported to have said—

"To seek knowledge is duty for every Muslim man and woman."

"Seek knowledge though if it is in China."[3]

Prophet recommended his young companions to study under non-Muslims of Medina. The second Caliph appointed a number of learned men to lecture in mosques on Islam. Hazrat Ali advocated for Ilm and condemned the 'Jehl' declaring that it is never proportionate, balanced and just. It

1. Ali, Amir, The Spirit of Islam, S.K. Lahiri & Co., Calcutta, 1902, p. 32.
2. Naqi, Maulana Syed Ali, Islam ki Hakimana Zindagi (Urdu), Neaz Publisher, Lucknow, 1932, p. 57.
3. Ibid.

either leads to exceeding the just limit or it results in checking from reaching the just limit."[4]

From the time of Prophet to the medieval period education beyond the primary level in the Islamic world was largely in the hands of theologians, jurists, philosophers or mystics. There was no organised and formal system of education as we find in the modern age. Further, education was confined mainly to the ruling elites and wealthy families. They could afford to make special arrangements for tutors at their houses or send their wards to the maktab situated at a neighbour's house or at the mosque, as per their convenience. After completing the elementary course at maktab (the) students were sent to the Madrasa for lesson (if they desired so) under recognised alims and scholars in subjects, viz., language, grammar, literature, rhetoric, the holy scriptures of Qur'an, tradition, jurisprudence, logic, philosophy, etc. A Khanqah or hospice of the mystic was also a centre of education.

When a boy was of four (years), four months, and four days, there began the 'Bismillah' ceremony. For this student (Talib-e-Ilm) was taken to a moulvi or alim or any saint who wrote on a white sheet of paper or on the board 'Bismillah' and then 'Alif', 'Be', 'Te', 'Se', 'Jim' and the boy was made to utter Bismillahir-Rahmanir-Rahim first, and then made also to repeat it. Thereafter the teacher prayed to God to make the boy a learned man. Cakes and sweets were distributed among people present there in the ceremony. Hazrat Nizamuddin Auliya and Hazrat Sharfuddin Yahya Maneri were approached to bless the boy by imparting the first instruction."[5]

Scholars from India or abroad were largely patronised by the Sultans or rulers of the time. Specialists taught either a single subject or only a book. After the completion of a course the ceremony of conferring academic distinction called Dastarbandi was held. The teacher, after a light refreshment or dinner, used to tie the dastar (turban) round the

4. Ali, Hazrat, Nahj-al-Balaghah (Urdu), Ahbab Publication, Lucknow, 1970, p. 912.
5. Rashid, A., Society and Culture in Medieval India, Firma K.L. Mukhopadhyay, Calcutta, pp. 150-51.

head of his pupil in gathering. Likewise the Sanad-e-Fazilat (degree of excellence or efficiency) was given to a student after he had attained perfection in a particular branch of knowledge of his choice.

The motive (of those students) of the recipient of education was not the achievement of a status in society, or of becoming a Qazi but of developing saintly habits and controlling one's carnal desires. Removal of illiteracy and advancement of knowledge were also the aims of education. While a good number of them acquired education for qualifying in the state service, but by and large this attitude was condemned by saintly people and was not favoured by the upper class.

Teachers and institutions were often patronised and subsidised by the state. Both the teachers and the students received stipends and rewards from kings and aristocracies. But these grants were not sufficient to meet their needs. Thus teachers and their pupils as a whole remained in economic hardship. Excepting (the) students from well-to-do families, others had to look after themselves and to do (their) work with their teachers. Those who were enthusiastically eager for education maintained themselves on their earnings. Many saintly scholars preferred to lead a simple and an austere life and refused to accept gifts or aid from the rulers and aristocracies, because (they were) of too much self-consciousness.

Obedience to and respect for the teachers were the ruling principles of the Muslim students. Good character and good behaviour on the part of the students was necessary, and insisted upon. The teacher gave due weight to the question of character and culture of those receiving lessons from them and they saw to it that their students were well-disciplined and attentive to their main duty which was the acquisition and advancement of knowledge.

Shukla says, "In all over Northern India the maktab, most often associated with the mosque, gave Muslim boys their first acquaintance with the Holy word and also some rudimentary literacy. Domestic instruction by the Maulvi Saheb arranged by men of substance for their own children where some children of more modest circumstances might also participate was also prevalent on a considerable scale."[6]

Downfall of the Mughal empire and the rise of British rule awakened the Muslim elite. Their political subjugation made them conscious of the future of their religion, culture and education, because (the) experience shows that every ruling group tries its best to suppress (the) non-ruling groups politically and amalgamate them religiously and socially by crushing their cultural and social institutions. In order to protect their identity Indian Muslims thought it best to spread mass education, But the Muslim intelligentsia could not decide unanimously on the form and content of education. Two main viewpoints emerged—one argued for the religious education (traditional religious education) and the other favoured a secular and modern education of the Western model. The protagonist of the former set up Darul Uloom, Deoband and the latter founded the Muslim University at Aligarh. Difference in the mode of thinking not only gave way to a different line of action but also created a gulf between the two groups which hampered the growth of Muslim education.

The Khilafat movement of 1920 played an important role in uniting the Indian Muslims. Muslims from all walks of life and of varied ideologies assembled (together) and gave a second thought and adopted a moderate educational policy. Two more universities developed making the total number of Muslim centres of education four: Muslim University, Aligarh as a secular seat of learning tending to modernity, University of Darul Uloom, Deoband as a purely religious one, University of Nadwat-ul-Ulema, Lucknow as more a religious and less a worldly teaching centre, and lastly Jamia Millia Islamia, Delhi as more a worldly and less a religious institution. Referring to this fact Aziz Ahmad mentioned three main ideological currents working among Indian Muslims of the British age which had their origin in the schools of Deoband, Nadwa and Aligarh.

6. Shukla, S., Indian Muslims and Education, in Muslims in India (ed.), Zafar Imam, Orient Longman, New Delhi, p. 209.

The rise of Muslim awakening and development of educational consciousness among them was caused mainly by the movement launched by Sir Syed Ahmed Khan (in the second half of 19th century) and Sir Mohammed Iqbal (the philosopher poet in the first half of the 20th century). The above two personalities brought about educational renaissance among Indian Muslims.

The Aligarh movement launched by Sir Syed Ahmad Khan and his associates produced a deep impact on the system of education. It was mainly concerned with the development of a rational outlook in respect of western education and creating a taste in Muslims for modern scientific education synthesized with Islamic culture. This movement was a watershed in the history of modern education of Indian Muslims which attracted a large number of Muslim youths from all corners and all sections of India. Illustrating this fact Shukla writes, "The gradual development of M.A.O. College at Aligarh into a major educational centre for Muslims in the country and its growth into a University constitutes an important element in the history of Muslim education. The Mohammadan educational conference and its annual sessions from 1898 owards along with occasional sessions of provincial conference propagated the idea of a Muslim University which fructified in 1920."[7]

During the days of ideological conflicts Iqbal appeared with his philosophy of education. He realized the importance of modern scientific education, but at the same time he was confident that Islamic ideals were essential for a Muslim to build his character and to preserve his ego. Thus his philosophy presented a fusion of Islam and modernism, in presenting a system of education and he tried to fuse science with religion. Education should be thoroughly imbued with the religious spirit. But (his) religion does not refer to orthodoxy and dogma. Such a synthetic educational philosophy of Iqbal made a profound impact on Muslims in general and a trend for Western education set in.

But even all these could not accelerate the growth of

7. Ibid.

general education among Muslim youths of the first three or four decades of the 20th century. This resulted in the educational bankruptcy of the Muslim masses. Mass upsurge against British colonialism, Quit India Movement, independence but partition of the country and last but not the least the abolition of zamindari badly affected the momentum of the spread of education among Muslim youth. Discussing the educational problem of Muslims Abid Husain writes, "As far the backwardness in general higher education which existed among the Muslims even before the partition of India, and has now been aggravated to a deplorable extent, it spells danger not only to their economic but also to their cultural, moral and spiritual life. In this critical period, when the Muslim mind is lost in the maze of contradictory values of culture and morality and conflicting theories of social and political organization, the community has an acute need for higher education."[8]

Similarly, Muslims also lag behind in technical and job-oriented education. The handicraft and cottage industries formerly monopolised by Muslim artisans, craftsmen and technicians are now going into the hands of non-Muslims because of the lack of scientific and technical education, as well as adverse psycho-social and politico-economic conditions. Abid Husain writes, "What is most unfortunate is that Muslim young men are averse to technical education which requires a great deal of hard work and application. Until recently workers in various handicrafts did not require any formal education but learned their trade in the traditional ways through practical work apprentices and became expert craftsmen. Many handicrafts for which great skill is needed were the (special) preserve of the Muslims. But since training in the various crafts has started on scientific lines and requires a certain standard of general education, the Muslims are being driven out from this field also from the artisan class, which has not had even elementary eduction for generations, it is useless to expect that they would send their children first

8. Husain, S. Abid, The Destiny of Indian Muslims, Asia Publishing House, Bombay, 1965. p. 230.

for general and then for technical education and in educated families which specialize in Government service, even those belonging to lower-middle class, generally consider all manual work below their dignity and do not want to give any technical training to their children, regardless of the fact that they may in future have to be condemned to unemployment or even to beggary. Some attention is being paid to higher technical education by the educated class Muslims."[9]

While discussing the causes of the present state of education among Muslims, Shukla makes responsible to two main factors as migrating of a large number of educated elite to Pakistan and continued communal hatred. He writes, "Migration of the educated elite in the Muslim community to Pakistan soon after partition had reduced the percentage of education in the community considerably....However, when after about twenty years the after-effects of partition were just about to be forgotten and a new spirit of enterprise in education as well as other spheres was just emerging, Hindu communal chauvinists launched their counter attack. This was evidenced in the slogans of Indianization and a spate of violent communal incidents organised against the Muslims with a view to eliminating economic, political or other social leadership among them."[10] These facts reveal that from the lack partly of desires and partly of recourses Muslims are lagging behind in elementary and higher technical education. Aversion to technical education based on snobbish prejudice should be discarded by all the Muslims. Abid Husain suggests, "To remove this the organised campaign, such as Sir Syed had started to break the spell of the so-called religious prejudice of Muslims against English education, is required."[11] He is also of (the) opinion that a check on the development of materialism resulting from purely technical education should be made by introducing moral values among the students.

9. Ibid., pp. 230-31.
10. Shukla, S., Indian Muslims and Education, In Muslims in India (ed.), Zafar Imam, Orient Longman Ltd., New Delhi, 1975, p. 212.
11. Husain, S. Abid, The Destiny of Indian Muslims, Asia Publishing House, Bombay, 1965, pp. 230-31.

Likewise, the backwardness in general higher education among Muslim youth spells danger to their economic, cultural, moral and spiritual life. Thus in this critical period the community has an acute need for higher education. Since without higher education Indian Muslims cannot tackle the difficult task on which depends not only their progress but their very existence.

Two severe blows, the partition and the abolition of zamindari system, awakened the Muslims from sweet slumber. But the decisions to be made were not easy because problems were numerous and complicated, situation was critical and the path was full of thorns and was hazy. Anyway, a process of regeneration started in this half-dead community and interest in education developed. Every section of the community now fully realises the importance of education, appreciates the acquisition of knowledge and tries to send their children to the academic institutions to receive knowledge as per their interest and ability. But it should be clear from the present day observations and experiences that the acquisition of knowledge is not for the sake of knowledge among present day Muslims. Its ultimate aim remains to get an employment and earn money. Thus Muslim education is job-oriented—whether technical or non-technical. They support the idea of doing business but they are found attached to the small and petty business due to lack of finance. They are rapidly being detached from the agricultural land because it requires serious physical labour and large monetary input which they cannot afford. Thus there is no way out for Muslims except gaining education in order to survive as a living community. Now the maktab and madrasa education is being replaced fast by Hindi or English medium schools and colleges because of a craze for secular rather than traditional education. A fundamental cause of this switch-over is a desire and necessity for a quick and a better economic place in the society. Referring to this fact Amir Ali states, "There is no demand now for Arabic or Persian education. A strong desire has grown up among all sections of the Mohammadan community for the study of the English language and literature."[12]

Likewise, Yusuf Ali's view also resembles very much to that of Amir Ali. According to him, "It may be said generally for the whole of India that 95 per cent of the students of this generation receive an education, even if it is not in English, of a kind wholly different from traditional education of a century ago."[13]

It appears from these observations that in present day education western influences are more positive. Students are preferring to be admitted in the institutions imparting modern education. Even the old institutions have tended slightly in the direction of modernization of its courses of studies.

Rural India has been educationally backward since long and the percentage of literacy in rural areas has been very low. The condition of literacy has been more pathetic especially in case of the female section living in the rural areas. After independence much attention has been paid to improve the condition of literacy in general and female education in particular. For this purpose various steps have been taken by the Government to provide facilities for female education. Girls schools and colleges have been established in a large number for educating the girls of those families in particular where co-education is not favoured. In case of Muslim community female education has been more difficult due to the institution of purdah sanctioned by Islam. The Muslim families observing and favouring purdah do not allow the young girls to go to the educational institutions and hence the Muslim girls are relatively more backward from educational point of view. In purdah observing families the young girls go out only with some elderly guardian and they are not allowed to move alone. This factor stands in the way of sending girls to educational institutions. But with

12. Ali, Amir, Muhammedan Education, History of Education in Bihar (ed.), Rai Bahadur Bhagwati Sahay, Bhagalpur University Press Ltd., Bhagalpur, 1928, p. 300.
13. Ali, Yusuf A., Muslim Culture and Religious Thoughts in Modern India and the West, in Philosophy of Education (ed.), L.S.S. O'Malley, Calcutta, 1941, p. 410.

the impact of various modern factors, a process of liberalisation of purdah has started and it has helped in changing the attitude towards female education. Even in village areas the traditional attitude does not exist in respect of educating girls. This change in attitude is not uniform in all village areas and there are differences in the degree of change in attitude and actual practice.

A few questions were put to the respondents regarding female education in particular and education in general. The first question put to respondents was, "Are you in favour of educating girls?" The responses obtained from the respondents are presented in Table 5.21.

Table 5.21

Attitude towards Female Education

N=158

Response	*Number*	*Percentage*
Favourable	102	64.56
Unfavourable	43	27.22
Undecided	13	8.22
Total	158	100 00

It appears from the above table that 64.56% of the respondents are in favour of educating girls. Only 27.22% are opposed to it and 8.22% are neither in favour nor against female education. Hence it may be interpreted that there is a significant change in the attitude towards female education and the majority favours the idea of educating girls.

Table 5.22 shows the distribution of the responses given in Table 5.21 on the basis of age.

It is evident from the table that age factor is significantly relevant to the variation in the response patterns. 100% of the respondants in the youngest age group of 20 to 30 years favour girls education. The percentage of response favouring girls education has consistently declined

Table 5.22

Age and Attitude towards Female Education

N=158

Age Group	*Favourable*		*Unfavourable*		*Undecided*	
	No.	*%*	*No.*	*%*	*No.*	*%*
20-30 yrs.	20	100.00	—	—	—	—
31-40 yrs.	22	84 61	2	7 69	2	7.69
41-50 yrs.	30	62.50	15	31.25	3	6.25
51+	30	46.87	26	40.62	8	12.25
Total	102		43		13	

with the rise in age. In the eldest age group of 51 years and above less than 50% of the respondents (46.87%) have favoured girls education. In all other age groups the majority has favoured girls education. But at the same time it is important to point out that even in the eldest age group the percentage of favour for girls education is higher than the percentage of negative response. On the basis of these findings it may be interpreted that younger generation is more rational and liberal than the older generations. Thus the dominance of tradition is gradually weakening with the passing of time and the new generation does not appear to be tradition-oriented in this regard.

Table 5.23 presents the classification of the same responses on literacy basis.

Table 5.23

Education and Attitude towards Female Education

N=158

Educational Category	*Favourable*		*Unfavourable*		*Undecided*	
	No.	*%*	*No.*	*%*	*No.*	*%*
Illiterate	24	57.14	14	33.33	4	9.52
Below Matric	42	53.16	29	36.70	8	10.12
Below Graduate	24	96.00	—	—	1	4.00
Graduate+	12	100.00	—	—	—	—

It is evident from the table that 100% of graduates and above, 96% of matriculates and above, 53.16% of below matriculates and 57.14% of the illiterates have favoured girls education. In case the percentage of response in the illiterate category is not considered. it can be interpreted that there is a consistent variation between the level of literacy and attitude towards girls education. Those who are more qualified are rational and the percentage of favour for girls education has risen with the rise in literacy level. It is also important to point out that in case of matriculates and above as well as graduates and above no respondent has opposed girls education. Hence it may be interpreted that education has rationalised the attitude of the people.

The next question put to the respondents was, "Are you in favour of co-education?" The responses collected from them are presented in Table 5.24.

Table 5.24

Responses showing Attitude towards Co-education

N=158

Response	*Number*	*Percentage*
Favourable	30	18.98
Unfavourable	112	70.88
Undecided	16	10.14
Total	158	

It is obvious from the table that majority of 70.88% is opposed to co-education and only a smaller section of 18.98% has favoured it. It means that most of the people favouring girls education do not favour educating boys and girls together in the same institution, rather they want separate institution for boys and girls. In other words, they are still dominated by the idea of seclusion of women.

Table 5.25 presents classification of the same responses on age basis.

It is evident from the table that in no case the majority is in favour of co-education. In all the age groups the majority

Table 5.25

Age and Attitude towards Co-education
N=158

Age Group	*Favourable*		*Unfavourable*		*Undecided*	
	No.	%	*No.*	%	*No.*	%
20-30 yrs.	6	30.00	11	55.00	3	15.00
31-40 yrs.	8	30.76	14	53.84	4	15.38
41-50 yrs.	10	20.83	31	64.58	7	14.58
51+	6	9.37	56	87.50	2	3.12
Total	30		112		16	

is opposed to co-education. The table further shows that the percentage of favour for co-education is slightly higher in the two younger age groups (30.00% and 30.76%) whereas it is considerably lower in the two elderly age groups (20.83% and 9.37%). It shows that the elderly age groups are more conservative than the younger generation; but in all cases the idea of educating boys and girls together is opposed by the majority.

Table 5.26 presents the classification of responses showing attitude towards co-education on literacy basis.

Table 5.26

Education and Attitude towards Co-education
N=158

Educational Category	*Favourable*		*Unfavourable*		*Undecided*	
	No.	%	*No.*	%	*No.*	%
Illiterate	—	—	42	100.00	—	—
Below Matric	8	10.12	60	75.94	11	13.92
Matric and above	12	48.00	9	36.00	4	16.00
Graduate+	10	88.33	1	8.33	1	8.33
Total	30		112		16	

It is evident from the table that no respondent in the illiterate group has favoured the idea of co-education. The percentage of favour for co-education has consistently increased with the rise in literacy level. Only in case of graduates the majority of 88.33% has favoured co-education. It shows that only in the highly qualified group the separation of boys and girls in educational institution is not essential. These response patterns clearly show the relevance of literacy level to attitude towards co-education and it may be interpreted that the factor of education has liberalized the attitude towards educating boys and girls in the same institution.

D. PURDAH

In Islam there exists a conspicuous concern for feminine modesty, both in matters of dress and demeanour. Such feminine veiling and seclusion are referred to as 'purdah' taken from the Persian literature. Modesty, decorum and chastity were emphasized in the Qur'an. A Muslim woman may wear whatever she pleases in the presence of her husband or among women friends. But when she goes out or when men other than her husband or close family are present she is expected to wear a dress which will cover all parts of her body, and which should not reveal the figure. Thus women were advised not to display their beauty. It was thought proper to keep women away from the gaze of outsiders. Among Indian Muslims, burqa has been common device for keeping women away from the gaze of male persons. Jacobson observed, "The concept of modesty (sharm) is central to the ideology of purdah as well as to all other rules governing women's dress and behaviour."[1] Shushtery writes, Purdah

1. Jacobson, Doranne, The Veil of Virtue: Purdah and the Muslim Family in the Bhopal Region of Central India, in Imtiaz Ahmad (ed.), Family Kinship and Marriage among Muslims in India, Manohar Book Service, New Delhi, 1976, p. 187.

has got a religious sanction in Muslim society.[2] The Prophet denounced such mode of behaviour and commanded that men and women must cover bodies, while offering prayer at Kaaba.

The revelant verse of Qur'an says, "O Prophet, tell your wives and daughters and the women of the believers to draw upon them their over-garments. That is more appropriate so that they may be recognized and not molested."[3] Women were also asked to cast down their eyes and guard their chastity and not to display their ornaments except those that were too apparent (such as on their hands and feet). God says, "Tell believers to avert their glances and to guard their private parts; that is purer for them. God is informed about anything they do. Tell believing women to avert their glances and guard their private parts and not to display their charms except what (normally) appears of them. They should draw their coverings over their bosom and not show their charms except to their husbands."[4] These facts clearly show that the practice of purdah has Islamic sanction. But it does not mean that no such system was found before the emergence of Islam. Saleema Noordeen says, "It is a mistake to consider the custom of seclusion of women to be an Islamic innovation. The ancient Greeks and Roman kept their women-folk separate from men."[5] Saiyed also writes, "Most major religions of the world have taken a keen interest in the position of women, and made various pronouncements concerning them."[6]

2. Shushtery, A.M.A., Outlines of Islamic Culture, Bangalore Publishing Co. Pvt. Ltd., Bangalore, 1937, p. 573.
3. The Qur'an, s. 33, v. 59.
4. The Qur'an, I. 24, v. 30-31.
5. Noordeen, Saleema, Purdah No Bar to Progress, The Muslims Review, V. XII, No. 5, Lucknow, 1933, p. 9.
6. Saiyed, A.R., Purdah, Family Structure and the Status of Woman: A Note on a Deviant Case, in Imtiaz Ahmad (ed.), Family Kinship and Marriage Among Muslims in India, p. 241.

Thus purdah was not quite unknown to the pre-Islamic people or in the ancient period. It was, however, chiefly confined to the aristocratic families. It becomes quite clear, when Jacobson writes that purdah or purdah-like behaviour is not restricted to Muslim women. She writes, "There is evidence that women were veiled and secluded among various pre-Islamic Mediterranean, Arab and Persian people, and in recent centuries many Hindus, Christians, Buddhists and other women of various regions of the globe have traditionally followed practices that closely resemble Muslim purdah observances."[7]

But Pandit Gauri Shanker Ojha argues that the purdah system started in India after the arrival of Muslims. He says, "At the time under review there was no purdah system, and the women of the royal household attended the court. The dramas of the time reveal no trace of purdah. The Arab traveller, Abu Zaid, states that women used to appear before Indians and foreigners, and accompanied their men-folks in social gatherings and amusements. The Kama Sutra mentions that women served in the army, and accompanied the Rajhas in their darbars, campaigns, pleasure parties, etc. It was after the advent of Muslims that purdah system was established in India. As the Musalmans became predominant in Northern India, the system of purdah and veil (ghunghat) spread rapidly. Where the influence of the Musalman was less, the purdah veils were not so well established."[8]

Similar remark has been made by Jawahar Lal Nehru. He opines that purdah seems to have grown in India during Moghal period when the upper classes of both Hindus and Muslims made it a status symbol and practised it in different

7. Jacobson, Doranne, The Veil of Virtue: Purdah and the Muslim Family in the Bhopal Region of Central India, in Imtiaz Ahmad (ed.), Family Kinship and Marriage among Muslims in India, Manohar Book Service, New Delhi, 1976, p. 171.
8. Ojha, Pandit Gauri Shanker, History of Medieval Civilization, in M. Habeeb (ed.), Indian Culture and Social Life at the time of the Turkish Invasion, Journal of the Aligarh Historical Research Institute, 1941, pp. 109-10.

parts of India."[9]

It is difficult to believe that the institution of purdah was unknown before the Muslims. Isolated instances may be cited in all the ages. Some form of veil was also prevalent among Hindu women. There was segregation of sex varying from community to community. It might be possible that the Muslims introduced certain rigidity in it. The underlying idea of keeping the damsels segregated was to avoid contact with men of opposite sex lest they should bring disgrace to the family. The common women-folk did not lead a secluded life. Many of them had to help their husbands in cultivation. They had to draw water from the well, went to the river for bath, collected cow-dung for making cakes for fuel, and such other household works compelled them to go out of their house. So they could not afford to remain indoors and their innate modesty would not allow them to gaze at strangers. Ashraf rightly says, "They moved the lapel of their sari or other head-dress slightly over their faces when they passed by a stranger."[10]

The advent of Islam made this system more strict and gave a divine sanction. Qur'anic proscriptions and Prophet's Tradition recommended some limitation to feminine activity and dress related to the observance of purdah by Muslim women. Qur'an emphasizes on chastity and modesty, proscribe illegitimate sexual affairs (zena) and prescribed punishment for such offence. The following verses throw light on the Islamic sanctions about purdah:

"O Ye who believe; enter not houses other than your own without first announcing your presence . . . . "

"Tell the believing men to lower their gaze and be modest. That is purer for them. Allah is aware of what they do."

"And tell the believing women to lower their gaze and be modest, and not to display their ornaments except that

9. Nehru, Pt. J.L., The Discovery of India, Signet Press, Calcutta, Sixth Edition, 1956, p. 197.

10. Ashraf, K.M., Life and Conditions of the People of Hindustan, Munshiram Manohar Lal, New Delhi, 1970, p. 139.

which is apparent, and draw their veils over their bosoms, and not to reveal their adornment save to their own husbands, or father, or husband's fathers, or their sons, or their husband's sons, or their brothers, or their brother's sons, or sisters sons, or their women, or their slaves, or male attendants who lack vigour, or children who know naught of women's nakedness. And then not stamp their feet so as to reveal what they hide of their adornment."[11]

A thorough study of the above-quoted verses shows that Islam has used the term purdah in a very broad sense. Thus the purdah is not a system of veil, burqa or ghunghat, rather it is more than this. This is why it is not simply ordained that private parts of the body should be covered, it also cautions against all such activities which are responsible for exciting sexual feelings and desires and so involves purdah of sight or gaze (hejab) too. It suggests that no part of a woman should remain uncovered excepting the face and the hands for prayers. But Islam permitted women to show any part of the body to the attending physician if needed. Islam likes the women to be simple, modest and selective in talking, meeting and behaving with others. Beautification and decoration of the body with ornaments, etc. is not discouraged, rather its open exhibition is prohibited.

Bafi has summarized the religious sanctions of purdah in the following ways:

1. To cover the whole body excepting the parts allowed to be exposed (face and portion of hands below the wrist).
2. To observe purdah in such a manner which might not become an adornment in itself.
3. Not to use thin and transparent garments (exposing nudity).
4. Not to use tight garments.
5. Not to use scented garments.

11. The Qur'an, S. XXIV, v. 30-31.

6. Not to use male garments.
7. Not to use garments similar to those of a kafir.
8. Not to use fashionable garments.[12]

The genesis and growth of purdah system reveal that there has been changes in the values and practices of purdah system in different periods of the history of Islam. The form in which it was present during Caliphate period could not remain the same in the medieval age. It grew from flexibility to rigidity and from liberality to orthodoxy with the passage of time. The present state of purdah and reaction against it in the modern age is the manifestation of its impracticability due to its rigidity and orthodoxy. This is why Muslim women at some places do not use it and at some places use it in a modified form."[13]

In traditional Indian society the planning of house construction was done keeping in view the need of keeping the women in seclusion. Referring to this Jacobson observed, "Proper observation of purdah requires certain architectural features, such as, wall in courtyard, private latrines."[14]

Such house designing having separate apartment for women also existed in the Muslim community of Bihar. This becomes evident from the observations made by Zeyauddin Ahmad. He says, "The ladies, particularly of high caste and economically well of Muslims, live in seclusion, i.e, in a section of house exclusively meant for them."[15]

12 Nasiruddin-al-Bafi, Mohammed, Islam Aur Asre Jadid (Urdu Journal), January 1973, Vol 5, No. 1, pp 43-44.

13. Dube, Leela, with Abdul Rahman Kutty, Matriliny and Islam: Religion and Society in the Laccadives, University of Saugar Monograph in Anthropology and Sociology, National Publishing House, Delhi, 1969, p. 24.

14. Jacobson, Doranne, The Veil of Virtue: Purdah and the Muslim Family in the Bhopal Region of Central India, in Imtiaz Ahmad (ed.), Family Kinship and Marriage among Muslims in India., Manohar Book Service, New Delhi, 1976, p. 189.

15. Ahmad, Zeyauddin. Marriage and Family among the Muslims of Bihar, in George Kurian (ed.), The Family in India—A Regional Review, Monton, Paris, 1974, p. 329.

But so far as the present day Muslim society in India is concerned, we find a great deal of relaxation in the observances of purdah. The ideal of purdah could not remain in practice in modern age as it was practised in the traditional society due to various factors at work. It has got a decreasing trend due to a number of factors such as modern education, eeonomic pursuit and the forces of modernization, etc. Raza is also of the opinion, "The outbreak of the first world war, nationalist movement started by Indian National Congress, spread of female education in particular and of education in general, growing contact with western culture, industrialization and urbanization and recently the setting up of the parliamentary system of democracy produced impacts on the attitudes and values of Indian Muslims also. The outlook changed and consequently sanctions and values gave way to rational approaches."[16]

The findings of different studies conducted so far in the South Asian countries of India, Pakistan, Bangladesh and Ceylon, etc., give us ample evidences of the declining trend of purdah system in the Muslim society. Ahmad, while discussing this aspect in the context of Bihar, writes, "Today with the abolition of zamindari system and spread of education among Muslim ladies, purdah system is fast vanishing."[17] Likewise, Raza is also of the opinion that present day Muslims of Bihar are discarding purdah. He says, "The existing trend seems to be different from ideal as well as traditional concept oi purdah and it violates the fundamental principle of purdah of sight and purdah of voice and movement."[18]

In the context of the observance of purdah in the district of Gaya, where this study has been made, Choudhry observes that purdah is being slowly discarded by the Muslims of the

16. Raza, S. Musi, Changing Pattern of Muslim Community in Bihar, unpublished Ph D. Thesis, Patna University, 1976, pp. 167-68.
17. Ahmad, Zeyauddin, Marriage and Family among the Muslims of Bihar, in George Kurian (ed.), The Family in India– A Regional View. Monton, Paris, 1974, p. 329.
18. Raza, S. Musi, Changing Pattern of. . . , p. 168.

district.[19] Likewise, Bhattacharya and Misra also support this viewpoint. The Committee on the Status of Women in India also finds that this custom is decreasing.

Thus the findings of different studies reveal that at almost all places there is a change in the custom and values of purdah.

In the village under study, which may be perhaps true for all the Muslim areas, females of different age groups wear several types of dresses. Girls above the age of seven or eight wear cloth covering them from shoulder to ankle, even in the hottest weather. Most unmarried girls wear shalwar, jumper and a dupatta over the head and bosom, although sometimes they wear saris also. Other common Muslim costumes are the gharara and sharara accompanied by a long dupatta. They generally keep their head and bosom covered with the dupatta or sari in the presence of the elders and males, and in public without fail. At the time of prayer women show modesty through demeanour as well as dress. It is expected from women to have their head covered and eyes downcast when they pass through men in the lanes or go out of their houses. Talking loudly and roaming widely is commented on, while flirting is known to be a most disliked activity. Women in the villages generally visit other's places after the sunset. Whenever they have to go out during day they put burqa (if the place to be visited is at some distance and the possibility is that others will see her) some member of the family must accompany her.

Findings

Purdah is an important institution in Muslim society. It is not only a social concept or a customary practice rather it is obligatory by religion for every adult female. The Qur'anic verses and Prophet's Tradition have time and again emphasized the observance of purdah by the believers. According to religious sanctions, observance of purdah is essential for

19. Chaudhry, P.C. Roy, District Gazetteer of Gaya, Patna, 1957, p. 166.

protecting the chastity of women and for putting a check on illegitimate sex relations and sex corruption. In the early days of Islam purdah was strictly observed in Muslim society. But the observance of purdah simply meant the seclusion of women from men, but it never meant the complete confinement of women to the four walls of the house. In fact the spirit of purdah carries the spirit of 'hejab', which simply demands a distinction between the two sexes and aims at putting a check of free mixing between male and female. The Islamic scholars have differed in respect of observing the extent of purdah. According to one section, the face and hands of the women may remain uncovered; whereas according to another section the face and hands should also be covered along with the other parts of the body.

The observance of purdah did not continue to exist in the same form throughout the history of Muslim society. It has been changing from age to age and from one region to another. Loval conditions of the regions and areas also influence the Muslim society in different respect including the observance of purdah. In the same way with the passing of time the changes took place in the attitudes, outlooks and approaches and consequently the patterns of purdah observance did not remain unchanged. In the early days of Islamic movement purdah was observed according to the sanctions of Sharia but gradually the traditional values and customary usages prevailed upon the religious sanctions and modification took place in the practice of purdah observance. In the traditional Indian Muslim societies purdah was extremely rigid. There was complete seclusion of women from the world outside. The extreme limit may be realised from this fact that alongwith the purdah of faces and body the notions of purdah of gaze and voice was also observed in the traditional society. Outside movements of women was rare phenomenon and only on important occasions like marriage, birth, death and illness in any of the families of relatives, the women could move completely veiled. The rules of purdah were relatively more rigid for unmarried and young married women than old women. This observance of purdaht was generally found in the Ashraf section of the Muslim society. The women of Atraf or Ajlaf section did not observe this purdah and they also moved outside for earning their livelihood either as domestic maid servant or as a wage earner or labourer in the agricultural field. In the Indian rural society the traces of this traditional purdah are still found, though a changing trend has developed with the spread of literacy and education, movement for the emancipation of women, impact of industrialisation and urbanisation and other related reformative movement in the Indian society.

Keeping this fact in view certain questions were put to the respondents of the village under study to collect information regarding the observance of purdah in the village. The first question put to the respondents was, "Do the females in your family observe purdah ? Hundred per cent of 158 respondents replied in affirmative and declared that the female members of their families observe purdah. Hence there was no use of framing table in respect of this response pattern showing no variation.

The next question put to the respondents was, "Which type of purdah is practised in your family ? To facilitate the respondents, three alternative response categories were also provided. The response categories were strictly traditional, religious and liberal. The respondents were asked to check either of the response categories for indicating the nature of purdah observed in their families. The responses collected from 158 respondents are presented in Table 5.27

It appears from the table that, on the whole, in 15.19% of the families of the respondents, the purdah is strictly traditional and in 26.59% of the families the religious purdah is observed, whereas in 58.22% of the cases liberal purdah is being observed. These findings clearly suggest that the majority of the families in the Muslim village observes liberal purdah. The lowest percentage has gone in favour of strictly traditional purdah. Hence it may be interpreted that traditional ties are gradually weakening in the village and a liberal outlook is emerging as the dominant outlook in respect of purdah observance. Thus a process of rationalisation of purdah observance has started in the village and most of the families observe neither strictly traditional nor religious, but

Table 5.27

Types of Purdah used by the Women in the Village

N=158

Type of Purdah	*Number*	*Percentage*
Strictly traditional	24	15.19
Religious	42	26.59
Liberal	92	58.22
Total	158	100.00

religious purdah. It may be due to the spread of literacy and education in village in general and in female section in particular. Moreover, contact with the urban life of the villages may be helpful in the development of a rational outlook. A higher degree of exposure to media of mas communication like radio and newspapers may also be an underlying force in the rationalisation of outlook. Moreover, the frequent visits to the shrines, dargahs, khanqahs situated outside the villages at distant places in different cities like Patna, Gaya, Biharshariff, Delhi, Ajmer, etc. by the villagers (both males and females) may also be instrumental in changing the outlook, because their trips are not exclusively holy visits but also partly pleasure trips providing opportunities to enjoy films, to see important places and buildings in the cities and to go to markets for shopping. Hence this movement outside the village facilitates a change in the outlook. This may be the reason for the dominant liberal outlook regarding purdah observances.

The same responses have been classified and tabulated in Table 5.28 on the basis of education.

This table presents the classification of responses on literacy basis. It is found from the table that in all four categories of the respondents the higher percentages of response have gone in favour of liberal purdah and the lowest

Table 5.28
Education and Observance of Purdah
N= 158

Educational Qualification	*Strictly traditional*		*Religious*		*Liberal*	
	No.	%	*No.*	%	*No.*	%
Illiterate	6	14.28	10	23.80	26	61.90
Below Matric	9	11.39	20	25.31	50	63.29
Matric & above	6	24.00	8	32.00	11	44.00
Graduation & above	3	25.00	4	33.30	5	41.66
Total	24	15.18	42	26.58	92	58.22

percentage of response in favour of strictly traditional purdah. On the basis of it one can interpret that the patterns of purdah observance in all the categories appear to be alike. Excepting this fact that in the two higher categories of educated respondents the percentage of response in respect of liberal purdah (44% and 41.66%) are lower than the corresponding percentages in the categories of below matric and illiterate (63.29% and 61.90). On the other hand, the percentage of response showing strictly traditional as well as religious purdah are higher in the categories of matriculates and above and graduate and above than in the categories of below matriculate and illiterate. It means that educated persons are more conservative and tradition-oriented than literates and illiterates. It shows an inverse relation between the level of literacy and the degree of liberalism.

The data collected about the nature and types of purdah used in the village (Table 5.27) have been classified and tabulated in Table 5.29 on the basis of caste.

This table presents the classification of responses on caste basis. It is found from the table that in both upper and lower caste categories the highest percentage of response (56.92% and 64.28%) has gone in favour of liberal

Table 5.29

Caste and Observance of Purdah

N=158

Caste Category	*Strictly traditional*		*Religious*		*Liberal*	
	No.	%	*No.*	%	*No.*	%
Upper Caste	20	15.38	36	27.69	74	56.92
Lower Caste	4	14.28	6	21.42	18	64.28
Total	24		42		92	

purdah and the lowest percentages of response (15.38% and 14.28% respectively) in favour of strictly traditional purdah. It means that a higher percentage of lower caste is observing liberal purdah, whereas strictly traditional as well as religious purdah is observed by higher percentage of upper castes. These findings do not suggest that the lower caste people or less educated people are more rational than the upper caste people. As already stated above, in the traditional society strict purdah was observed by Ashraf section (comprising the upper castes) and a liberal purdah was found in the Atraf or Ajlaf section (comprising the lower castes). The same practice appears to be prevalent even today in the village because a relatively more free movement of the women in lower castes is found than in the upper castes. It is also important to point out that illiteracy or literacy is mostly found in the lower castes whereas upper caste people are relatively more educated. This may be the reason for observance of liberal purdah by higher percentages of families in the categories of literates and illiterates. But at the same time it is also important to point out that the traditional practice continues unchanged. Even in the upper castes or categories of educated families the majority is observing liberal purdah. It is definitely an index of change in attitude and outlook and liberalization of the practice of purdah observance.

Further the data have been classified on the basis of income category in Table 5.30.

Table 5.30

Income and Observance of Purdah

N=158

Income Category	*Strictly traditional*		*Religious*		*Liberal*	
	No.	*%*	*No.*	*%*	*No.*	*%*
Up to 1500	6	18 18	7	21.21	20	69.60
1501-3000	9	15.78	16	28 07	32	56.14
3001-4500	7	13 46	14	26.92	31	59.61
4501 +	2	12.50	5	31.25	9	56 25
Total	24		42		92	

This table presents the classification of responses on income basis. It is found from the table that in the lowest income group the highest percentage of response (69.60%) has gone in favour of liberal purdah and the lowest percentage of respone in favour of strictly traditional purdah (18.18%). In the next higher income category of 1501 to 3000 the highest percentage of response (56.14%) has gone in favour of liberal and then next (28.07%) position to liberal purdah and the lowest percentage of response in respect of traditional purdah (15.78%). In the third income group the highest percentage of response has gone in favour of liberal purdah (59.61%) and the lowest percentage in favour of strictly traditional purdah (13.46%). Only about 27% favoured religious purdah. In the highest income group the highest percentage of response (56.25%) is in favour of liberal purdah and the lowest percentage of response in favour of strictly traditional purdah (12.5%), while, on the other hand, 31.25% practised religious purdah. These response patterns do not show a consistent variation with the variations in income level. Hence the incomes of the families do not appear to be relevant to the types of purdah observed.

Another question put to the respondents was in respect of the reasons of purdah observance. They were asked to state why do the Muslim women observe purdah. The responses obtained from them are presented in Table 5.31.

Table 5.31

Reasons of Observing Purdah

N=158

Reasons	*Number*	*Percentage*
Personal likeness	46	29.12
Social values	49	31.01
Religious obligation	63	39.87
Total	158	100.00

It is evident from the above table that about 40% of the respondents' female members observe purdah due to religious obligation, whereas 31% maintain that social norms and values are the reasons of purdah observance and according to 29% personal liking is responsible for purdah observance. It means that the most important reason is religious sanction. A low percentage of Muslim women observe purdah because of personal liking for it. The majority of 71% of women observe purdah under some pressure or obligation whether social or religious. Hence it may be interpreted that the observance of purdah is not an ingradient of personality in most of the cases. The normative and religious sanctions regulate the behaviour patterns and purdah is observed. Thus it appears that in the Muslim families in village the purdah is not personally cherished and is not observed due to adequate institutionalization of norms but due to social pressures and religious obligations. The respondents were also asked to give the reasons for changes in the pattern of purdah observance as compared with purdah observed in the traditional societies of the past. This fact has come to light that liberal purdah is being observed by majority of the families and it is definitely an index of changing trend in purdah observance. The reasons of observing purdah mentioned by the respondents are presented below along with the frequencies and percentages of response in Table 5.32.

Table 5.32

Reasons of diminishing Purdah Observance

N=158

Reasons	*No.*	*Percentage*
Economic	36	22.79
Socio-cultural	29	18.36
Modern education	41	25.95
Freedom & fashion	32	20 25
Lack of religiosity	20	12.65
Total	158	100.00

It is found from the table that the most important reason mentioned by 26% of respondents is modern or western education. The next higher percentage of response has gone in favour of economic reason. 20% of the respondents have mentioned freedom and fashion as the reason for the liberalization of purdah, whereas according to 18% socio-cultural reason and according to 13% lack of religiosity are the reasons of observance of liberal purdah in the present age. On the basis of these findings it may be interpreted that education is considered to be the most important reason for a rational outlook in respect of purdah observance. It is obvious that the spread of western education is developing a rational outlook and weakening the hold of conservative and orthodox outlook. Hence the traditional practice of strict purdah is becoming less prevalent and liberal purdah is becoming dominant practice. The economic reason is the second important reason. A large number of men have migrated from village for earning their livelihood. Moreover in certain cases the women are also earning to supplement the family income. Hence the economic reason has become an important reason. The persons working outside the village are exposed to urbanism and hence rationalisation of their outlook continues to liberalisation of purdah in their families. The reason of freedom and fashion also refers to the migration of families from villages to towns and visits to holy shrines as well as excursion trips. These factors facilitate the impact of fashion and freedom of movement contributing to the liberalisation of purdah.

6

Economic Relations

Islam recognizes the man's desire of economic well-being and urges its followers to carry on their struggle for existence. Dignity of labour is rated very high and self-reliance is preferred to dependence. It does not restrict efforts, at material progress. It regards a certain standard of material provision as an indispensable condition for the evolution of the desirable social pattern. It expects the individual to make all efforts at its achievement. It ordains society to guarantee such provision to each individual in all circumstances. But it limits the economic activities because exclusive devotion to economic development may result in the neglect of other aspects of human life. Thus a Muslim should always be conscious of the fact that a materially prosperous life is not an end in itself. The value of everything is determined by the contribution it makes towards the life hereafter. It is actually the virtue and goodness that count and which should be the centre of our attention even in our economic activities, but it does not mean asceticism or negation of economic ends. It is not separated and cut off from life rather passes through the activities of practical life. This attitude simply means a check upon the unwarranted flow of what is called 'Economic rationality' in the capitalistic economy. The Islamic individual is to be mindful of other ends, like the remembrance of God, propagation of truth and goodness, help to the poor and needy, while he is engaged in economic pursuit.

A special feature of the Islamic spirit is that it calls upon the believers (its people) to co-operate with one another. Economic goods are means to living, while life itself is a means to please God and achieve success in the life and hereafter. Every Muslim is anxious to achieve this success which involves co-operation in each and every walk of life. Thus the entire life becomes a co-operative movement towards the achievement of a common goal.

According to the philosophy of the Qur'an all human activities should be directed towards the achievements of Falah—a comprehensive term devoting all-sided-welfare of this life as well as that of the hereafter. From Islamic and social point of view there is no way of achieving the welfare of the one without co-ordinating it with the interests of the others. The society that neglects the hereafter can never achieve welfare in this life; and it is only through the welfare of the worldly life that the welfare of the other world could be expected to adorn human achievements. Economic, political, social and spiritual objectives and ideals are legitimate in so far as they contribute to the achievement of wealth. Islam condemns materialistic approach in the most severe terms. Economic enterprise and productive efforts in themselves are not the point of attack rather the approach to fulfil this aim. This shows that material well-being is an assential constituent of Falah. Conditions of starvation, pressure of need and factors that agitate against peace of mind and normal activity of the human body cannot create a climate favourable for the attainment of the life-end.

Islam encourages productive efforts and made it a duty. The immediate ends that Islam regards proper for man's economic activities can be enumerated as follows:

1. Fulfilment of one's needs in moderation.
2. Meeting family liabilities.
3. Provision for future contingencies.

4. Provision for posterity.
5. Social contribution to the cause of Allah.

Fulfilment of One's End

Food, drink, clothing, shelter, medical care and education come under this category. A person who feeds himself well, wears decent clothes and supplies himself with a comfort with a view to making himself more efficient, more useful in the service of the God, is welcome to the society of Islam. But after a certain limit, consumption of these items may turn into extravagance, which is prohibited. Similarly, a person may allow himself only so much comforts and luxuries that may not lead to indulgence in luxuriant living. Thus Islam takes every precaution to ensure against extravagant expenditure and wilful squandering of wealth beyond the limits and requirements of a reasonable standard of life. These two cases, that of extravagance and indulgence in luxuries, are nearly independent of mental attitude of the persons, being explicitly prohibited by Qur'an. The reason behind these injunctions is that they can serve no good purpose. Contrary to this, total abstinence from the permissibles is shunned and condemned and asceticism is totally rejected. The Qur'an says, "And eat and drink, but be not prodigal, Lo, the squanders were ever brothers of the devil."[1]

Islam forbids certain items of consumption. It forbids hard drinks, gambling, wearing of pure silks and use of gold as ornaments by the male, as well as the use of gold and silver utensils. It forbids dancing and sculpture, bearing few exceptions, assigns a descent and honourable place to women in society, and forbids the free mixing of the two sexes in society. Hence Islam rejects the unbalanced and luxurious living.

Meeting Family Liabilities

Islam has regarded one's legal duty to support his wife

1. The Qur'an, XVII, pp. 26-27.

and children, and the parents if they require help. In special circumstances other near relations also become entitled to support. Besides these there are many directives from the Prophet enjoying consideration of such dependents. He says:

> "Begin (chastity) from your own person. Pass over the surplus to your family and if there is any more after providing for your family, give to your kinsmen . . . ."

These duties and the above exhortations act as incentives persuading the individual to earn more than his personal requirement.

Provision for Future Contingencies

Islam also recognizes the genuine human need to provide for the future and store or deposit for the bad days. The Prophet often advised to his companions not to spend all they had, even in the cause of Allah, for the future does need some provision. Once the Prophet told to a companion, "Keep some of your property to yourself for it is advisable unto you." Thus it is clear that though Islam has permitted to save for the future contingencies, it disallows hoarding of wealth. Thus the question of accumulation of wealth does not arise and, hence, capitalism is contrary to its nature.

Provision for the Posterity

Islam, being aware of the human motive, allows to leave behind something upon which one's dependence could fall back when death withdraws his support from them. For this a clear cut law of inheritance has been presented in Qur'an. Thus here also Islam encourages to earn, keep and save wealth; but it discourages the craze to pass on huge treasures to posterity.

Social Service

Islamic sanctions reveal that after having satisfied with one's own wants and those of the dependents, and having saved something for the rainy days and for posterity, one is not to sit idle and give up all enterprise and activity. A Muslim is to strive his best and contribute as much as possible for the social services and the cause of Allah. He should put all his energies to service of the society and religious causes. Qur'an says, "And strive with your wealth and your lives in the way of Allah."[2]

Thus Islamic laws are not confined to spiritualism only rather it is close to the practical human life. It encourages human economic values to earn livelihood for self and the society. The social man has been ordained to live and work in co-operation and contribute according to their abilities. It is the sacred duty of the followers to maintain life in an efficient and reasonable manner. Consequently, the production of the necessities is the duty of all.

Justice, benevolence, honesty and truthfulness are the highly valued characteristics in Islam. Islam enjoins that these values must be honoured in all walks of life, especially in business, transactions and entrepreneurial matters. Fraud, deception, exloitation of innocents and weaks, deceptive salesmanship and false statements, information or publicity are strictly prohibited. "To exploit the person who confides (in you) is akin to usury."[3]

Laws concerning adulteration, false weights and measures, advertisements, etc. were also made during the early Islamic period to ensure moral uprightness and justice in business and industry.

Likewise, gamblous transactions, based on pure speculation, and involving great risk and uncertainties have been disallowed by Islam.

Business deal should be based on co-operation and

2. The Qur'an, sura IX, verse 41.

3. Behqi, Alsanan Alkubra, Vol. 5, Hyderabad, 1353 A.H , p. 348.

mutual agreement, and not on coercion. Complete willingness of both the parties is one of the primary requirements in the transaction of business and commerce.

But in the event of higher social purpose, or necessary individual interests, forced transactions have been approved. Forced purchase by state in case of emergency, or exception to the above rule in case of the right to pre-emption have been allowed.

Economic Enterprise

Islam has given the individual rights of property and freedom of enterprise. According to Islam all the resources of nature are thrown open to utilization by man so that he might lead a contended life. God declares, "And We have given you (mankind) power in the earth and appointed for you therein a livelihood "[4]

Islam looks upon wealth as a means to living, 'Your wealth which Allah has made a means of support for you."[5]

"And when prayer is ended, then disperse in the land and seek of Allah's bounty. . . . ."[6]

God encourages economic activities and right to property for the fulfilment of personal and social needs. God as the real owner of everything in the universe, has made the individual his trustee. Besides, the individual, the society and the state also own property and exercise the rights of ownership. State is the guardian of individual's rights with powers to intervene, circumscribe and in some cases take away the individual right to property with a view to protecting social and individual interest of vital importance.

Natural resources related to the common interest of man, such as, the rivers, the mountains, the sea and the space; and the collective goods, such as, the roads, bridges, etc., are not to be owned by individuals. Any individual can own the

4. The Qur'an, S. VII, V. 10.
5. Ibid., S. IV, V. 5.
6. Ibid., S. LXII, V. 10.

objects rightly acquired through purchase, inheritance or original possession of unowned objects. But the possession must usefully employ the object possessed, failing which it would be void and in such a case the state may regulate such acquisition in the larger interest of society. Every one has a right to use his property for earning more money through commerce, industry and agriculture, etc. None has the right to destroy, squander away or use one's property for illegitimate purposes. In all these activities a code of conduct has to be observed.

Islam rendered the right of property with certain obligations towards others. The first obligation of the individual after meeting his own requirements is towards family, relatives and kins. A poor and needy relative has more rights to be supported by his well-to-do relatives. Offer hospitality to guests and helping the needy who seeks assistance is also obligatory.

Zakat

There is the legally fixed Zakat (Tax) on almost all forms of wealth. This is a collective measure sanctioned by Islam for making individual activities serve the social good and the society look after the individual interests. Implicitly it discourages amassing, hoarding and accumulating of wealth for no purpose rather than to show off and claiming superiority, to satisfy one's ego, or with a view to indulgent living. Thus Zakat is the tax against such wealth surplus to one's own requirements. In other words, Zakat is not charity. It is a right of the have-nots in the wealth of the haves. The Qur'an says, "And in whose wealth there is a right acknowledged for the beggar and the destitute."[7] The Prophet declares that it is a measure designed to transfer part of the wealth from the haves to the have-nots in society.

Zakat covers almost every kind of wealth—cash and bullion, stocks and inventories, agricultural produce, cattle, mineral wealth, etc. Exemption limits and rates have been fixed once for ever. As a permanent provision in Islamic law

7. The Qur'an, LXX, 24-25.

this redistributive measure is necessitated by the unequal distribution of abilities, which in turn cause unequal opportunities.

Interest

Like all the Prophets of the past, Mohammad too denounced 'interest' as something utterly incompatible with the principles of Islamic social and economic justice. The very concept of interest has no place in Islam, because it is unclean, debasing, criminal, a most dreadful sin, so it is totally forbidden. . . . [8]

Ahmad Ali opines, "The most important reason for banning interest is that since it is the lending of money for gain alone, without any risk, or as a consumption loan proper made to the needy person, it must be considered absolutely loathsome and unfair, and, so should be banished from the thoughts of man."[9]

God, disliking interest-based loan, recommends all sorts of interest-free assistance to the needy. He says, "If Ye lend unto Allah a goodly loan (interest-free loan) He will double it for you and will forgive you..."[10]

Borrowing of loan has not been outrightly condemned. When no immediate means exist, and only when repayment is possible, at a future date, is borrowing allowed.

Regarding the non-payment of loan Imam Jafer-al-Sadiq says, "One who borrows but does not intend to repay is like a thief."[11]

The Prophet says, "For the affluent to evade repayment of his loan (debt) is tyranny."[12]

In case of the inability to pay the debt and relieve the debtee from difficulties, Islam made the state responsible,

8. Ali, S.A., Economic Foundations of Islam, Orient Longmans, Calcutta, 1964, p. 160.
9. Ibid.
10. The Qur'an, S. XVI, V. 71.
11. Mustadrak-al-Wassaell, p. 259.
12. Ibid.

in certain circumstances, for paying off the debts of its citizens. A creditor should allow the debtor ample time to pay off his debt, that is till his circumstances improve, provided the loan has not been squandered in sinful ventures.

Trade

Islam has emphasized the importance of trade and commerce. Trade, according to Islam, is the basic fact of economic life and it has been ranked first among all the legitimate occupations and professions. Depicting the importance of trade, Tradition says, "One who gives up trade loses two-thirds of his wisdom (so), do not give up trade as it causes a a loss of wisdom. Follow your pursuit for the maintenance of your family, and let it be the other way round."[13]

It is required that an agreement he entered into freely without compulsion, coercion or under duress, and thoughtfully, so that a possible after-thought does not necessitate its cancellation. Further Islam recognizes the freedom of action of sellers and buyers, the buyers have the fullest measure of freedom of choice, and there is no restriction on sellers in choosing the market.

While discussing the business morality and commercial ethics, Prophet suggests, "It is graceful to treat all customers alike, the humble is akin to the great, and wealthy to the beggar. In settling the price, the haggler, meaning justice should be done between those who do and those who do not demand a reduction in price. Not that the price should be reduced for those who demand it, and not for those who do not."[14]

Qur'an explicitly opposes unfair trading, "O my people! Give full measure and full weight in justice, and wrong not people in respect of their goods. And do no evil on earth, causing corruption."[15]

13. Mustadrak-al-Wassaell, p. 2.
14. Ibid.
15. The Qur'an, S. XI, V. 85.

These pronouncements of Qur'an, Hadis and Imams are helpful codes of business conduct to which all merchants should follow. But in actual practice none of the Muslim or non-Muslim businessmen of the present age remembers these principles and adopts its honest practices. It is because everyone has lost contentment and acquired materialistic lust of life.

The Prophet has also emphasised the importance of cottage industries. He says, "The spinning wheel is an excellent occupation for the good woman, so it is good to teach women spinning."[16] This has been suggested to break idleness and add to the family income.

The history reveals that the Muslim community has always been enthusiastic in trade and commerce. Actually it were these Muslim merchants and traders who carried their goods far and wide and left the impression of Islam wherever they visited. Referring to this fact, Shushtery says, "At the advent of Islam, the Prophet and most of his early converts were merchants, exporting goods from Hejaz into Syria and importing from Syria to Hejaz."[17]

Land and Agriculture

Besides trade and commerce, Islam has also laid great emphasis on agriculture. Being a real owner of all the creations, land belongs to Allah, and man is His trustee."[18]

Islam has also classified the land according to its nature and discussed the question of its ownership. It takes up the problems of farming, rights of landlords and cultivators and tenants, forced labour, rent collection and fixation of rent, etc.

On the whole it appears that Allah is interested in maintaining the principle of owners as Himself and man as His trustee, though, it appears that in regard to land the

16. Mustadrak-al-Wassael, Vol. 2, p. 206.
17. Shushtery, A.M.A., Outlines of Islamic Culture, Bangalore Publishing Co. Pvt. Ltd., Bangalore, 1937, p. 147.
18. Mustadrak-al-Wassael, Vol. 2. p. 358.

Imam is granted the right of ownership by Allah, and man is allowed the use of the land in the pleasure of the Imam."[19]

On the imposition and fixation of land rent Islam has also put some light. According to it, rent is a function of the capacity of the cultivator and the principle of justice.

Likewise, Islam is against the use of force in collecting rent, such as, confiscation of cattle or other belongings of the peasants, who, when in difficulties, is to be kindly treated.

In this connection Hazrat Ali's directive to his revenue officer clarifies the Islamic attitude towards rent collection, "...Remember, while collecting rent of food, animals used for cultivation (draught animals), and their slaves, do not touch belongings of any one, be he a Muslim, a Jew or Christian...."[20]

In the same way we find that the rights of the tillers of the soil are not left at the mercy of the landlords, and a tradition requires landlords to collect rent for each plot of land rented out separately, this means that the tiller is saved from having to pay the cash rent agreed upon from the produce of other plots, if the crop on the particular plot fails; the proposition is extremely fair. So, rent in cash or kind will have to be collected only in respect of the particular plots, other plots, even though rented out by the same landlord, cannot be touched.

From these facts it must be noted that the economic code of Islam is totally based on the attitude of welfare and justice. Nowhere the haves or the sovereigns are let loose to use tyranny and show injustice to the poor and the masses. Further it shourld be noted that what Islam preached 1400 years ago, is still being realized fresh and fruitful. Most of the nations today are making laws against usury, tyranny of landlords, relaxation in the payment of land tax and the abolition of the system of bonded labour.

Still, we cannot claim that the Muslims, atleast of today, and of any part of the world, are a true adherent to Islam.

19. Ali, S.A., Economic Foundations of Islam, Orient Longmans, Calcutta, 1964, p. 186.
20. Nahjul Balagha, print III, item, 51, pp. 90-91.

They have forgotten the qualities of a good trade and a good farmer. They are not polite, sincere, serious, honest, either in the pursuit of trade and commerce or in agricultural farming. This is a fact beyond any doubt that a large number of landed Muslim peasantry is converting into landless rural mass, and the business of Muslims is moving in a deteriorating direction. As a whole, Muslim economy is in a sinking trend. These differences are confirmed from the facts collected in the present study.

The basis of economy in rural India has been agricultural occupations. The main occupation of the rural people has remained cultivation for centuries and it has served as the basis of economic life. But in the present century the spread of literacy and education has changed the attitude and outlook not only in respect of social life but also in respect of economy. A large number of villagers are receiving education and after completing education they find some job and work in offices. Moreover, a considerable number of villagers have migrated to industrial areas to work as industrial wage-earners. Thus both educated sections of rural society are getting jobs in industrial and urban areas. This change in occupation is changing the mode of economic life. Even in the field of agriculture changes are taking place due to introduction of agricultural innovations, i.e., tractor, tube-well, chemical fertilizers, pesticides and improved seeds. These agricultural innovations have opened a new era of cultivation in the rural areas. The increased production has also resulted in widening economic relations with the world outside the village. In this way significant changes are taking place in rural economy. As the present study is concerned with the analysis of village community the study of economy of the people under study and the changes therein is of vital importance. Hence certain questions were put to the respondents for collecting information about their economic life, choice of occupation, trend of economic development and changing economic relations, etc.

Finding

For analysing the present economic condition of the

people under study various questions were put to them. One of the questions asked from them was, "Indicate your level of satisfaction with your present economic condition." The respondents were required to give their responses in either of the four categories of fully satisfied, unsatisfied, and highly dissatisfied. The responses obtained from them are presented in Table 6.1.

Table 6.1

Respondents' Level of Satisfaction with their present Economic Condition

N=158

Level of Satisfaction	*Frequency of Response*	
	Number	*Percentage*
Fully satisfied	5	3.17
Satisfied	43	27.22
Not satisfied	72	45.56
Highly dissatisfied	38	24.05
Total	158	100.00

It is evident from the above table that the highest percentage of respondents (45.56%) is unsatisfied with the present condition. The second higher percentage of response is in respect of satisfied (27.22%). 24.05% of the respondents are highly dissatisfied and only 3.17% are fully satisfied. On the whole 30.37% have expressed satisfaction and 69.63% have expressed dissatisfaction. It suggests that the majority of the respondents is not satisfied with the existing economic condition and faces economic hardships.

The same responses have been classified on income basis in Table 6.2 for analysing the level of satisfaction in different income groups.

It appears from this table that in the two lower income groups no respondent is fully satisfied. In the income group of 3000 to 4500, 1.92% and in the highest income

Table 6.2
Income and Level of Satisfaction
N=158

Income Category	*Fully satisfied*		*Satisfied*		*Dissatisfied*		*Highly dissatisfied*		*Total*
	No.	%	*No.*	%	*No.*	%	*No.*	%	
Up to Rs. 1500	—	—	2	6.06	14	42.42	17	51.51	33
Rs. 1500-3000	—	—	14	24.56	31	54.38	12	21.05	57
Rs. 3001-4500	1	1.92	22	42.30	20	38.4[illegible]	9	17.30	52
Rs. 4500+	4	25.00	5	31.25	7	43.75	—	—	16
Total	5		43		72		38		158

group of above 4500, 25% are fully satisfied with the present economic condition. As regards the response in respect of satisfaction, it is 6.06% in the lower income group, 24.56% in the next higher income group, 42.30% in the third higher income group and 31.25% in the highest income group. Thus the percentage of satisfaction has consistently risen in the first three income groups with the rise in income level though it has declined in the highest income group. The responses showing dissatisfaction do not show any consistent variation with the variation in income level. But in case of highly dissatisfied the percentage of response has consistently declined with the rise in income level and no respondent in the highest income group has expressed complete dissatisfaction. It shows a relevance of income level to the level of dissatisfaction. But on the whole dissatisfaction is prevailing in all income groups and the families having higher income are also dissatisfied due to one reason or the other.

Table 6.3 presents the analysis of responses on caste basis.

It is found from the table that no respondent in the lowest age group and the next higher age group has expressed full satisfaction. Only 5% of the respondents in the third age group and 4.86% in the eldest age group have expressed full satisfaction. As regards simple satisfaction with the present economic condition, the table does not show any consistent variation in response patterns along with the variation in age. The same is found in case of dissatisfaction and complete dissatisfaction. Hence it may be interpreted that age is not significant variable in this regard.

Another question put to the respondents was, "What form of aid you require for your economic upliftment ?" The responses obtained from them are given in Table 6.4.

It is evident from the table that the respondents were provided with different alternative responses showing economic aid and they were required to choose any one form of aid. The respondents were asked to mention that economic aid which they required most and which was given priority by them. Thus each respondent has mentioned only one type of aid on priority basis. It appears from the table that the

Table 6.3

Caste and Level of Satisfaction

N=158

Caste Category	*Fully satisfied*		*Satisfied*		*Dissatisfied*		*Highly satisfied*		*Total*
	No.	*%*	*No.*	*%*	*No.*	*%*	*No.*	*%*	
Upper Caste	5	3.84	36	27.69	63	48.46	26	20.00	130
Lower Caste	—	—	7	25.00	9	32.14	12	42.85	28
Total	5		43		72		38		158

Table 6.4

Aid required by the Respondents for their Economic Upliftment

N=158

Aid Category	*Response Frequency*	
	Number	*Percentage*
Agricultural Aid	47	29.75
Aid for Cottage Industry	5	3.17
Aid for Business	41	25.95
Aid for Technology	12	7.59
Any other job	53	33.54
Total	158	100.00

highest percentage of response has gone in favour of any other job. 33.54% of the respondents declared that they needed some different job for their economic upliftment. It means that these respondents are not satisfied with the present job or engagement and feel that there should be complete change in their job or occupation. The next higher percentage of response has gone in respect of agricultural aid (29.75%) and then in favour of aid for business (25.95%). Aid for technical training is preferred only by 7.59% and aid for cottage industry by 3.17%. On the basis of these findings it may be interpreted that the villagers under study are more inclined towards some other job. It may be due to the fact that a large number of villagers work outside and are employed in one service or the other. Agriculture also appears to be an important occupation for them because it has been given priority by a considerable percentage. Business appears to be less important than service and agriculture for the villagers. They are less enterprising and hence the least interested in developing cottage industry.

The responses analysed in Table 6.4 have been classified on the basis of literacy or level of education in Table 6.5.

Table 6.5

Education and Aid Required by the Respondents

N=158

Level of Education	*Agricultural Aid No./%*	*Aid for Cottage Industry No./%*	*Aid for Business No./%*	*Aid for Tech. Training No./%*	*Any other job No./%*	*Total*
Illiterate	12 28.57	3 7.14	12 28.57	1 2.38	14 33.33	42
Below Matric	29 36.70	1 1.26	17 21.51	1 1.26	31 39.24	79
Below Graduate	5 20.00	1 4.00	9 36.00	4 16.00	6 24.00	25
Graduate+	1 8.33	—	3 25.00	6 50.00	2 16.66	12
Total	47	5	41	12	53	158

It is evident from the table that 28.57% of the illiterates, 36.70% of below matriculates, 20% of under-graduates and 8.33% of graduates and above have shown preference for agricultural aid. It means that the educated and more qualified persons are less interested in agriculture, whereas literates and illiterates are more interested in getting agricultural aid. The reason is quite obvious. Those who receive education want to get some job outside the village, more preferably in the town and do not prefer agricultural occupation. Hence they are less inclined towards receiving agricultural aids. But the responses in respect of some alternative job also show that a higher percentage of respondents in the literate and illiterate categories have shown preference than the respondents in the under-graduates and graduates category. It means that change in job is also less preferred by educated persons than the literate and illiterates. In case of graduates the highest percentage of response has gone in favour of aid for technical training (50%) and the highest percentage of response in the category of under-graduates has gone in favour of aid for business (36%). It means that the graduates are more interested in getting technical training, whereas under-graduates are more interested in doing business and hence they need financial help for business. Hence it may be interpreted that the under-graduates prefer business occupation. It may be because they may not like to do cultivation and at the same time they are not expected to get a suitable job. On the other hand the preference for technical training by the graduates may be due to this feeling that after training they may get better job and the financial position may improve.

Table 6.6 presents the classification of the same responses on the basis of educational background.

It appears from the table that those engaged in cultivation, 50% of them want agricultural aid, 23.63% favour aid for business, 20% have a preference for some other job and only 2.77% desire technical training and 1.38% desire aid for cottage industry. In case of respondents engaged in business 50% desire aid for business, 30% for some other job, 10% for technical training and 10% for aid in cottage industry. Those who are service-holders among them 41.66% want to change

Table 6.6

Occupation and Aid Required by the Respondents

N=158

Occupation Category	*Agrl. Aid*	*Aid for Cottage Industry*	*Aid for Business*	*Aid for Tech. Training*	*Any Other Job*	*Total*
	No /%	*No./%*	*No /%*	*No./%*	*No /%*	
Cultivation	36(50)	1(1 38)	17(23.61)	2(2.77)	16(22.22)	72
Business	—	1(10)	5(5))	(10)	3(30)	10
Service	—	—	2(16.66)	5(41.66)	5(41.66)	12
Multiple occupation	—	1(6.25)	6(37.5)	—	9(56.25)	16
Nothing (dependent)	9(25)	1(2.77)	5(13.88)	3(8.33)	18(50)	36
Total	47	5	41	12	53	158

their job, whereas the same percentage desires technical training. Only 16.66% have expressed their priority for business aid. As regards the labour class, 56.25% have preference for change of job, whereas 37.05% desire aid for business and 6.25% want aid for cottage industry. Among the respondents engaged in multiple occupation, 16.66% want agricultural aid and the same percentage wants some other job, 8.33% of these respondents desire aid for cottage industry and the same percentage wants technical training. Those who are dependents or doing nothing, 50% of them want some job, 25% need agricultural aid, 13.88% desire aid for business, 8.33% prefer technical training, 2.77% have opted for aid for cottage industry. Thus it appears that those who are in specific occupations have more liking for the aid related to their own occupations because they feel that the related aid may be more helpful in their economic upliftment.

The next question put to the respondents was concerned with an enquiry into the satisfaction or dissatisfaction with the present occupation and desirability to change the occupation. The responses obtained from the villagers are presented in Table 6.7.

Table 6.7

Responses showing Degree of Satisfaction with the Present Occupation and Likeness to Change

N=158

Response	*Satisfied*	*Not satisfied*	*Want to change*	*Do not want to change*	*Unable to change*	*Total*
Number	41	117	75	22	61	158
Percentage	25.95	74.06	47.46	13.92	38 60	100.00

It is evident from the table that only 25.95% of the respondents are satisfied with their occupation, whereas 74.06% of the respondents are not satisfied. It suggests that the majority does not feel satisfied with the present occupation. The table further shows that 47.46% of the respondents want to change the occupation, whereas only 13.92% are not willing to change their occupations. It is important to note that 25.94% are satisfied with the occupation but only 13.92% do not want to change their occupations. It means that many of those satisfied with their occupations are also willing to change. It is also found from the table that 38.60% of the respondents declared that they were unable to change the occupation but the circumstances do not permit them to do so. It may be due to hereditary obligation or due to illiteracy or due to old age or lack of alternative job that these respondents cannot change their occupations in spite of desire for the change. Thus the respondents may also be put in the category of those who want to change the occupation. In this way a very low percentage is in favour of not changing their occupation.

The responses presented in Table 6.7 are classified in Table 6.8 on the basis of occupation.

It is found from the table that in all occupational categories the percentage of respondents expressing dissatisfaction is higher than the percentage expressing satisfaction. It means that whether it is the occupation of cultivation, business, service, labour or multiple occupation, the majority is not satisfied. Those who are dependent are generally of old age and among them also the majority is not satisfied with the present occupation. Their views are in respect of the occupation of their sons or of supporting members of the family. The table further shows that only in case of cultivation and dependents the majority of the respondents wants to change the occupation. In case of labourers 50% have expressed their desire to change. The table further shows that only in case of business category and multiple occupation category the majority has declared that change is not favoured. It means that they are satisfied with their present occupation. In case of service also a considerable percentage (41.66%) appears to be satisfied because it does not want to change the occupation. Those respondents who have expressed their inability to change the occupation are relatively in lower percentage in all

Table 6.8

Occupation and Degree of Satisfaction with the Present Occupation and Likeness to Change

N=158

Occupation Category	*Satisfied* No./%	*Not satisfied* No./%	*Want to change* No./%	*Unable to change* No /%	*Do not want to change* No./%	*Total*
Cultivation	27	45	41	27	4	72
	37.5	62.25	56.94	37.5	5.55	
Business	4	6	2	6	2	10
	40.00	60.00	20.00	60.00	20 00	
Service	5	7	2	5	5	12
	41.66	58.33	16.66	41.66	41.66	
Labour	—	16	8	5	3	16
	—	100.00	50.00	31.25	18.75	
Multiple-occupation	1	11	3	7	2	12
	8.33	91.66	25.00	58.33	16,66	
Nothing (Dependent)	4	32	19	11	6	36
	11.11	88.88	52.77	30. 55	16.66	
Total	41	117	75	61	22	158

categories. In case of service category 41.66% and in case of business category 20% have declared that they cannot change their occupation. In other categories the percentages are still low.

Table 6.9 presents the classification of the given responses in Table 6.7 on the basis of the level of education.

It appears from the table that in no category of the respondents the majority is satisfied with the present occupation. But the table suggests that a higher percentage of respondents in the educated categories has expressed satisfaction. 44% of the under-graduates and 41.66% of graduates have expressed satisfaction with the present occupation, whereas 21.42% of illiterates and 20.25% of under-matriculates are satisfied with the present occupation. Hence it may be interpreted that educated section has greater satisfaction than the uneducated section. It shows the relevance of the level of education to the satisfaction with the occupation. The same relevance is found in analyzing the responses showing dissatisfaction. 78.57% of the illiterates and 79.74% of literates are not satisfied with their present occupation, whereas 56% of the under-graduates and 58.33% of graduates are not satisfied. It means that a higher percentage in the uneducated categories has expressed dissatisfaction than the percentage showing dissatisfaction in the educated categories.

The table further shows that 59.52% of illiterates, 46.50% of under-matriculates, 52% of graduates and 41.66% of graduates want to change the occupation. It means that a consistent rise of fall in the percentage of response is not found along with rise in the level of literacy and education. But the pattern of response showing no desire to change suggests that the percentages of response are relatively lower among uneducated categories than in educated categories. 33.33% of graduates and 20% of under-graduates do not want to change, whereas only 10.12% of under-matriculates and 11.90% of illiterates do not want to change occupation. It also suggests a higher level of satisfaction in the educated categories than in the uneducated categories. The response in respect of

Table 6.9
Education and Degree of Satisfaction with the Present Occupation and Likeness to Change
N=158

(*Number/%age*)

Level of Education	*Satisfied*	*Not satisfied*	*Want to change*	*Unable to change*	*Not want to change*	*Total*
Illiterate	9(21.42)	33(78 57)	25(59.52)	12(28.57)	5(11.90)	42
Below Matric	16(20.25)	63(79.74)	32(40.50)	39(49.36)	8(10.12)	79
Below Graduate	11(44.00)	14(56.00)	13(52.00)	7(28.00)	5(20.00)	25
Graduate+	5(41.66)	7(58.33)	5(41.66)	3(25.00)	4(33.33)	12
Total	41	117	75	61	22	158

inability to change occupation do not show a consistent variation with the variation in literacy level.

The respondents were also asked to give their choice of occupation for themselves as well as for their family members. They were asked to mention one occupation which they like. The responses gathered from them are presented in Table 6.10.

Aable 6.10

Respondents' Likeness for Occupation

N=158

Occupation	*Response Frequency*	
	Number	*Percentage*
Cultivation	37	23.42
Business	43	27.22
Service	73	46.20
Cottage Industry	5	3.16
Total	158	100.00

It is found from the table that the highest percentage of response (46.20%) has gone in favour of service. The next higher percentage of 27.22% has gone in favour of business and 23.42% have expressed their choice for cultivation. Only 3.16% mentioned cottage industry as their liked occupation. It suggests that nobody wants to remain a labourer or engaged in any multiple occupation or dependent on others. It is also evident that only three occupations of service, business and cultivation are liked. Moreover, among these three occupations the most liked occupation is service and the least liked occupation is cultivation. It is also important to point out that at the time of the study 72 respondents were engaged in cultivation, whereas only 37 respondents gave their choice for this occupation. It means that many of the cultivators do not want to continue this occupation. On the other hand, at the time of data collection only 10 persons were in business but 43 respondents expressed their choice for this occupation. In the same way 12 respondents were in service at the time of study but 73 had a liking for this occupation. It means that many of the respondents who are not in service or business desire to enter this occupation.

Certain questions were put to the respondents regarding agricultural operations and cultivation by Muslims. One question asked from them was, whether they think that the rural Muslims of the present day are backward in agriculture. Hundred per cent of the respondents accepted that rural Muslims are backward in agriculture in the present age. These respondents were further asked to give reasons for this backwardness. These responses are given in Table 6.11.

Table 6.11

Responses showing Reasons for Agricultural Backwardness of Rural Muslims

N=158

Reasons	*Response Frequency*	
	Number	*Percentage*
Lack of fund	48	30.40
Lack of manpower	7	4.45
Lack of hard labour	13	8.22
Lack of interest	17	10.75
Lack of profit	23	14.55
Lack of economic holding	10	6.32
Lack of co-operation	12	7.59
Lack of facilities	28	17.72
Total	158	100.00

It appears from the table that in all eight reasons of agricultural backwardness have been given by the respondents. These reasons are—lack of fund, manpower, hard labour, interest, profit, economic holding, co-operation and other facilities. Among these eight reasons the most important reason is lack of fund expressed by 30.40% of the respondents. The next important reason is lack of facilities mentioned by 17.72% of the respondents. The third reason is lack of profit mentioned by 14.55% of the respondents. Thus it appears that the main reason of agricultural backwardness mentioned by the respondents appears to be economic in nature. Whether it is lack of fund or lack of profit or lack of facilities, each of them has an economic relevance.

The next question put to the respondents was, "Have you ever been exposed to the following media of agricultural instruction and guidance?" The responses are presented in Table 6.12.

Table 6 12

Exposure to the Media of Agricultural Instruction and Guidance

N=72

Media	*Response Frequency*	
	Number	*Percentage*
Krishi Mela	1	1.40
Agrl. Demonstration and Training Centre	3	4.18
Block Farming Centre	3	4.16
Chaupal	34	47.22
Krishi Samachar Patra	—	—
Village Discussion Group	19	26.38
None	12	16.66
Total	72	100.00

This question was put only to those 72 respondents who are engaged in agriculture. The table shows that out of these 72 respondents doing cultivation, 12 are exposed to any medium of agricultural instruction and guidance. It means that 16.66% of these cultivators are not exposed to agricultural innovations whereas 83.33% are exposed to one or the other medium of agricultural instructions and guidance. The table further shows that the highest percentage of respondents

(47.22%) is exposed to chaupal, i.e., the radio programme on agriculture. The next higher percentage (20.33%) is exposed to village discussion group or Gram Vichar Goshti. Only 4.18% are exposed to agricultural demonstration and training centre or to block farming centre. 1.40% of the cultivators is exposed to Krishi Mela. It means that the most important medium of agricultural instruction and guidance for the respondents is the radio programme on agriculture (chaupal). The next important media is village discussion group. The other media do not appear to be significant.

Another question put to the respondents was, enquiring into the usefulness of agrarian programmes. The responses obtained in this respect are presented in Table 6.13.

Table 6.13

Response showing the Usefulness of Agrarian Programmes

N=72

Usefulness	*Response Frequency*	
	Number	*Percentage*
Highly useful	7	9.72
Useful	19	26.40
Not so useful	28	38.88
Can't say	18	25.00
Total	72	100.00

This question was put only to 72 respondents engaged in agriculture. 25% of them are not definite about the utility of agrarian programmes introduced by the government in the present age. But the majority of 75% accepts some degree of usefulness. The highest percentage (38.88%) feels that these programmes are not so useful. Only 9.72% have described the programme highly useful and 26.40% as useful. It means that a considerable section of those related to agriculture accepts the utility of agrarian programmes. It shows the impact of these programmes on the villagers under study.

The next question asked to the respondents was concerned with the reasons for not using advanced agricultural implements and items. The responses obtained from them are presented in Table 6.14.

Table 6.14

Responses showing the Reasons for not using Advanced Agricultural Implements and Items
N=72

Reasons	*Response*	
	Number	*Percentage*
Lack of Fund	38	52.80
Lack of Information	3	4.18
Lack of Confidence	3	4.16
Lack of Availability	5	6.94
Fear of Theft	11	15.27
Lack of Training to Use	1	1.38
Lack of Interest	5	6.94
Any other	6	8.33
Total	72	100.00

It is evident from the table that the most important reason for not using agricultural innovations is the lack of fund. The next important reason appears to be fear of theft or loss mentioned by 15.27%. Other reasons like lack of availability, lack of interest, lack of information, lack of confidence and lack of training are mentioned by very low percentages of respondents. The majority of 52.40% mentioned the lack of fund as the basic reason. Thus the most important reason appears to be economic hardship and poverty.

Another question put to the respondents was about the changes in the area of landed property inherited by their parental generation. The responses obtained from them are presented in Table 6.15.

Table 6.15

Changes in the Area of Land Inherited by the Parental Generation

N=158

Holding Condition	*Response Frequency*	
	No	*Percentage*
No change	7	4.44
Increased (by purchase)	12	7.60
Reduced (by sale)	139	87.96
Total	158	100.00

It is evident from the above table that 87.96% of the respondents declare that the area of such landed property has been reduced by sale. Only 7.60% of the respondents declare that the area of landed property has been increased by purchase, whereas 4.44% have retained the same area of landed property. Thus in general the economic condition has declined and in most of the cases the people have been compelled to dispose off certain portions of their inherited land.

The next question enquired into the reasons for the sale of inherited landed property. The responses are presented in Table 6.16.

It is evident from the table that the highest percentage of response suggests the sale of landed property on the occasion of marriage in the family (26.61%). The next higher percentage of response shows the sale of land for meeting daily expenses as well as festival expenses (25.17%). 18.70% declared that the land was sold because of the extravagancy of the elders of the family, 13.66% declared that the land was sold for investment in business. The responses showing other reasons are in very low percentages. These responses suggest that the important reason for the sale of land has been economic in nature. But at the same time lack of control over expenditure and luxurious habits also appear to be significant reasons. The responses suggest that the elderly members of the

Table 6.16

Reasons for the Sale of Inherited Lands
N=139

Reasons	*Response Frequency*	
	Number	*Percentage*
Sold out to meet marriage expenses	37	26.61
Sold out for education	4	2.87
Sold out for treatment	3	2.15
Sold out for meeting daily and festival expenses	35	25.17
Sold out because it was not under control	9	6.46
Sold out because it was not cultivable	6	4.31
Sold out because the elders were extravagant	26	18.70
Sold out for investing in business	19	13.66
Total	139	100.00

family were not much careful about future and they remained more concerned with their present and enjoyed their days, even at the cost of declining economic condition. This situation is very much similar to the conditions prevailing among old aristocratic and zamindar families of Bihar which are facing economic crisis these days due to unplanned and uncareful luxurious life of the past.

The next question put to the respondents was, "Which of the following factors do you think to be important to lead a happy life?" The responses obtained from the respondents are presented in Table 6.17.

It is evident from the facts that the highest percentage of response has gone in favour of material achievement (43.67%). 15.82% of the respondents have mentioned esteem and prestige as the factors contributing to a happy life.

Table 6.17

Factors Responsible for a Happy Life
N=158

Factors	*Response Frequency*	
	Number	*Percentage*
Material achievement	69	43.67
Contentment	19	12.04
Spiritualism	12	7.59
Simplicity	15	9.49
Esteem and prestige	25	15.82
Higher post and status	18	11.39
Total	158	100.00

Contentment has been mentioned only by 12.04% and simple living by 9.49%. The factor of higher post and status mentioned by 11.39% is also nearer to material comfort. Hence it may be interpreted that the dominant view about happy family life is materialistic in nature. It shows the declining influence of religion and spiritualism.

The next question put to the respondents was concerned with the conditions of borrowing cash or kind from others. The responses are presented in Table 6.18.

Table 6.18

Conditions of Borrowing Cash or Kind
N=158

Borrowing Category	*Response Frequency*	
	Number	*Percentage*
On Interest	67	42.42
Without Interest	82	51.89
Don't Borrow	9	5.69
Total	158	100.00

The responses given in the above table suggest that the majority of 51.89% takes interest-free loan, whether in cash or in kind from other members of the community. 42.42% of the respondents borrow cash or kind from others on interest and the remaining 5.69% do not borrow at all. These responses suggest that the general practice of borrowing cash or kind is not interest bound though a considerable section pays interest on the loans taken in cash or in kind.

The 67 respondents who take loan on interest were asked to give reasons for taking such loans. The responses obtained from them are presented in Table 6.19.

Table 6.19

Reasons for Borrowing Money on Interest

N=67

Reasons	*Response Frequency*	
	Number	*Percentage*
Marriage	19	28.37
Illness	5	7.47
Agriculture	9	13.43
Business	16	23.88
Education	3	4.47
Festivities	7	10.44
Household Expenditure	8	11.94
Total	67	100.00

It appears from the above table that the most important reasons for taking loan on interest are marriage in the family (28.37%), investment in business (23.88), for the purpose of agriculture (13.43%), and for household expenses (11.94%). The other reasons mentioned by the respondents are festivities (10.44%), illness (7.47%), and education of children (4.47%). All these responses suggest that the economic hardship compels for taking loan on interest and the money is borrowed mostly for necessities and not for luxuries.

7

Political Relations

The basic principle of Islamic polity is that, both individually and collectively, human beings should waive all rights of legislation and all power to give commands to others. No one should be allowed to pass orders or issue decrees in his own right and no one should seek to accept the obligation to carry out such decrees and obey such orders. None is obliged to abide by them. The right vests in Allah alone. The main characteristics of the Islamic law, according to the Qur'an, are as follows:

1. No person, clan, class or group, nor even the entire population of the state as a whole can lay claim to sovereignty. God alone is the real sovereign and all others are his subjects.
2. All legislative power too vests in God. The believers cannot frame any law for themselves nor can modify any law which God has laid down.
3. The Islamic stage must be founded upon the law laid down by God through His Prophet. The government which runs this state shall be entitled to obedience in its capacity as a political agency set up to enforce the laws of God and only in so far as it acts in that capacity.

In order to fulfil various needs of its members the society evolves different institutions. These institutions derive their authority, moral or legal, from the will of their members. Islam recognizes and approves of all the institutions functioning to the will of Allah—Sharia. The state is one of the important institutions in society which performs a number of social functions with its political power and capability to enforce decisions. The state is above the individuals and, to a great extent, above all the other institutions of society. It is a socially necessary human institution distinguished by supreme power and universally recognised authority in the society concerned. The state creates suitable conditions enabling its individuals to lead a good life. Thus different types of states emerged in different stages of human history, corresponding to its aims and methods to fulfil it.

The primary objective of the Islamic state is the establishment and preservation of a social order based on Islamic injunctions with a view to enabling men to live the Islamic way of life. Islamic state ensures freedom from fear so that man may repudiate false gods and dedicate themselves to the true sovereign. There are obligatory duties of the state according to the Islamic law. They include Jehad, propagation of Islam, education and moral regeneration, dispensation of justice, maintenance of law and order in general, protection of all the material and spiritual interests of the Islamic people. The state requires and has a right to acquire the resources and power needed for the effective discharge of those functions. The Islamic state negates any conflict or ill-will between its members and puts a premium on co-operative living.

According to the Islamic law the details of the functions of the Islamic state are to be worked out by the Muslim society whose general will is the final arbiter of the power and jurisdiction of the Islamic state within the boundaries defined by the Qur'an and the Sunnah. The government of the Islamic state is installed through free choice by citizens who have the right to dismiss it. The affairs of the state must be conducted by consultation, decisions being taken according to the democratic procedure, subject to the constraints provided by the specific laws in the Qur'an and Sunnah. Every citizen must have easy access to an independent judiciary.

The state has to ensure observance of the obligatory Islamic injunctions, and enforce the Islamic law. It should see to it that the individuals do not transgress the limits set upon the rights of ownership and enterprise, that they fulfil the obligations involved and exercise their rights in a manner harmonious with the interest of the society. This applies to all rights and every human activity.

The Islamic state is that which can be run only by those who believe in the prescriptions of Divine Law; whose whole life is spent in the observance and enforcement of the Law, who not only agree with its programmes and fully believe in it but thoroughly comprehend its spirit and are acquainted with its details. Islam does not recognize any geographical, linguistic, or colour bar in this respect. It puts forward its constitutions, purpose and programme of reform before all men. But those who do not accept it are not entitled to have any voice in shaping the policy of that state. They can live in that state as subjects (Dhimmi), and his life, property and honour will be fully protected, and if he is capable of any service, he will be provided.

The Structure of the Islamic State

In Islam God alone is the real sovereign, and anyone who holds power and rules in accordance with the laws of God would be the viceregent and will not be authorised to exercise any powers other than those ordained by God. The power and rulership of the earth has been promised to the whole community of believers, there is no reservation in favour of any family, class or race. Every believer is a Caliph of God in his own capacity and he is individually responsible to God. In this regard the Prophet has said, "Every one of you is a ruler and every one is answerable for his subjects. And one Caliph is in no way inferior to another." Some special features of the government in a Islamic state have been enumerated below:

1. The leader (Ameer) will be selected on the basis of the religious virtues one has and who enjoys the full confidence of the Muslim public. After selection he will exercise full authority in all respects, and will be obeyed so long as he follows the laws of God and His Prophet.

2. The leader or governor will not be above criticism. Every citizen will have full right to criticise his private or public affairs. In the eyes of law he will be just an ordinary citizen who may be deposed and punished.

3. There will be an advisory council of trusted Muslims which would guide the leader of the state as and when necessary.

4. The decision of the council will generally be made by the majority of votes. But Islam does not regard number as a criterion of truth and rectitude. It holds that the opinion of a single person may be sounder than the unanimous opinion of the entire council, and if this is so, there is no reason why truth should be given up only because its supporters are in a minority and error be accepted merely because it has the support of a large majority. Hence the leader has the right to concur either with the majority or the minority and is further entitled to disagree with the whole of the council and decide matters according to his whim.

5. Election for the post of a leader or membership of the council is not made democratically in the modern sense of the word. Because for any post none is allowed to put forward his candidature himself and try to secure it from the media of publicity and propaganda or such other means. The leader shall be chosen by the public themselves on the basis of his virtues by consensus.

6. The members of the Islamic Advisory Council will express their opinions independent of the party

consideration. They should only side with the truthful and the just.

7. In Islam judiciary has been made entirely independent of the executive. A judge (Qazi) should implement and enforce God's law in society as a representative of God. A leader should not interfere in any form with the affairs of justice from him, whether the Caliph or the pauper.

Law

Islamic law comprises injunctions emanating from Islamic world view. The provisions of Islamic Law (Sharia) are purposive, related to both phases of man's life, viz., the immediate earthly life and the life hereafter. A comprehensive statement of this purpose is tazkiya (purification-cum-growth). Moral and spiritual growth of man, leading to welfare in this life as well as in the life after death is the ultimate aim of Shariah."[1]

"The Qur'an gives certain laws, foundational and basic in nature on which the Islamic society should be organized. The laws relate specially to the family—the ultimate basis of social life (marriage, divorce, inheritance, will, etc.); but incidentally many other matters have been referred to. With regard to political organization only two broad observations are made: the rest is left to the secular instincts and legislative activity of mankind."[2]

The chief sources of Islamic law are Qur'an and the Sunnah. In the third place the consensus (Ijma) of jurists and competent thinkers of an age is also a means of discovering Islamic Laws. Systematic inference from texts ranks fourth. Besides these four sources some other methods of discovering the law of God in matters not covered directly or

1. Ibn Qazzim, Ilm-al-Muwaqqin, Vol. 3, P. I, Matba Muniriah, Egypt, n.g., p. 29.
2. Nizami, Khaliq Ahmad, Some Aspects of Religion and Politics in India During the 13th Century, Asia Publishing House, Bombay, 1961, p. 34.

inferentially by the texts are also prevalent, like Istihsam, that is defining the law in accordance with what is good. Compliance with laws enacted by the Islamic state is a religious duty of its Muslim citizens, but not being final and immune from error, they can be subjected to criticism and sought to be changed.[3]

On the whole, four schools of law stand out prominently in the history of Islam: The Hanafite, Malikite, the Shafi-ite, and the Hanbalite. The sources utilized by these jurists for building up the legal structure of Islam were—the Qur'an, the Ahadis, the Ijma, and the Qiyas.

Khalifa Omar, Usman and Ali propagated the Islamic spirit of democratic government and maintained balanced socio-political order. But that fourth Khalifa, Hazrat Ali could rule only less than five years because of opposition he met with and his assassination later on by the Moawiya and his kinsmen. After his execution Hasan was elected Khalifa, but finding himself too weak, he abdicated in favour of Moawiya. The four early Khalifa lived simple lives and carried out their administrative duties in a paternal spirit and all their steps were directed to the welfare of their subjects. Their humble dwellings served the purposes of palaces, and they held their Durbar in mosque, where all the Muslims, white and black, master and slave, could approach them and place grievances before them. They had neither vazirs nor ministers to serve them and attended in person even to minor matters pertaining to the administration. They also distributed booty, settled disputes—criminal and civil. But this method of governing could not last long. When the Umayyad came to power, they adopted the Roman and sometimes the Iranian systems of administration.

India under Islam

The Arabs and Iranians were connected with India as traders long before the advent of Islam. But, on the whole, India was not influenced by Islam till the appearance of Sultan

3. Ibid., p. 35.

Mahmood. Then after numerous other kings appeared and disappeared on the Indian political scene. Then starts Moghul period in India with the estabishment of the first kingdom by Babur. The Moghul administration was based upon the military system of Turko-Moghals, which was modified by their contact with Persians and Indians. Justice in the modern sense was not expected and known. Nobles were kept in obedience and loyalty not because they considered such loyalty would bring prosperity and power to the community and race, but for the reason that the king was powerful and could force them to remain loyal. The Arab thinkers argue that kingship was necessary institution for the maintenance of social order. They did not hesitate to declare that even an unjust and oppressive monarchy was better than unlicensed freedom. Prof. Ashraf says, "In short, the Muslims were faced with a choice between monarchy and anarchy, and they wisely chose the former."[4] He has designated as 'Zillullah', the shadow of Divine being. This, however, did not stop divine honours from being paid to a Sultan, or a monarch from ruling over people 'as a God in human form'. In India also no attempt was made to conceal this position. People had to prostrate themselves before the Sultan of Delhi when he was present, and to stand up even when his name was mentioned as a mark of solemn reverence; when at a distance from Delhi, they bowed towards the seat of Sultanat. Ashraf says that the position of the Sultan was made easier in the Indian environment by the submissiveness of the masses of the people and the Hindu institution and political traditions."[5]

The fall of Moghal Empire and the appearance of the British on Indian political scene gave a severe jolt to the politico-economic and socio-cultural life of Indian Muslims. Muslims of India as a whole had a profound dislike for the British government as well as for western learning and culture. But the situation compelled them to remain under British rule and learn their teachings. Southern and Western Indian

4. Ashraf, K.M., Life and Conditions of the People of Hindustan, Munshiram Manoharlal, New Delhi, 1970, p. 29.
5. Ibid., p. 33.

Muslims took a lead and the north-eastern Muslims followed them gradually.

The Ulemas and Sufis hated the western culture more intensely, and regarded the English as the enemies of Islam and the friends and patrons of Christianity. Thus Muslims in general and feudal and religious classes in particular became a bitter critic and enemy of the English due to various political, economic and socio-cultural motives. Muslims and Hindus of such a temper combined together and fought against the Britishers for national independence in 1857. But the plan could not succeed. This revolt once more convinced the Britishers of the hostile and unreliable character of Muslims. So they hanged thousands of Muslims even on the slightest suspicion of being implicated in the movement, and confiscated the jagirs and properties of many others. Besides, they now replaced Muslims by Hindus in government service anywhere they liked.

In the nineteenth century the impact of the new age gave rise to three trends of thought and action among three regular movements, vis-a-vis, secular communalism, religious nationalism, and secular nationalism. The advocates of all the three concepts aimed at bringing about changes in various departments of life, the only difference being that some wanted change from a modern liberal point of view and some from a revivalist point of view. These movements, under the pressure of prevailing circumstances, ultimately became purely political.

After about a century in 1947, the movement of independence launched by Hindus and Muslims achieved independence. But the Indians paid heavily for it, because Britishers' policy of 'divide and rule' succeeded in dividing India into two nations—India and Pakistan. Both Hindus and Muslims paid heavily. In reality the plight of the Muslims during 1947 and the following years was and, to some extent, still is, worse than that of 1857. Pre-partition as well as the post-partition effects created an atmosphere of suspicion, hatred and coercion between the two communities. A section of the majority community always remained in a mood to fan the hostility and take revenge on the Indian Muslims. Again, after a few years the zamindari and jagirdari system was abolished. This ruined the economy of upper and middle class Muslims. By this time neither the Muslims had entered sufficiently into modern education in agriculture, business and trade and in government services etc., nor the new government wished to protect their prestige and support them psychologically, economically and socio-culturally.

In India, after the independence, a democratic political order has been formed which proclaims in values of equality, liberty and fraternity. Irrespective of caste, class and creed everyone may enjoy the freedom of action and speech, right to vote and form a popular government. Such a democratic government is characterised as the 'government of the people, by the people and for the people.' Indian Muslims in general claim that democracy is completely in accord with Islamic teachings and that Islamic society under the Prophet and the righteous Khalifas was a model democratic society.

But a comparative analysis of the Islamic democracy and the modern democracy shows many a basic differences. First, in a modern democratic state the people elect their representatives who, after being a majority, form the government and rule over them. These representatives frame laws according to their conveniences and administer it over them. Practice of favour to one's supporters and disfavour to opponents is a special feature of such government. Islamic democracy adopts somewhat different principle and practice in election, administration, legislation, etc. It follows only those laws contained in Qur'an. The ruler cannot do anything according to his wishes. If so, it shall be un-Islamic, and hence such a ruler may be replaced. Commenting on modern democracy, Lari says, "Modern political theory exalts 'the general will'." Democratic government attempts to put that general will into practice by making law out of the policy voted for by 'the majority' (which need only be 51%) leaving null and void the will of the minority (which may be that of as many as 49% of the voters). The minority is thus not 'free' at all, even though in some cases its will may be sensible, and in the circumstances right. But "Government by the will of the people" will never voluntarily strip it of sanctity and splendour with which it has endowed "the general will, giving that concept precedence over all other material and spiritual values."[6]

Thus Islam gives primacy to the will of the God or Divine Law, rather than to the mere majority of people. Because, it is believed man cannot frame laws suited to human condition, or justly cure the troubles that arise. Modern slogans of "Liberty and Equality", and "the Public Will" are charming words used by politicians to win support for their laws, which, in fact, represent the interest of the politicians and their supporters rather than of the masses. Likewise, the terms 'communism' and 'socialism' are also not in accordance with the Islamic social and political values. Anyway, the second generation of Muslims after 1947 has got a more liberal and secular outlook on life. With a democratic political consciousness they are making headway in the Indian politics, whatever the party may be. And this is a fact that the communal outlook on politics will ruin the nation, Hindus and Muslims alike.

Findings

The political climate of India has been changing fast since the very beginning of the present century. The nationalist movement started by Indian National Congress, the emergence of Muslim League and Hindu Mahasabha on communal patterns, the growing influence of communism, trade union movements and peasant movements have been of vital significance in developing a new political climate in the country. Along with struggle for the freedom of the country, the Indian National Congress also struggled for the emancipation of women and for improvement in conditions of literacy and education. The improvement in literacy and the participation of women in outdoor activities also contributed to the development of political consciousness among Indian masses. After the achievement of independence the parliamentary system of democracy facilitated the common people to

6. Lari, S.M.R.M., Western Civilization Through Muslim Eyes, Biddles Ltd., Britain, 1977, p. 54.

participate in politics not only as a voter but also as a candidate as well as a campaigner or organiser of election campaign. The general elections and mid-term polls held in the country have provided ample opportunities for the villagers and masses in general to take part in politics and to develop an interest in political activities and performances of various political parties. The common people have also developed some degree of political consciousness along with varying degrees of political participation.

In the light of above-given facts it was desirable to find out to what extent the people in the village have been exposed to political climate and to what extent they have developed an interest in political activities. For analyzing political consciousness and political participation of the villagers under study, certain questions were put to the respondents. One question put to the respondents was, "Are you a member/office bearer of any social, political, religious organisation?" The responses collected from the respondents are presented in Table 7.1.

Table 7.1

Respondents' Affiliation with Social/Political/Religious Organisation

N=158

Organisation	*Membership*		*Ordinary Member*		*Office Bearer*	
	No.	%	*No.*	%	*No.*	%
Social	45	28.48	40	88.88	5	11.11
Political	7	4.44	5	71.42	2	28.57
Religious	25	15.82	14	56.00	11	44.00
None	81	51.26	—	—	—	—
Total	158	100.00	59		18	

It is evident from the above table that majority (51.26%) of the respondents are not associated in any capacity with any type of organisation. But 48 73% of the respondents are associated with one or the other type of organisation, either as an ordinary member or as an office bearer. The table further shows that the highest percentage of association is with social organisation (28.48%) and the lowest percentage of association is with political o-ganisation (4.44%), while 15.82% of the respondents have their association with religious organisation. The table further shows that 88.88% of the respondents associated with social organisation are ordinary members, whereas remaining 11.11% are office bearers. Among those associated with political organisation, 71.42% are ordinary members and 28.57% are office bearers. In the same way among the respondents associated with religious organisation, 56% are ordinary members and 44% are office bearers. These data suggest that the villagers are conscious of joining organisations of one type or the other. It is also important to point out that the village under study is quite large having waqf institution, madrasa, schools, clubs, library and other socio-cultural organisations. Hence association with social or religious organisation is in a higher percentage. But at the same time the association with political organisation not only as an ordinary member but also as office bearer shows the persistence of political awareness.

The next question put to the respondents was, "To which party you think to be your well-wisher?" The responses obtained from the respondents are presented in Table 7.2.

The respondents mentioned different parties whom they think to be their well-wisher. For a precise classification the names of the different parties have not been mentioned. On the other hand, the broader categories of rightist parties, leftist parties and reactionary parties have been shown in the table. The category of rightist party includes the parties like Congress (I), Congress (S). Congress (J), Janata Party and Lok Dal. The category of leftist party includes the parties like C.P.I., C.P.I. (M) and Forward Block. Reactionary parties include Bhartiya Janata Party, Jamaat Islami, C.P.M. (ML) and the like.

Table 7.2

Political Consciousness of the Respondents

N=158

Parties	*Number*	*Percentage*
Right Parties	68	43.05
Left Parties	23	14.56
Reactionary Parties	6	3.79
Undecided	35	22.15
None	2[illegible]	16.45
Total	158	100.00

It is evident from the table that 22.15% of the respondents could not mention any specific party as their well-wisher and 16.45% of the respondents do not regard any party as their well wisher. It means that 38.60% of the respondents do not think any specific party which may render services to them. The table further shows that 43.05% of the respondents have mentioned rightist parties, 14.56% have mentioned leftist parties and 3.79% have mentioned reactionary party. Hence it may be interpreted that the villagers are more inclined towards rightist forces and a low percentage feels associated with leftist forces. The reactionary parties do not have any important place in the village. It is also important to point out that the village under study is in naxalite belt in the Jehanabad sub-division of Gaya district. But in spite of this fact the attachment with the reactionary party is insignificant. It may be due to the fact that the respondents are Muslims and the naxalite movement is mostly favoured by various groups of Harijans. On the whole the data suggest that the political parties have their impact on the villagers.

For analyzing the political consciousness of the villagers on the basis of the responses given in Table 7.2, the same responses have been classified on literacy basis in Table 7.3.

Table 7.3

Education and Political Consciousness

N=158

Level of Literacy	*Right parties*	*Left parties*	*Right reac.*	*Undecided*	*None*	*Total*
Illiterate	13(30.97)	7(16 66)	2(4·76)	11(26.19)	9(21.42)	42
Below Matric	32(40.50)	10(12.65)	3(3.79)	21(26.58)	13(16.45)	79
Below Graduate	15(60.00)	3(12.00)	1(4.00)	3(12.00)	3(12.00)	25
Graduate+	8(66.66)	3(25.00)	—	—	1(8 33)	12
Total	68	23	6	35	26	158

It appears from the above table that the percentage of response declaring no party as well-wisher has consistently declined with the rise in literacy level. The highest percentage (21.42%) is in the illiterate group and the lowest (8.33%) in the category of graduation and above. In the same way the percentage of response showing indecision is the highest in case of illiterate and literate categories, whereas it is nil in the highly qualified category. Thus these response patterns show the relevance of literacy to political consciousness.

The table further shows that percentage of response favouring rightist parties has consistently risen with the rise in literacy level, whereas the percentage of response favouring leftist parties has declined with the rise in the level of education excepting the percentage of response in the highly qualified category. These variations in response patterns show a relevance with the variation of the level of literacy. The highly qualified villagers are more attached with rightist and leftist parties but none of them has an appreciation for the reactionary parties.

Table 7.4 presents th classification of the responses on the basis of occupation.

It is evident from the table that cultivation is the most important occupation in the village. The next important specific occupation is labour or wage-earning. Other occupations held by the villagers are business, service, multiple occupations and other unspecified occupations. It is evident from the table that the highest percentage of favour for the rightist parties is in the business category (60%) and more or less the same in case of cultivators (59.72%). But among wage-earners only 18.75% have mentioned rightist parties as well as the same percentage thought leftist parties as their well-wisher. In this category the highest percentage of response is in respect of undecided (31.25%) and the second highest (25%) in the column of none. It shows that majority of the wage-earners do not mention any specific party. It is important to note that among service holders the highest percentage has favoured leftist parties (41.66%) and only 33.33% have mentioned rightist parties. As most of the service holders are educated, it may be interpreted that leftist parties are more

Table 7.4

Occupation and Political Consciousness

N=158

Occupation	*Right parties*	*Left parties*	*Right Reac.*	*Undecided*	*None*	*Total*
	No./%	*No./%*	*No./%*	*No /%*	*No./%*	
Cultivation	43	5	1	12	11	72
	59.72	6.94	1.38	16.66	15.27	
Business	6	1	1	2	—	10
	60.00	10.00	10.00	20.00	—	
Service	4	5	—	2	1	12
	33.33	41.66	—	16.66	8.33	
Labour	3	3	1	5	4	16
	18.75	18.75	6.25	31.25	25.00	
Multiple occupation	4	2	1	3	2	12
	33.33	16.66	8.33	25.00	16.66	
Others	9	7	2	11	7	36
	25.00	19.44	5.55	30.55	19.44	
Total	68	23	6	35	26	158

favoured by educated people. It is also evident from the table that only in case of service holders no respondent has mentioned any reactionary party. Hence it may be interpreted that the service holder class is more conscious than the cultivators, businessmen and wage-earners.

Another question put to the respondents was regarding the form of government they like. For collecting responses from the respondents the different forms of government were explained when needed. The responses thus collected, have been presented in Table 7.5.

Table 7.5

Form of Government liked by the Respondents

N=158

Form of Government	*Number*	*Percentage*
Parliamentary Democracy	62	39.26
Presidential Democracy	26	16.46
Totalitarian	9	5.69
Islamic Democracy	20	12.65
Undecided	41	25.94
Total	158	100.00

It is evident from the above table that the highest percentage of response is in favour of parliamentary democracy (39.26%). The second highest percentage of response has gone in favour of presidential form of government (16.46%). In spite of the fact that the respondents are Muslims only 12.65% have favoured Islamic democracy. A smaller section of 5.69% have expressed its liking for totalitarian form of government. Moreover, a considerable section of the villagers (25 94%) has remained undecided. In the light of these findings it may be interpreted that parliamentary system of democracy is still supported by most of the people and other forms of government are less liked.

The responses analysed in Table 7.5 have been classified on the basis of level of literacy in Table 7.6 with the objective of finding out the relevance of literacy to the response patterns.

It is evident from this table that the percentage of response supporting parliamentary form of democracy has consistently risen with the rise in the level of education. The same is the pattern of response supporting presidential form of government. But in case of totalitarianism zero per cent of graduates and above have shown its liking whereas in the remaining three categories the percentage of response has consistently risen. The highest percentage of response in favour of Islamic democracy is found in case of illiterate (19.04%) and the lowest percentage in case of graduates and above (8.33%). Excepting the category of below matriculation the percentage of response has declined with the rise of level of literacy. The table further shows that 40.47% of the illiterate and 30.37% of under-matriculates are undecided whereas no respondent of the two higher categories has expressed indecision. It means that illiterates and literates have a lesser degree of appreciation or evaluation of different forms of government than matriculates and graduates. It also shows the relevance of literacy level to political consciousness.

The next question put to the respondents was about the functioning of gram panchayat in that area. The responses obtained from the villagers are given in Table 7.7.

It is evident from the table that the majority of the respondents is not satisfied with the functioning of the gram panchayat because 52.53% of the respondents have described the functioning as bad. Only 32.92% of the respondents have praised the functioning of gram panchayat. It may, therefore, be interpreted that the common people are not happy with the working of gram panchayat in the area. The reason for the satisfaction or dissatisfaction with the working of gram panchayat is evident from Table 7.8 which shows the responses of the villagers regarding the type of persons being elected to the gram panchayats.

Table 7.6

Education and the Likeness for the Form of Government

N=158

Level of literacy	*Parliamentary Democracy* No./%	*Presidential Democracy* No./%	*Totalitarian* No./%	*Islamic Democracy* No./%	*Undecided* No./%
Illiterate (42)	12(28.57)	3(7.14)	2(4.76)	8(19.04)	17(40.47)
Below Matriculation (79)	32(40.50)	10(12.65)	5(6.32)	8(10.12)	24(30.37)
Below Graduation (25)	12(48.00)	8(32.00)	2(8.00)	3(12.00)	—
Graduation+	6(50.00)	5(41.66)	—	1(8.33)	—
Total	62	26	9	20	41=158

Table 7.7

Responses showing the Functioning of Gram Panchayat

N=158

Category of response	*Number*	*Percentage*
Good	52	32.92
Bad	83	52.53
Undecided	23	14.55
Total	158	100.00

Table 7.8

Persons Elected in Gram Panchayat

N=158

Category	*Number*	*Percentage*
Honest and active	25	15.84
Wealthy	14	8.87
Bad elements	47	29.74
Casteists	26	16.45
Social workers	20	12.65
Politicians	26	16.45
Total	158	100.00

It is evident from the above table that the highest percentage of response (29.74%) has gone in respect of bad elements. The second highest percentage of response (16.45%) shows that casteists and politicians are elected to the gram panchayats. These typologies of persons are negative attributes. Hence on the whole 62.64% of the respondents have declared that evil elements are elected to the gram panchayats and the election of these evil, partial, selfish or corrupt elements may be responsible for the dissatisfactory functioning of Panchayati Raj. Only 15.84% of the respondents have stated that honest and active persons are elected and only 12.65% have declared that social workers are elected. Hence it may be interpreted that the villagers have the feeling that real representatives are not being elected to the gram panchayats. The evil forces of caste, money and might are instrumental in panchayat elections and hence the gram panchayats are not working up to the expectations of the people. This view of the villagers about the working of gram panchayat also reveals the persistence of political awareness and political consciousness.

8

Cultural Relations

A. BELIEFS, RITUALS AND FESTIVITIES

Since the early phase of human life religion has played a vital role in organizing human groups and in developing orderly ways and manners in human societies. Till the scientific achievements and technological developments in the present century the institution of religion remained an unchallenged reality of social life and continued as a basic institution of society regulating social, economic and political activities of small as well as large social systems. After scientific achievements and technological developments, rise of communism and modernity the necessity of religion in social life has become a debatable issue. But the fact is that even today religion enjoys a prominent place in the major part of the human population. Even in societies denying the existence of super-natural power and divine forces religion is not completely uprooted and one can find people holding religious beliefs and performing religious observances even in communist societies. Thus religion is a universal institution, though every individual cannot claim to be guided by religious sanctions. Broom and Selznick have rightly remarked: "Religious beliefs and practices exist in every known society, from the most simple and isolated to the most complex and urbane. Not all individuals are religious, but some form of religious behaviour is found in all human communities."[1] It appears from this remark that religion is a universal institution and it exists in every society. More or less the same view-point has been expressed by Anderson and Parker in the following words: "Religion is a universal experience with man."[2] Belief in super-natural power is of central importance in every religion. It is found that alongwith a belief of super-natural power a system of worship is also associated with every religion. Anderson and Parker have mentioned four primary components of religion. These components are—(1) belief in super-natural forces, (2) man's adjustment to super-natural forces, (3) acts defined as sinful, and (4) some method of salvation."[3] It mean that when a belief in super-natural power develops and adjustment to the belief is also essential and consequently a system of worship develops. The concepts of right and wrong give birth to the notions of sinful acts and acts leading to salvation. The behaviours conforming to religious sanctions lead to the attainment of salvation whereas the behaviours violating religious sanctions are believed to be sinful acts. There is a divine reward for the former and a divine punishment for the latter.

The universality of religion as an institution does not mean that the patterns of religious beliefs are also the same everywhere. There are differences in the forms and patterns of religious sanctions, In the words of Broom and Selznick, "As important as the universality of religion is its remarkable diversity. Some religions believe in a single supreme being, others are polytheistic. In some prevalent societies religion

1. Broom, Leonard and Selznick, Philip, Sociology: A Text with Adapted Readings, Row Peterson & Co., Evanston, Ill., 1955, p. 301.
2. Anderson, Walfred A. and Parker, Fredrick B., An Introduction to Sociology, Affiliated East West Press Pvt. Ltd., New Delhi, 1966, p. 195.
3. Ibid., p. 196.

centres around spirits, forces and demons that are often capricious, wilful and malevolent."[4]

The functional importance of religion may also be described in the context of social cohesion. The cohesive function of religion has been of such a great significance in society that Durkhiem declared that "the idea of society is the soul of religion."[5] Referring to this function he says, "The functions that religion does for society are often of opposing types. Seen in the short run they seem contradictory; in the long range of history they may be complementary, the one supplying stability and the other providing for change. Religion generally supports the social norms, re-assuming the people that their ways are right and their causes just, but at the same time the great religious prophets have all been critics of their societies."[6] Thus it appears that religion functions not as a unifying force and a divisive force in society. The divisive functions take place when two or more intolerant religions or two or more intolerant sects of the same religion exist in the same society. Moreover, in case of the emergence of a new religion challenging the already existing religion also generates a conflict and develops a division in the society. As remarked by Stewart and Glynn, "Religion becomes a divisive force in history when a society is faced with conflicting and mutually intolerant religions or conflicting and mutually intolerant interpretations of the same religion. Religion also has been divisive at other times, as when a new religion began to spread in a society whose institutions and values were incompatible with its doctrines."[7] Maxweber recognized six major religions of the world and included in this list the religions of Christianity, Islam, Hinduism, Buddhism Judaism and Confucianism. Among these religions the last one has lost its importance in

4. Broom, Leonard and Selznick, Philip, Sociology: A Text with Adapted Readings, Row Peterson & Co., Evanston, Ill., 1955, p. 301.
5. Durkheim, Emile, Elementary Forms of the Religious Life, trans., J.W. Swain, Free Press, Paris, 1947, p. 419.
6. Ibid., p. 202.
7. Stewart, E.W. and Glynn, J.A., Introduction to Sociology.

the very region of its origin due to the impact of Buddhism and later on the rise of communism in China. Moreover, among the other five religions the followers of Christianity are largest in number and the second largest number is that of the followers of Islam. In addition to Arabia, the place of origin, Islam is followed in almost all parts of the world and in a large number of Asian and African countries the Muslims are in majority. It is also important to point out that among these major religions of the world Islam is the latest.

In the light of the above analysis it appears that Islam is a major religion and its followers are found in Asia, Africa, Europe and America. The religion appeared in Arabia about 1400 years ago and it is believed by the Muslims that Mohammad was deputed by God to preach this religion to humanity and he was to act as a divine messenger. Prophet Mohammad presented the teachings of the people of Mecca, then to Arabia and ultimtely to the entire humanity. The sanctions of this religion suggest that Islam preaches monotheism and advocates the existence of only one supreme divine authority known as Allah. The two basic sources of Islamic sanctions are the Holy Qur'an (Divine Revelation to the Prophet) and Traditions or Hadis (the sayings of Prophet himself). Moreover, the life of the Prophet is believed to be a model for the Muslims and an expression of the sanctions of Islam in the actual practice. Commenting on the distinctive features of Islam as a religion, Mohammad Mazharuddin Siddiqui remarks, "The distinctive characteristics of Islam as a world religion are its simplicity, its explicitness and its highly realistic attitude towards human problems, leaning neither towards excessive optimism or excessive pessimism, and enjoying moderation and balance of mind in all things."[8]

"Islam recognizes that social and external conditions which have great influence in shaping man's conduct and character, and, therefore, tries to set right the social, political and economic system in consonance with its own spiritual and moral ends",[9] Siddiqui says further. It appears from this

8. Siddiqui, Mohd. Mazharuddin, What is Islam, p. 20.

9. Ibid., p. 20.

remark that Islam deals with the realities of life. It does not lay emphasis on spiritualism only; rather it recognizes the importance of worldly life. It does not direct its followers to withdraw from worldly life and to lead an ascetic life; rather it permits the Muslims to participate in community life and to labour hard for earning livelihood. Thus Islam embraces both spiritualism and materialism and maintains that at every stage and in every conduct, a man should abide by Islamic sanctions. The concept of legitimate or illegitimate, 'halal' or 'haram' should be the guiding principle in performing any task or in doing work.

According to the interpreters of Islam, a person offering Namaz but not looking after his children and other dependents is not a true Muslim and he is not liked by Prophet and God. The real spirit of worship in Islam lies in obeying God and observing Islamic sanctions in all walks of life. Thus the teachings of Islam include sanctions about economic life, social life, political life and living together in the community. It defines the relations among the Muslim brethren and also between Muslims and non-Muslims. Thus the Islamic sanctions cover the totality of man's life and define the role and conduct of Muslims on different occasions. In short, Islam does not stand for the killing of the self but for control over the self Character building is of central importance in Islam.

In the light of the above analysis it appears that Islam came as a system of philosophy to be observed in actual practice. It exists as a way of life. The preachings of Islam were not expected to be accepted only in theory; rather these were required to be observed in practice. It is claimed by the Muslims that the life of the Prophet was a practical demonstration of observing Islamic sanctions. In the beginning of Islamic preachings, those who embraced Islam during the lifetime of Prophet observed Islamic sanctions to the best of their capacity. Thus in the early days Islamic sanctions were followed by the Muslims. But gradually the impact of environmental conditions, other cultures of the world and various other factors influenced the ways of life in Muslim society and certain changes took place in relation to the early period of Islam. Moreover, with the passing of time, Islam was also divided into various sects. Some of these sects differed on fundamental principles and others on minor points. The major division of Islam is into two sects of Sunnis and Shias. The basic difference between the two sects lies in respect of succession issue after the death of the Prophet. The Sunnis hold that Ali, the cousin and son-in-law of the Prophet, was the fourth successor (Caliph) after Abu Baker, Umar and Usman, whereas according to Shia sect, Ali was the first successor. Shushtery has pointed out, "The Shias differ from the Sunnat Jamaat in regard to the successor to the Prophet."[10]

In addition to these two major sects, another important sect in Islam is known as Wahabis or Ahle-Hadis. Referring to this sect, A.M.A. Shushtery has pointed out, "This sect was founded by Mohammad, son of Abdul Wahab, born in Central Arabia in 1691. He wanted to revive the simplicity of Islam. He bases his reform in interpreting the teachings of the Qur'an with the help of Tradition and private judgments without binding himself to the opinions expounded by the four orthodox Imams."[11] The Muslims came to India as traders and the Muslim missionaries were established before the invasion by Mohammad Bin Qassim. Before this invasion the Musltms living in this country were not supported by any propagation of Islam. Gradually Islam was accepted by a considerable section of Indian society because this religion believed in equality of Muslims whereas the traditional Hindu society denied equal right to all its followers. The conversion of Hindus into Islamic fold was not mainly due to the capturing of political power by the Muslims but by the Muslim missionary activities. This view has been supported by Shushtery.[12]

The developments taking place in the Islamic world in general and in India in particular resulted in a significant

10. Shushtery, A.M.A, Outlines of Islamic Culture, Bangalore Publishing Co. Pvt. Ltd., Bangalore, 1937, p. 28.

11. Ibid., pp. 28-29.

12. Ibid., p. 240.

change in the life of the Indian Muslims. The indigenous population embracing Islam could not part with its traditional ways, manners and the rituals and customs. Through this indigenous population, the rituals, superstitions and customary observances of traditional Indian society were introduced in the Muslim society and the foreign section of the Indian Muslim society also could not escape from the impact of traditional life. Consequently the Muslim society in India gradually became a tradition-oriented society much divorced from the spirit of Islamic sanctions.

The spread of Islam in India was influenced by the traditional culture and consequently Islamization and Indianization continued to operate together. The ideal sanctions of Islam were not strictly observed in everyday life and deviation from Islamic sanctions was seen in every sphere of life, religion, family, social hierarchy, education, rule and status of women and political system. The rise of aristocratic class in Muslim community and the distinction among the followers of the same religion on the basis of wealth and material power were against Islamic sanctions. But, gradually a distinction was made on the basis of property, occupation and economic interest, birth and educational attainments. But the distinction was not sufficient to constitute a caste system such as it existed in Hindu society. It was possible for an individual to rise from a lower to a higher class.

In the light of the above discussion it can be stated that the social structure prevailing in the Muslim society of medieval India was much different from the ideal social structure.

The changes in social life and outlook of the people were also reflected in the performances and celebrations of the festivals of Muslim society. The important festivals observed by Muslims are Muharram, Shab-e-Baraat, Idul-Fitr and Idul-Zoha. Among the festivals Idul-Fitr and Idul-Zoha are observed by Muslims throughout the world, whereas Muharram and Shab-e-Baraat are not observed as a religious festival by a section of Muslim society. The patterns of observing these festivals suggest that the Indian culture and other environmental factors have deeply penetrated into the community life of the Indian Muslims since the medieval age.

As regards the festival of Muharram, it is observed in the memory of the martyrdom of Imam Hussain, the son of Hazrat Ali and the grandson of the Prophet Mohammad. He died fighting at Kerbala against Yazid, the son of the usurper Moaviah to the Khilafatship of Islam. Imam Hussain sacrificed his life and his companions (including children, youths and old people) for serving the cause of religion and rejecting the illegitimate Khilafat of Yazid. This festival is observed by the Muslims in general and Shias in particular. As the festival is in the memory of the tragic events of Kerbala, it is a mourning festival. There are different ways of mourning the martyrdom of Imam Hussain in different parts of the country. Majalis are held where the tragic events are recited in prose and poetry. Elegies are recited by the people to mourn the death of Imam Hussain and his companions. Both men and women attend such programmes maintaining purdah. When the tragic events are described tears roll down on the face of the listeners and they express their sorrow and grief over the tragic death. Generally the Shi'ite women wear black dresses and avoid to wear red, pink and yellow garments because these colours are believed to be the index of joy. Moreover, they abstain from using cosmetics and participating in entertaining programmes. The married women do not wear bangles and do not apply sendur in the partition of the hair. Among Indian Shias marriage or any other such joyful functions are not performed during the mourning period. Moreover, the general Muslims observe Muharram through taking out 'Akhara' in which bands of different types are used. It is obvious that there is no religious sanction prohibiting people from performing marriage or participating in entertainments or wearing bangles or other such activities. It is the concept of Indian tradition and the observation of Muharram in this manner.

Indian society has been characterised as faith-oriented society. Religious beliefs and mythological sanctions dominated over traditional social life for centuries in this country. The Muslims living in India have a religion of their own which was brought from Arabia and Persia. But after living for centuries in this country their religious life and related rituals and beliefs have not been the same as sanctioned by Islamic ideology. Under the impact of traditional social life and Hindu culture, significant changes have taken place in their everyday life including rituals, beliefs and religious practices. The faith in Islam is unaltered, but beliefs in ghost and other such spirits among orthodox Muslims is an addition under the impact of traditional Hindu culture. In the same way, the performances in the field of religion have been coloured by the contents of traditional Indian culture. The observances of Shab-e-Baraat, Id, Baqrid and Muharram, etc. are primarily religious in nature but these religious performances have been influenced by the elements of Indian culture. Moreover, the rituals on the occasion of marriage, death, birth ceremony, aqiqa and circumcision (khatna) are not purely Islamic in nature. Local customs, traditions, orthodox beliefs and superstitions have been inculcated into these rituals and ceremonies.

In the present age changes are taking place in traditional way of life and rituals, beliefs and religious peformances. The Muslims are exposed not only to the process of modernization but also to re-Islamization. Various religious organizations like Jamaat-e-Islami, Tablighi Jamaat and other such organizations are working for removal of the evil practices and developing the firm faith in Islamic ideology. The teams of the preachers are moving in remote village areas for this purpose. Religious preachings and ceremonies are organised by such visiting teams. Under the impact of these movements the mullahs leading Friday prayers also preach on the same lines. These reformative struggles are also proving instrumental in re-Islamization and bringing about changes in a ritual, beliefs and religious practices. The impact is not uniform in all areas and hence it is important to find out to what extent the villagers under study have been exposed to the processes of modernization and re-Islamization and what are the changes taking place in these aspects.

Findings

As all the respondents covered by the present study are Muslims, they believe in Islamic sanctions and fundamentals of the religion of Islam. But whether they are Muslims only in faith or also in practice is an important aspect of the study concerning religious life, rituals and festivities. Certain practices in Muslim Society are basically religious and constitute the forms of worship in Islam. The important forms of worship are five times prayer a day, fasting for a month, payment of zakat or divine tax from personal savings, offering sacrifice or Qurbani on the occasion of Idul-Zoha and performing Haj pilgrimage at Mecca at least once in life, by those who can afford. Hence a question put to the respondents was, "How seriously do you practise the following fundamentals of Islam ?" The fundamentals mentioned to the respondents were prayers, fasting, zakat, qurbani and haj, as indicated from Table 8.1.

It appears from the table that the respondents were provided with four categories of response for the different forms of worship. These different categories were, 'seriously', 'normally', 'occasionally' and 'unable to perform'. The table shows that 39.87% of the respondents offer nimaz seriously, 30.37% normally, 22.15% occasionally and 7.59% never due to one reason or the other. It means that a considerable section is punctual in offering nimaz while a little lower percentage is in the habit of offering nimaz occasionally. On the whole, 70.14% of the respondents are in the habit of offering nimaz regularly or almost regularly. It suggests that the majority not only believes in this Islamic fundamental but also practises it in daily life. As regards the fasting, 77.84% are normally in the habit of fasting. Only 8.22% stated that they did fasting occasionally and 4.3% declared that they were unable to do fasting due to one reason or the other. Thus 87.33% are in the habit of observing fast, regularly or almost regularly and a very low percentage of the respondents abstain from fasting. Non-observance of fast may be due to old age, illness, poor health or lack of will in observing fast. Hence it may be interpreted that in comparison

Table 8.1

Practice of the Fundamentals of Islam by the Respondents

N=158

Fundamentals	*Seriously*	*Normally*	*Occasionally*	*Unable to perform*	*Total*
	No./%	*No./%*	*No./%*	*No./%*	
Prayer	63(39.87)	48(30 37)	35(22.15)	12(7.59)	158
Fasting	123(77.84)	15(9.49)	13(8.22)	7(4.43)	158
Zakat	87(55.06)	22(13.92)	—	49(31.01)	158
Qurbani	55(34.81)	53(33.54)	13(8.22)	37(23.41)	158
Haj	4(2.53)	—	—	154(97.46)	158

to nimaz, the people are more adherent to the practice of fasting. The responses in respect of zakat show that 55.06% are serious in giving zakat, whereas 13.92% normally pay this divine tax. 31.01% are not able to pay zakat. It means that the earning of these people is too small to save anything and hence they are not bound to pay zakat. But the data suggest that about 69% of the families pay zakat either punctually or regularly. They have the facility of offering grains in zakat and hence they do it in a higher percentage. In respect of qurbani, 34.81% declared that they are punctual whereas 33.54% normally perform qurbani. Only 8.22% do it occasionally and 23.41% are unable to perform qurbani due to one reason or the other. It is thus obvious that more or less the same percentage performs sacrifice, offer zakat and go for nimaz. As regards the performance of Haj, only 2.53% have performed it and they were also serious in going for Haj pilgrimage. The remaining 97.46% have not performed Haj pilgrimage as yet due to one reason or the other. As Haj pilgrimage to Mecca involves heavy expenses and, moreover, there are other technicalities in getting permission for Haj pilgrimage so the large majority fails to perform this form of worship.

In the light of above findings it can be stated that on the whole the people living in the village are religious minded. The imprint of their faith is also found in their everyday life. They are Muslims not only by faith or ideology but also they practise Islamic sanctions in daily life and perform the prayers either regularly or almost regularly.

The next question put to the respondents was regarding their participation in religious gatherings like 'milad', 'waaz', 'tabligh' and 'urs'. They were also asked to indicate their frequency of participation in terms of regularly, occasionally. The responses obtained from them are given in Table 8.2

It appears from the table that the highest percentage of response showing a regular participation in respect of 'milad' is 20.25%. In the same way the highest percentage of occasional participation also in respect of 'milad' is 48.73%. The second highest percentages showing regular and

Table 8.2

Participation of the Respondents in different Religious Gatherings
N=158

Occasions	*Regularly*		*Occasionally*		*Rarely*		*Total*
	No.	%	*No.*	%	*No.*	%	
Milad	32	20.25	77	48.73	49	31.01	158
Waaz	24	15.18	42	26.58	92	58.22	158
Tabligh	23	14.15	33	20.88	102	64.55	158
Urs	19	12.02	32	20.85	107	67 72	158

occasional participations are in respect of 'urs' (12.02% and 20.85%). Hence it may be interpreted that milad is the most important religious gathering for the villagers in which they have the highest frequency of participation. The second important religious gathering appears to be 'waaz' showing the second highest frequency of participation by the villagers. Gathering concerning 'tabligh' stands third in importance and 'urs' appears to be the least important among these religious gatherings in which the frequency of participation is the lowest.

The same responses presented in Table 8.2 above have been classified on the basis of level of education in Table 8.3

It is evident from the table that among illiterates the highest percentage of regular participation in respect of 'milad' is 45.33%. In case of below matriculates the highest percentage of regular participation in respect of 'tabligh' gatherings is 22.88%. In case of graduates the highest percentage of regular participation found in case of 'milad' is 16%. In case of graduates the highest percentage of regular participation is in case of 'milad'. Thus excepting under-matriculates the highest percentage of regular participation in each category is in respect of 'milad' and hence it can be interpreted that there is no significant variation in the frequency of participation with this variation of literacy level. The reason for most

Table 8.3

Education and Participation in Religious Gatherings

N=158

Level of Education	*Milad*			*Waaz*			*Tabligh*			*Urs*			*Total*
	Reg.	*Occ.*	*Rar.*	*Reg.*	*Occ*	*Rar.*	*Reg.*	*Occ.*	*Rar.*	*Reg.*	*Occ.*	*Rar.*	
Illiterate	19	14	9	8	13	21	5	8	29	9	8	25	42
	45.33	33.33	21.42	19.04	30.95	50.0	11.90	19 04	62.04	21.42	19.04	50.52	
Below Matriculate	7	40	32	12	17	50	18	21	40	7	17	55	79
	8.86	50.63	40.50	15.18	21.51	63 29	22.88	26.58	50.63	8.86	21.51	69.62	
Below Graduate	4	16	5	3	9	13	—	4	21	2	4	19	25
	16.00	64.00	20.00	12.00	36.00	52.00	—	16.00	84.00	8.00	16 00	76.00	
Graduate +	2	7	3	1	3	8	—	—	12	1	3	8	12
	16.66	58.33	25.00	8.33	25.00	66.66	—	—	100.00	8.33	25.00	66.66	
Total	32	77	49	24	29	92	23	33	102	19	32	107	158

Reg.=Regularly. Occ.=Occasionally. Rar.=Rarely.

frequent participation in 'milad' may be its frequent organisation and arrangement in the village. The individual families hold 'milad' on different occasions like 'aqiqa', 'khatna' (circumcision), marriage, success in examination, appointment in a service, economic transaction like purchase of land or house, recovery from illness, birth of awaited child, death of a relative in addition to the 'milad' which is generally held on the occasion of the birth anniversary of the Prophet. In attending 'waaz', 'tabligh' or 'urs' gatherings the people are required either to go outside or to organise it on collective basis. Hence such gatherings themselves are infrequent and consequently the participation in these gatherings occasional or rare.

Table 8.4 presents the classification of responses on the basis of income.

It is evident from the table that in case of the lowest income group of up to Rs. 1500 the highest percentage of response showing regular participation is in respect of 'waaz' (39.39%) whereas in the two next higher income groups the highest percentages of response showing regular participation are in respect of 'milad' (21.05% and 17.3%). In the highest income group the same percentage of regular participation is found in all the four types of religious gatherings (12.5%). Thus it can be interpreted that there is no consistent variation in the percentage of regular participation in 'milad' with the variation in income level. The same is the education in respect of regular participation in respect of other religious gatherings. Hence the degree of participation in the religious gatherings is not relevant to the variation in income level.

Another question put to the respondents was, "Which of the following do you think to be responsible for anything happening against you?" The respondents were given a list of superstitions and rational causes, i.e., God, own deed, luck, circumstances and enemy. The responses obtained from them are presented in Table 8.5.

It appears from the table that the highest percentage of response has gone in respect of God. 59.50% of the respondents think that God is responsible for the events

Table 8.4

Income and Participation in Religious Gatherings
N=158

Income	Milad			Waaz			Tabligh			Urs			Total
	Reg.	Nor.	Occ.	Reg.	Nor.	Occ.	Reg.	Nor.	Occ.	Reg.	Nor.	Occ.	
Up to Rs. 1500	9	13	11	13	10	10	7	11	15	9	9	15	33
	27.27	39.39	33.33	39.39	30.30	30.30	21.21	33.33	45.45	27.27	27.27	45.45	
Rs. 1501-3000	12	34	11	5	16	36	9	10	38	5	11	41	57
	21.05	59.64	19.29	8.77	28.67	63.15	15.78	17.54	66.66	8.77	12.29	71.92	
Rs. 3001-4500	9	24	19	4	13	35	5	8	39	3	9	41	52
	17.30	46.15	36.53	7.69	25.00	67.30	9.61	15 38	75.00	5.76	17.30	76.92	
Rs. 4500 +	2	6	8	2	3	11	2	4	10	2	3	11	16
	12.5	37.5	50.0	12.5	18.75	68.75	12.5	25.00	62.5	12.5	18.75	68.75	
Total													158

Table 8.5

Which of the following do you think responsible when something happens against you?

N=158

Causal Attribute	*Number*	*Percentage*
God	94	59.50
Own Deed	23	14.56
Luck	22	13.93
Circumstances	13	9.22
Enemy	6	2.79
Total	158	100.00

and happenings against them. In other words, the majority of respondents owes everything to the divine power. The next higher percentage of response has gone in favour of 'own deeds' (14.56%). It means that according to these respondents their own actions and deeds are responsible for any untoward happening. In this way these people have a belief in 'Amal', i.e., the personal deeds and actions. Luck has been mentioned as the cause for such happenings by 13.93% of the respondents, and, thus, belief in superstition stands third in importance. 9.22% of the respondents have held circumstances responsible for such happenings and only 2.79% have blamed enemies. Thus the rational explanation is given by the lowest percentage. The most important explanation is faith-oriented, holding God and personal deed responsible for mishappenings. Superstitions appear to be the second important reason. Hence it may be interpreted that rationality in this respect is still less significant and the faith and superstition are more powerful.

The responses analysed in Table 8.5 are presented in Table 8.6 on the basis of the level of education.

It appears from the table that in each category of the respondents the highest percentage of response has gone in favour of God or divine power. But the percentage of response in favour of God or divine power has consistently declined

Table 8.6

Education and Understanding of Happenings
N=158

Level of Education	*God*		*Own Deed*		*Luck*		*Circumstances*		*Enemy*		*Total*
	No.	*%*	*No.*	*%*	*No.*	*%*	*No.*	*%*	*No.*	*%*	
Illiterate	28	66.66	4	9.52	6	14.28	2	4.76	2	4.76	42
Below Matriculate	52	65.82	10	12.65	8	10.12	5	6.32	4	5.06	79
Below Graduate	10	40.00	6	24.00	5	20.00	4	16.00	—	—	25
Graduate +	4	33.33	3	25.00	3	25.00	2	16.66	—	—	12
Total	94		23		22		13		6		158

with the rise in the level of education. On the other hand, the percentage of response showing rational explanation and holding circumstances responsible for mishappenings has consistently risen with the rise in literacy level. Hence there appears to be a relevance between response pattern and literacy level. Less educated are more faith oriented than educated respondents and highly educated are more reason-oriented than the lowly educated respondents. Thus education appears to be a factor contributing to the rationalization of attitude and outlook.

The same responses were classified on caste basis and are presented in Table 8.7.

It is evident from the table that in both upper and lower caste categories the majority holds divine power or God responsible for mishappenings. The percentage of response is slightly high in the upper caste (60%) than in the lower caste (57.14%). The responses holding circumstances responsible are slightly higher in upper caste than in lower caste (8.46% and 7.14% respectively). Hence it may be interpreted that there is no consistency between variation in caste and the variation in response patterns. Thus caste is not significantly relevant.

Another question put to the respondents was, "Do you believe in superstitions like sorcery, ghosts and spirits?" The responses are presented in Table 8.8

It appears from the table that the majority of 74.69% of the respondents have replied in negative, 14.56% have accepted a belief in these superstitions and 10.75% have remained undecided. Hence it can be interpreted that only a smaller section of the villagers believe in superstitions and the majority has expressed a disbelief.

The responses analysed in Table 8.8 are presented in Table 8.9 on the basis of the level of education.

It appears from the table that in all the four categories of the respondents the negative response is in the highest percentage. The variation in the percentage of response is not consistent with the variation in the literacy level. The same is

Table 8.7

Caste and Understanding of Happenings

N=158

Caste	*God*		*Own Deed*		*Luck*		*Circumstances*		*Enemy*		*Total*
Category	*No*	*%*	*No*	*%*	*No.*	*%*	*No.*	*%*	*No.*	*%*	
Upper Caste	78	60.00	20	15.38	16	12.30	11	8.46	5	3.84	130
Lower Caste	16	57.14	3	10.71	6	21.42	2	7.14	1	3.57	28
Total	94		23		22		13		6		158

Table 8.8

Belief in Superstitions like, 'Ganda', 'Taweez', 'Totka', 'Tona', etc.

N=158

Response Category	*Number*	*Percentage*
Yes	23	14.56
No	118	74.69
Undecided	17	10.75
Total	158	100.00

true for the percentages of response showing disbelief or indecision. Hence the level of education is not relevant to the belief in superstitions. The illiterates as well as the highly qualified respondents have replied in negative in an overwhelming majority.

It is found that in the upper caste only 11.53% of the respondents believe in superstitions, whereas in the lower caste category 28.57% have this belief. On the other hand, in the upper caste 80.76% and in the lower caste 46.42% have replied in negative. Hence it may be interpreted that upper caste people are less superstitious than the lower caste people. Moreover, the percentages of response showing indecision suggest that 25% of the respondents in the lower caste and 7.69% in the upper caste have not said anything definitely about their belief or disbelief about superstition. It also suggests that upper caste people are more rational and, hence, caste variable is relevant in this regard. Superstition is relatively more important in lower caste category than in the upper caste category.

Table 8.9

Education and Belief in Superstitions, like Taweez, Ganda, etc.

N=158

Level of Education	*Yes*		*No*		*Undecided*		*Total*
	No.	%	*No.*	%	*No.*	%	
Illiterate	7	16.66	29	69.04	6	14.28	42
Below Matriculate	10	12.65	63	79.74	6	7.59	79
Below Graduate	4	16.00	18	72.00	3	12.00	25
Graduate +	2	16.66	8	66.66	2	16.66	12
Total	23		118		17		158

Table 8.10

Caste and Belief in Superstitions like Ganda, Taweez, etc.

N=158

Caste Category	*Yes*		*No*		*Undecided*		*Total*
	No.	%	*No.*	%	*No.*	%	
Upper Caste	15	11.53	105	80.76	10	7.69	130
Lower Caste	8	28.57	13	46.42	7	25.00	28
Total	23		118		17		158

The same responses have been classified on age basis in Table 8.11.

The table shows that the percentages of response expressing belief in superstition are not consistent with the variation in age. But the percentages of negative response have consistently risen with the rise in age and the percentages showing indecision have consistently declined with the rise in age. The younger people appear to be more superstitious and more in the stage of indecision than the elders. This finding shows the relevance of age variable but in a negative direction, because the younger people are expected to be more rational than the older people.

Another question was concerning belief in superstition like sorcery, ghost, witch and 'kichin' (churail), etc. These evil spirits found place in traditional Indian society and had an importance in the life of the village people. Hence this question was asked to find out whether the same level of superstitions still persists or there has been a change in the outlook. The responses obtained from the respondents are presented in Table 8.12

It appears from the table that 61.39% of the respondents have replied in negative. It means that the majority of the villagers do not believe in such superstitions. Only

Table 8.11
Age and Belief in Superstitions, like Ganda, Taweez, etc.
N=158

Age Group	*Yes*		*No*		*Undecided*		*Total*
	No.	%	*No.*	%	*No.*	%	
Up to 20 yrs.	4	15.38	16	61.53	6	23.07	26
21 to 35 yrs.	5	17.85	19	67.85	4	14.28	28
36 to 50 yrs.	6	15.00	30	75.00	4	10.00	40
51 and above	8	12.50	53	82.81	3	4.68	64
Total	23		118		17		158

Table 8.12

Belief i n Superstitions like Sorcery, Ghost, Witch, Kichin, etc., etc.

N=158

Response Category	*Number*	*Percentage*
Yes	48	30.37
No	91	61.39
Undecided	19	8.24
Total	158	100.00

a smaller section of 30.37% do believe and the remaining 8.24% are undecided.

The same responses have been presented in Table 8.13 on the basis of the level of education.

It appears from the table that the percentages of response showing a belief in these superstitions are higher in the categories of illiterates and under-matriculates and relatively lower in the categories of under-graduates and graduates. In the same way the percentages of negative response are higher in the two more qualified categories than in the categories of under-matriculates and illiterates. These facts suggest that educated people are less superstitious than uneducated people. Thus the factor of education is relevant to the degree of superstition.

Table 8.14 presents the classification of responses on occupation basis.

It appears from the data in this table that the highest percentage of response expressing belief in superstitions is in the category of labour respondents (37.5%) and the lowest in case of service holders (16.66%). The highest percentage of negative response is in case of service holders (66.66%) and

Table 8.13
Education and Belief in Superstitions, like Ghost, Sorcery, etc.
N=158

Level of Education	*Yes*		*No*		*Undecided*		*Total*
	No.	*%*	*No.*	*%*	*No.*	*%*	
Illiterate	11	26.19	25	59.52	6	14.28	42
Below Matriculate	29	36.70	42	53.16	8	10.12	79
Below Graduate	6	24.00	16	64.00	3	12.00	25
Graduate+	2	19.66	8	66.66	2	16.66	12
Total	48		91		19		158

Table 8.14

Occupation and Belief in Superstitions, like Ghost, Sorcery, etc.
N=158

Occupation Category	*Yes*		*No*		*Undecided*		*Total*
	No.	%	*No.*	%	*No.*	%	
Cultivation	20	27.77	44	61.11	8	11.11	72
Business	3	30.00	6	60.00	1	10.00	10
Service	6	16.66	8	66.66	2	16.66	12
Labour	6	37.05	7	43.75	3	18.75	16
Multiple Occupation	6	50.00	4	33.33	2	16 66	12
Dependents	11	30.55	22	61.11	3	8.33	36
Total	48		91		19		158

the lowest in the category of multiple occupation (33.37%) and then in the labour category. Thus it appears that those in service are the least superstitious. It may be due to their frequent contact with the world outside and due to the impact of modern forces like urbanism, industrialism and media of mass communication. The labourers are confined to the rural areas and are least exposed to the modern forces. Hence they are more superstitious.

Table 8.15 presents the classification of same responses on age basis.

It is evident from the figures in the table that the percentages of response showing belief in superstitions are not consistently varied with the variation in age. But the percentages of negative responese has risen with the rise in age excepting that the same percentage of negative response is in the last two age categories. Thus age variable is not much relevant, rather it has a lower degree of relevance to the variation in age. Moreover, according to this variation the elderly group appears to be less superstitious than the younger generation. This pattern of response is different from what is normally expected from the old and new generations.

The villagers in the tradition-oriented society are less exposed to modern outlook for treating ailments and diseases. They are either superstitious or faith-oriented in this regard. The superstitious people go to some mulla or pandit or ojha for the cure of any disease. The faith oriented people pray to God for recovery. But those who are rational consult modern physicians during illness. As the village under study is a Muslim village having a tradition of its own, an enquiry was made in respect of the present outlook of the people regarding treatment for a disease. They were asked what do you do when any member of your family falls sick ? The responses obtained from them are presented in Table 8.16.

It appears from the table that the highest percentage of response has been in favour of praying to God as well as consulting modern physician (39.87%). The next higher percentage is using folk medicine (29.74%). Only 20.26% go to doctors for advice and treatment, 6.97% go to

Table 8.15

Age and Belief in Superstitions, like Ghost, Sorcery, etc.
N=158

Age Group	*Yes*		*No*		*Undecided*		*Total*
	No.	%	*No.*	%	*No.*	%	
Up to 20 yrs.	9	34.61	11	42.30	6	23.07	26
21 to 35 yrs.	10	35.71	15	53.57	3	10.71	28
36 to 50 yrs.	11	27 05	25	62.05	4	10.00	40
51+	18	28.12	40	62.05	6	9.37	64
Total	48		91		19		158

Table 8.16

Action taken for the Relief of a Patient

N=158

Action Category	*Number*	*Percentage*
Go to Maulvi/Mulla	11	6.97
Go to Doctor	32	20.26
Use folk medicines	47	29.74
Pray to God for relief	5	3.16
Pray to God as well as consult physician	63	39.87
Total	158	100.00

some maulvi or mulla for taking some 'taweez' or 'ganda' or other such superstitious means of treatment. On the basis of these response patterns it may be stated that a very low percentage is only superstitious or faith oriented. In case the percentages of response in the second and the last categories are combined, it may be interpreted that 60.15% of the respondents consult doctors whereas the combining the fourth and the last categories suggest that 43.03% pray to God for relief and treatment. Thus the majority of the respondents have developed a rational outlook and is exposed to modern means of treatment. But the impact of faith in God is quite significant and hence the two are combined together in seeking relief from disease. The highest percentage of respondents take medical treatment but at the same time pray to God for the recovery from the illness. Hence faith and rationality both have been combined by them.

The same responses are classified on literary basis in Table 8.17.

Table 8.17

Education and Actions taken for the Relief of a Patient

N=158

Level of Education	*Go to Maulvi or Mulla*		*Go to Doctors*		*Use Folk Medicines*		*Only Pray to God*		*Pray God & Go to Doctor*		*Total*
	No.	*%*	*No.*	*%*	*No.*	*%*	*No.*	*%*	*No.*	*%*	
Illiterate	8	19.04	6	14.28	11	26.19	3	7.14	14	33 33	42
Below Matriculate	3	3.79	15	18.98	33	41.77	2	2.53	26	32.91	79
Below Graduate	—	—	7	28.00	2	8.00	—	—	16	64.00	25
Graduate+	—	—	4	33.33	1	8.33	—	—	7	58.33	12
Total	11		32		47		5		63		158

It is evident from the table that in all categories of respondents excepting the under-matriculates the highest percentage of response is in respect of the synthetic approach of prayer and medical treatment. In case of under-matriculates the highest percentage of response is in respect of the use of folk medicine. The percentage of response showing the consultation with the doctors only has consistently risen with the rise in literacy level and the percentage of response has consistently fallen with the rise in literacy level in respect of only praying to God. No respondent of the graduate or post-graduate category stated that prayer to God was the only means adopted. These facts show the relevance of literacy level to variation in response pattern.

Table 8.18 presents the classification of response on income basis.

It is evident from the table that percentage of response in respect of praying to God as well as consulting physicians has consistently risen with the rise in income level in respect of going to 'maulvi' or 'mulla' or only praying to God. It suggests that lower income people are more faith-oriented or orthodox than the people of higher income. It may be due to the economic hardship of low income group. The poor people are not in a position to afford medical treatment and, hence, they depend on prayers and superstitious devices; whereas the well-to-do persons take medical advice in a higher percentage because they can afford to do so.

Another question put to the respondents was, "What steps do you take when faced with any type of calamity or problem ?" The responses obtained from them are given in Table 8.19.

It appears from the table that the highest percentage of respondents (39.88%) pray to God for being relieved of any calamity or problem. The next highest percentage (36.70%) takes help from others in such hours of crisis. Only 10.76% of the respondents face the problem with courage; whereas 8.23% depend on the luck and 4.43% use fortune stones or taweez, etc. to get rid of calamities. Thus it appears that faith-oriented approach is quite significant in solving

Table 8.18

Income and Actions taken for the Relief of a Patient

N=158

Income Category	*Go to Maulvi or Mulla*		*Go to Doctors*		*Use Folk Medicine*		*Only Pray to God*		*Pray God & Go to Doctor*		*Total*
	No.	*%*	*No.*	*%*	*No.*	*%*	*No.*	*%*	*No.*	*%*	
Up to Rs. 1500	4	12.12	6	18.18	10	30.30	3	9.09	10	30.30	33
Rs. 1501-3000	5	8 77	11	19.29	19	33.33	2	3.50	25	35.08	57
Rs. 3001-4500	2	3.84	10	19.23	15	28.84	—	—	25	48.07	52
Rs. 4501+	—	—	5	31.25	3	18.75	—	—	8	50.00	16
Total	11		32		47		5		63		158

Table 8.19

Protectionary Steps against Natural Calamities
N=158

Recourse Category	*Number*	*Percentage*
Pray to God	63	39.88
Face with Courage	17	10.76
Take help from others	58	36.70
Depend on Luck	13	8.23
Use Stone/Taweez	7	4.43
Total	158	100.00

crisis and problems in the village life. But at the same time a considerable section uses rational approach of taking help from others and facing the situation with courage. Thus the people mostly stand at the junction of rationality and faith. If this is also taken into consideration, the tri-juncture of superstition, faith and rationality reflects people's outlook.

Table 8.20 classifies the same responses on education basis.

It is evident from the table that the percentage of response in favour of taking help from others has consistently risen with the rise in literacy level. In other response categories such a consistency is not found. Hence it may be interpreted that the level of literacy is partly relevant to the variation in response patterns.

Table 8.21 presents the classification of the same responses on income basis.

It is evident from the table that the percentage of response showing help from others has consistently risen with the rise in income level. In other response category such a

Table 8.20

Education and Protectionary Steps against Natural Calamities

N=158

Recourse Category	*Illiterate*		*Below Matriculate*		*Below Graduate*		*Graduate & above*		*Total*
	No.	*%*	*No.*	*%*	*No*	*%*	*No.*	*%*	
Pray to God	17	40.47	37	46.83	7	28 0	2	16.66	63
Face with courage	4	9.52	7	8.86	4	16.0	2	16.66	17
Take other's help	13	30.95	28	35.44	11	44.0	6	60.00	58
Depend on Luck	5	11.90	5	6.32	2	8.0	1	8.30	13
Use Stone/Taweez	3	7.14	2	2.53	1	4 0	1	8.33	7
Total	42		79		25		12		158

Table 8.21

Economic Level and Recourse to Protection against Natural Calamities

N=158

Recourse Category	*Up to Rs. 1500*		*Rs. 1501-3000*		*Rs. 3001-4500*		*Rs. 4501 & above*		*Total*
	No.	%	*No.*	%	*No.*	%	*No.*	%	
Pray to God	14	42.42	25	43 85	20	38.46	4	25 00	63
Face with courage	5	15.15	6	10.52	4	7.69	2	12.05	17
Take other's help	6	18.18	20	35.08	24	46.15	8	50.00	58
Depend on Luck	6	18.18	4	7.01	2	3.84	1	6.25	13
Use Stone/Taweez	2	6.06	2	3.50	2	3.84	1	6.25	7
Total	33		57		52		16		158

consistency is not found. It is also evident from the data that in lower income groups relatively higher percentages pray to God, whereas in higher income groups lower percentage of respondents adopt this measure. Thus the lower income groups appear to be more faith-oriented than the two higher income groups.

Table 8.22 presents the classification of the same responses on caste basis.

Table 8.22

Caste and Steps against Natural Calamities

N=158

Recourse Category	*Upper Caste*		*Lower Caste*		*Total*
	No.	*%*	*No.*	*%*	
Pray to God	53	40.76	10	35.71	63
Face courageously	13	10.00	4	14.28	17
Seek other's help	52	40.00	6	21.42	58
Depend on Luck	8	6.15	5	17.85	13
Use Stone/Taweez	4	3.07	3	10.71	28
Total	130		28		158

It is evident from the table that responses showing dependence on luck or facing with courage or use of fortune stones are in higher percentage in the lower castes than in the upper castes. In other response categories the percentages of response are higher in the upper castes than in the lower castes. It suggests that superstition is more powerful among lower caste people whereas rationality is more important in the upper caste people. The difference in the percentages of response showing prayer to God suggests that low caste people are less faith-oriented than upper caste people.

B. WAQF INSTITUTION

'Waqf' or 'Habs' is an Arabic masdar which literally means 'detention', 'to prevent', or 'to restrain'. In sharia, it connotes the tying up of property in perpetuity so as to prevent it from becoming the property of third person.[1] According to the Control Act, 'Waqf' means the permanent dedication by a person professing Islam.

The origin of this institution is to be sought in the strongly marked impulse to charitable deeds which is characteristic of Islam. The Qur'an contains a specific provision concerning waqf, but it abounds in injunctions in the matter of charity.

Historically, the origin of waqf is traced to the traditions of Prophet. Shibli Naumani cited a tradition of the Prophet to show that the first Muslim waqf came into existence in the first year of Hijra. The land on which the Prophet laid the foundation of Masjid Nabvi in Medina (in A. H.) belonged to two orphans. The Prophet wished to purchase the land and insisted to pay the price, but the orphans said, "No! By God we will not take the price, we will take it from God." Thus came into existence the first waqf of Islam.[2]

Another tradition regarding the origin of waqf has been cited by Fyzee:

"Omar had acquired land in the canton of Khyber and proceeded to the Prophet and sought his counsel to make the most pious of it, (whereupon) the Prophet declared, "tie up the property and devote the usufruct to human beings, and it is not to be sold or made the subject of gift or inheritance; devote its produce to your children, your kindered, and the poor in the way of God."[3]

Gradually many waqfs came into existence. Their supervision and administration were totally in the hands of Mota-

1. Heffing, Encyclopaedia of Islam, Vol. II, p. 1096.
2. Naumani, Shibli, Seerat-un-Nabi, Vol. II, Azamgarh, 1352 AH, pp. 129-30.
3. Fyzee, A.A.A., Outlines of Muhammadan Law, London, 1964, p. 265.

vallis. During the times of Umayyads, however, the supervision over the administration of waqfs was entrusted to kazis. According to Hitti, sometimes kazis directly administered "pious foundations and the estate of orphans and imbeciles."[4]

The number of waqfs became so large during the times of Samanids that a separate department—Diwan-e-waqf—was established for their effective supervision.[5]

Earliest description of waqfs, created in India during the reign of Mohammad of Ghaor (probably around 1185-95 A.D.) is found in the Insha-i-Mahru, written during the time of Jalal Uddin Firoz Khilji (1290-96) A.D.).[6]

A farman of Sher Shah Suri (of Bihar) throws light on how waqfs were administered locally by the village Mulla. The farman says:

"The villagers should build a mosque in every village and should attach productive land to it as waqf. The income of this village should be utilised in making arrangements for it. The management of this village should be entrusted to a group of men according to the population of that village so that everyone of them might try to look after it....The Hindus are also granted waqf by the Government, according to the above mentioned principles. . . . A school should also be attached to it so that the students might be instructed there in the Qur'an and the principal tenets of religion. The Hindus are also authorised to control and manage their own school. . . ."[7]

It is apparent from the facts mentioned in farman that the institution of waqf had started in India with the arrival of Muslim rulers. It also reveals the nature and function of

4. Hitti, Philip K., The History of Arabs, London, 1940, p. 225.
5. Mohammad, Abu Bakr bin Jaffer, Narshakhi, Tarikhe Bukhara, f. 28V, Royal Asiatic Society MSS, Cited in Rashid, S. Khalid, Waqf Administration in India, Vikas Publishing House Pvt. Ltd., 1978, p. XIX.
6. Ibid, p. 1.
7. Hasan Ali Khan, S.A. Rashid, and R.P. Tripathi, Tawarikh-e-Daulat-e-Sher Shahi, in Medieval India, Quarterly, Vol. I, July, 1950, No. 1, pp. 62-63.

waqf as well as the fact that the Muslim rulers also encouraged waqf for Hindus. This should also be noted that in Bihar too this system started very early. This is why it is observed that in most of the cases every mosque in the villages has got some landed property too.

On the eve of independence, the position of waqfs was far from satisfactory. Except in the case of a few states, the waqfs in the rest parts of the country were governed by the Mussalman Waqf Act, 1923, which was found to be wanting in many respects. Following the partition in 1947, many mutawallis and other persons at the helm of wakfs affairs migrated to Pakistan.

The Waqf Act, XXIX of 1954 is a landmark in the history of waqf administration in India. By constituting a non-official Board vested with considerable authority and power by imposing precise obligations upon mutawallis and making their violation a penal offence, by vesting in the State Government the supervisory responsibility relating to waqfs and by conferring authority on the Central Government to lay down a comprehensive administrative structure to ensure proper administration of waqfs in the country.

In the pre-independence period in Bihar the Muslim Independent Party drafted in 1945 a Waqf Bill in concurrence with the leaders of the provincial Jamiat-al Ulema and the local Amarat Sharia. After the bill was notified to the legislature, the Congress Government of the province drafted a fresh Bill on the lines of the former and introduced it in the legislature in 1946. The Ulema of Bihar made great efforts to adopt the provisions of the Bill to Islamic principles. Eventually the legislature enacted the Bihar Waqf Act, 1947. It now stands replaced by the Central Waqf Act, 1954.[8]

In the early thirties, a new experiment was attempted in a few states of the country by leaving the supervision of waqfs in the hands of nominated or elected representatives of the community. The community thus found a forum of self-

8. Mahmood, Tahir, Muslim Personal Law, Vikas Publishing House Pvt. Ltd., New Delhi, 1977, p. 80.

supervision and administration with no excessive state control. Thus the Waqf Board came to be established in different States of the country. In Bihar it was formed in the year 1947.

Apart from the Waqf Boards, the three other important agencies connected with waqf administration were constituted on Central and State levels. These are—(1) the Central Waqf Council, (2) the Waqf Section, Government of India, and (3) the local Waqf Committees. The first one is mainly advisory in character while the other two actively participate in the administration of waqf.

At least in the present times the state of the waqf property is in very bad condition. The waqfs everywhere in India are facing certain serious problems. Hafiz Mohammad Ibrahim said, "Of the many serious problems relating to waqf with which we are faced today, one complicated problem arises from the illegal occupation of waqf properties by trespassers. This is one of the results of partition following which numerous people left, or were forced to leave, for Pakistan abandoning waqf properties. A large number of these properties were taken over by the Custodian. Places of worship and of special sanctity are being returned to Waqf Boards but many among these properties also are in illegal possession and litigation may be necessary to secure their clearance."[9]

One of the most important problem before the waqfs is the mismanagement done by its mutawallis. Rashid observes that there are many ways in which mutawallis mismanage or misappropriate waqf properties: incorrect account of income; fabrication of bogus vouchers for amounts not spent; donations, subscriptions or nazranas not accounted for, illegal alienation of waqf properties, and some "pugrees" extracted from the tenants; rent at high rates realised from the tenant but receipts for lower amounts issued and the balance pocketed

9. Waqf Administration, a pamphlet published by the Muslim Waqfs Section, Ministry of Irrigation & Power, Govt. of India, 1961, p. 12.

as black money; compensation bonds for abolition of zamindari, jagirdari or inam prepared in their own names and sold by them for personal benefits, and son on."[10]

In order to set the matters right many actions ought to be done. One important among these is that the mutawallis should be educated to realise that they are holding a sacred trust and they must exhibit a high standard of rectitude.

Encroachment on graveyard is one of the most serious problems facing waqf administration in the country today. There are greater chances on encroachments on those graveyards, which lie in the hearts of big cities and in which burial is no more allowed by the Municipal authorities, or the village graveyards where Muslim population is nil or very thin. It is a general case in the state of Bihar.

A number of mosques are also illegally occupied in various parts of the country and are being used either as gaushala, houses or schools. Iron girders, bricks, doors and other materials of old dilapidated mosques are being carried away by unauthorised persons.

It is obvious from these facts that in the Muslim community Waqf institution has been of vital importance. A number of wealthy and religious minded persons made their entire property or a part of it as waqf or trust for some religious or virtuous objectives. Their intention was to create a permanent source for the noble and religious cause in the society. According to the provision of the Act two waqf boards, i.e., the Bihar Subai Sunni Majlis-e-Awqaf and the Bihar Subai Shia Majlis-e-Awqaf were constituted to look after the Sunni and Shia Awqaf respectively. These Waqf Boards are working under legal sanctions and all the waqf estates meant for charity purposes are governed by it. But it is also important to note that in spite of this legal provision and institutional supervision of the waqf estate a large part of waqf property has been sold out and is still being sold out. The waqf estates are in bad shape and the trustees or mutawallis are managing these waqf estates not according to the waqf deed

10. Rashid, S. Khalid, Waqf Administration in India, Vikas Publishing House Pvt. Ltd., New Delhi, 1978, p. 151.

but according to their self-interest. Personal benefits are being derived from these religious trusts and charity funds.

The village under study has remained a dominantly Muslim village from the very beginning and a number of families in the village were landlords or big cultivators. Hence several waqf estates were enacted in the village. According to the gathered information the total area of the cultivable land covered by these waqf estates comes to about 35 bighas and the total income of these waqfs comes to about Rs. 10,000 per annum. The waqfs were created in the village for the maintenance of village mosques, madrasas (religious schools) and for the religious functions and performances during the months of Ramazan and Muharram. Some of the waqf estates also provided for helping the poor families on the occasion of the marriage of girls and for the strangers coming to the village (musafirs). The investigator, through conversation and interview with the village people found that the waqf estates are not functioning satisfactorily and the mutawallis are not acting according to the real spirit of the waqf deeds. In many areas the waqf deed is being ignored. The masjid and madrasa are not getting their due share and the help to the poor families has become a rare phenomena. The information gathered about the working of a waqf from the respondents also suggests that the waqf estates are in pathetic conditions these days and this noble institution is not rendering the service satisfactorily. On the other hand it is being misused and misappropriated. It is evident from Table 8.23.

Table 8.23
Responses showing the Condition of Village Waqf Property
N=158

Condition	*Response Frequency*	
	Number	*Percentage*
Good	74	46.84
Bad	63	39.87
Can't say	21	13.29
Total	158	100.00

It is evident from the above table that only 46.84% of the respondents stated that the waq fproperty is in good condition. It means that the majority of the respondents does not feel that the waqf estates are working properly. 39.9% of the respondents declare that the waqf property is in bad shape, whereas 13.3% could not give any definite opinion. Hence it may be interpreted that the majority is not satisfied with the working of the waqf estates. This fact is further evidenced by Table 8.24.

Table 8.24

Responses showing the Level of Satisfaction with the working of the Waqf Estates

N=158

Category	*Response Frequency*	
	Number	*Percentage*
Yes	13	8.23
No	19	12.03
Can't say	126	79.74
Total	158	100.00

The above table shows the views of the respondents regarding this fact whether the mutawallis use waqf properties for their personal gains. The table suggests that only 12.3% of the respondents declared in negative, whereas 8.23% of the respondents replied that the properties are used for personal benefits, while 79.74% of the respondents did not give any opinion. Their neutrality may be either due to their relationship with the mutawallis or the members of waqf committee, because they did not like to have a bitterness with the persons concerned for telling the truth. Their neutrality and silence also speak of the misappropriation and personal gain out of the waqf properties. Because such a large majority in the village cannot be ignorant of the state of affairs regarding a waqf.

The respondents were also asked whether the waqf properties should be given under the supervision of the state government for their development. The responses obtained from the respondents are presented in Table 8.25.

Table 8.25

Responses in favour of or against the handing over of Waqf Estate to Government

N=158

Category	*Response Frequency*	
	Number	*Percentage*
Yes, it should be handed over	11	6.96
No, it should not be handed over	106	67.10
Can't say	41	25.94
Total	158	100.00

It appears from the table that the majority of 67% is opposed to the taking over of waqf estates by the Government. Only a small section of 6.96% has favoured this idea. It means that even those who are not satisfied with the conditions of the waqf estates are opposed to its being taken over by the state government. It may be either due to this fear that the waqf property may not be used for the religious purposes after its being taken over or due to this fear that the government may not bring about any improvement. Thus nationalisation of waqf estates is opposed and on this basis it can be interpreted that the community favours the existing system of waqf management as provided in the waqf deed.

The respondents were further asked whether they favour the idea of diverting waqf funds on those items not mentioned in the Waqf Deeds. The responses obtained from them are given in Table 8.26.

Table 8.26

Responses showing the Opinion on Diversion of Waqf Funds on Items not mentioned in the Waqf Deeds

N=158

Category	*Response Frequency*	
	Number	*Percentage*
Yes	19	12.03
No	108	68.35
Can't say	31	19.62
Total	158	100.00

It appears that only 12% of the respondents have favoured the idea, whereas 68% have opposed it, and 19.62% have remained neutral. It means that the large majority is opposed to the diversion of the funds and favours the idea of sticking to the provisions of the waqf deeds. Hence it may be interpreted that the majority still feels that the sanctity of waqf and waqf deed should be maintained, and holds the view that religion does not permit to use waqf income over those items not desired by waqif (executor of the waqf deed). 'Mansha-i-Waqif' (will of the deed executor) should be honoured and the waqf assets and income should be concerned with items only.

The respondents were also asked whether they would like to execute waqf deed out of their own properties. The responses obtained from them are presented in Table 8.27.

Table 8.27

Responses showing Opinion regarding the Execution of Waqf Deed out of one's own Property

N=158

Category	*Response Frequency*	
	Number	*Percentage*
Yes	18	11.40
No	119	75.31
Can't say	21	13 29
Total	158	100.00

The table suggests that only 11.40% of the respondents have expressed their willingness to create waqf whereas the majority of 75.31% does not like it. 13.29% did not say anything definitely. These respondents were the persons having no property to execute waqf deed. It shows that the idea of creating a waqf is not completely opposed. The majority does not like it but there is a percentage willing to execute waqf deed. It is important to point out that waqf has been created in all ages by a very small percentage and hence in this context the percentages of response favourable to the idea of creation of waqf is quite significant. People still have a faith in the utility of waqf estates and realise that charitable tasks may be performed through waqf estates, provided these waqf estates are managed honestly and effectively. In spite of the pathetic condition of the waqf estate in the village the people have not lost their confidence in the utilitarian aspect of the waqf institution.

9

The Winds of Change

In the preceding chapters various aspects of the community life of the village have been analysed to study the social structure of the village. These aspects have been discussed on the basis of the facts collected from the field, which throw light on the existing social, economic, political and cultural relations as well as the institutional aspects of purdah, marriage, family, religious performances, beliefs, rituals and festivities and waqf, etc. The analysis of factual data in the preceding chapters helps in understanding the changes in social structure in relation to tradition oriented village life. It is evident from the discussions in the earlier chapters that the village under study is a Muslim village having the background of zamindari and aristocratic living of the past. The upper caste Muslim families living in the village dominated over low caste Muslims as well as over low caste Hindus settled at the outskirts of the village. Their domination over the weaker section of the society was due to their economic supremacy and because of the aristocratic nature of social life. In the past the patterns of living in the village were determined by religious sanctions and traditional practices. The observance of tradition was a common practice but care was taken that the traditional practices do not violate the basic principles of Islam. Yet deviations from

Islamic sanctions in various aspects of Muslim life were not unknown in the traditional society, for instance, Islam sanctions and permits the re-marriage of the widows and divorced women but in actual practice in the traditional society these re-marriages were rarely performed. In the same way Islam stands for taking the consent of both the partners for the performance of marriage but the actual consent of the bride was not even thought of in the past and in the case of bridegrooms it was not common. The consent taken from the two partners at the time of nikah was simply a ritual and not the obtaining of real consent. Thus it appears that traditional norms and values were in supreme command and deviations from ideal sanctions of Islam took place in the traditional society.

The facts collected from the field suggest that a wind of change has started blowing in the tradition-oriented village and the social structure is gradually changing due to changes in relational and institutional aspects of community life.

The study of stratification in the village community, analysed in Chapter 5A, throws light on social hierarchy and attitudes of the people in respect of discriminatory behaviour and inequalities found among Muslims, though Islamic sanctions do not support any form of stratification or social hierarchy among the believers in Islam. Descent or heredity is not at all a consideration for determining the place and position of the individual in an Islamic society. Only piety and virtuous qualities are the bases for differentiating the people. But this differentiation is not associated with the distribution of social status. But in the traditional Muslim society this ideal sanction of Islam did not remain operative. The Islamic norms became ideal and the operative norms recognized distinction between man and man on the basis of lineage and descent. The Muslim society like the traditional Hindu society got divided into different status groups on the basis of lineage and descent. Syed, Shaikh, Mallick, Pathan, etc. were the different lineages claiming foreign breed, whereas the occupational groups like Rayeen, Rangrez, weaver, Kalal, Churihara, etc. were of indigenous breed. Among the lineage of foreign breed also there was a hierarchy of status, the Syeds being at the top and the remaining upper castes were having different positions and statuses in different localities. The lower section of the society constituted the indigenous population and different occupational groups or castes were accorded different statuses and positions. Thus there was a complex system of hierarchy and stratification in the traditional Muslim society.

In the Muslim village under study the traditional community was divided into different castes characterized by differences in rights, privileges, social ranking and social prestige. The aristocratic families of the areas around the village under study mostly belong to Mallick and Syed categories or castes, and the Mallick caste ranked next to Syeds. The Shaikhs occupied the third social rank and the fourth position went to the Pathans. Among lower castes there was no clear-out hierarchy but these castes were occupying much inferior positions in relation to the upper Muslim castes. The discriminatory behaviour with the low caste people were observed on the occasions of marriage, festivals and other socio-cultural gatherings. In the religious gatherings like waaz and milad the low caste Muslims sat behind the upper caste Muslims. On the occasion of Id and Friday prayers also the low caste Muslims stand behind the forward lines, mostly occupied by high caste people. Thus not only on social occasions but also on religious occasions the sense of superiority and inferiority remained at work. The upper caste Muslims did not invite low caste people on the occasion of any function in their families. In case the lower caste Muslims wanted the presence of some high caste persons on the occasions of functions in their families they went to these people personally and expressed their desire and requested for the same. In case any member of high caste attended such function the low caste family felt elevated and gave due regard and respect to such persons.

But in the present age the situation is changing. The distance between upper and lower caste Muslims is narrowing and greater frequency of interaction is found. On the occasion of milad, waaz and other such gatherings the low caste people are not very much particular in occupying last rows, rather many of them sit with high caste people without any hesitation. In the same way, on the occasion of prayers in the mosque the lines for upper caste and lower caste people are now not distinctly differentiated. Although sense of superiority on the basis of lineage is still persisting but not with the same zeal and consciousness. Persons of lower castes enjoying better economic positions and having educational background are being treated at par with the members of upper caste people. A wealthy and educated upper caste Muslim family prefers to have social interaction with a wealthy and educated lower caste Muslim family and not with a poor and educationally backward upper caste Muslim family. Thus the trend of class consciousness and class identification is developing. Only on the occasion of settling marriages of their sons and daughters still the lineage is a basic consideration, the upper caste people do not like marital relations with low caste people. No marriage in the village was reported between the high caste Muslim boy or girl with the counterpart in the lower Muslim caste. Hence the caste restrictions and lineage distinctions are taken into consideration only on the occasion of fixing marriages. In other aspects of community life this distinction is gradually diminishing. The low caste people are not at all in favour of caste distinction. In the traditional society also they might have not been in its favour, but they could not dare to express their feelings. But they declare it today openly that such distinctions are wrong and unjustified. This very declaration shows a change in social climate and the weakening ties of social stratification. The upper caste people still favour social hierarchy and are not ready to part with all social distinction, although they are opposed to any discriminatory behaviour on the basis of lineage and descent. They hold the view that the lineage should not be the determinant of a person's status or position but the personal qualities and achievements should determine the status of a person. It shows a change in the attitude and outlook of the villagers. The system of ascribed or inherited status prevalent in the traditional society is not favoured by them, rather they are favouring the system of achieved status.

With the change in attitude and actual practices

regarding ascribed and achieved system of status and the association of personal status and prestige with wealth and education, the society has facilitated social mobility. Social hierarchy is still persisting but the traditional form of rigid stratification is not in practice. On the other hand a trend is developing to facilitate the emergence of flexible social stratification. This change in the patterns of stratification and social hierarchy is an index of change in the social structure of the village community.

Marriage, family and kinship constitute an important aspect of social relations in the village life. In these institutions changes are taking place in different ways and at different levels. As regards the age at marriage, there appears to be a significant change in respect of the actual practice as well as the attitudes and values. Even in the past child marriage was not in practice in the village. But early marriages were common. Most of the girls married before attaining the age of 15 or 16 years. In the case of the lower stratum of the village the girls were married relatively earlier than the girls belonging to the families of the upper stratum. In the same way most of the boys were also married in early age, within twenty years. As the boys were not to look for a job or to wait for settling in life, they were married earlier. But these days the age at marriage has considerably been raised both in respect of girls and boys. Mostly the girls are being married after attaining the age of 15 or 16 years, generally before crossing the age of 20 years. Cases of girls being married in the age group of 20 to 25 years are also found. The majority of the villagers feel that the ideal age for marrying a girl is between 15 to 20 years, but in spite of this prevailing attitude girls are also being married after 20 years of age. Thus in relation to the prevailing attitudes, late marriages are also being performed. The reasons for late marriages are generally economic hardship and non-availability of suitable matches. In the past the boys were available even in early ages for marriage. But now some of them are engaged in receiving education and in search of jobs for settling in life. Consequently the age of boys at marriage has been raised. This raising of age at marriage of the boys has inevitably resulted in raising the marriage age of the girls. Moreover the abolition of zamindari system, migration of people to Pakistan and the developments taking place in the post-independence era have adversely affected the economy of the village. The people having aristocratic background did not like to work hard and, hence, with the fall in economic conditions, they are faced with economic hardships. Consequently the parents faee a lot of difficulties in arranging dowries and other marriage expenses. This factor, therefore, seems to be mainly responsible for raising the age at marriage for the girls. Whatever may be the reason, a clear change is found in this regard and the marriage age of both boys and girls has been raised. This is not only a change in practice rather the attitudes of the villagers have also changed in this respect. They are mostly now opposed to early marriage which was favoured in the traditional society. In the past there was no engagement for the girls after attaining puberty and hence the parents wanted them to get married as early as possible. But in the present age the families belonging to the upper and middle strata of the society want their daughters to receive education at least up to matriculation. The parents of middle and upper class families do not like to send their daughters in the school situated in the village for education in the higher classes. After schooling for a few years during the childhood, arrangements are made for private coa.hing of the girls at their residence and they appear from the school for secondary school examination mostly as a private candidate. This private coaching takes a little more time and the girls generally pass the matriculation examination after 16 or 17 years of age. After passing matriculation examination these girls are generally married and, hence, the marriage age is automatically raised. Thus it may be stated that the tradition-oriented approach is changing into reason-oriented approach regarding the age at marriage. The prevailing circumstances like looking for a job by the boys, arrangement for dowry, procurement of a suitable match and competition among brides' fathers for getting promising grooms are also responsible for raising the age at marriage.

The changes in marriage and family life are also found in respect of the attitude towards the re-marriage of the widows and divorced women. In the traditional society of the past such re-marriages were not appreciated in the upper and middle strata of the Muslim community in the village and in most of the cases the widows spent their whole life in widowhood. Divorce was a curse and such women were looked down upon in the society. Re-marriage of divorced women was not found in the past, but in the present age the attitude has considerably changed. On the one hand the people now realise that in case the adjustment between the two partners is not possible then there should be a divorce. Moreover, favourable attitude towards re marriage of widows and divorced women is also found. It is an index of change in attitude and outlook. But it is also important to point out that even today such marriages are uncommon in the village. In a very few cases childless widows of lower age have been re-married. Moreover the cases of re marriage of divorced women were not reported by the villagers in the near past. Hence it appears that any significant change in actual practice has not taken place, though the attitude has been rationalised.

All believers in Islam are equal, and the Islamic sanctions do not divide the Muslim community into different endogamous groups. But under the impact of traditional culture the Muslims also developed a caste-like hierarchy in the community life and the concept of superior and inferior prevailed on the basis of birth and descent. The purity of blood was given due importance and the Muslims also performed marriages within the same caste or category. In case of upper caste Muslims, the marriages were performed between Syed and Shaikh in certain areas. But generally the Syeds preferred to marry within their own castes. In general the practice of inter-caste marriage was not favoured. In the same way in the lower stratum of the Muslim society the marriages were generally held within the caste or sub-caste. Marriage between the members of upper and lower caste was not thinkable. But the present data show that inter-caste marriage is not totally opposed by many of them. The educated people are now favouring such marriages. Hence it can be stated that education is rationalising outlook and, with the rise in the level of literacy and education, the favour for inter-caste marriage is increasing. Thus the traditional practice of marriage within the caste only is not favoured. This rationalisation of outlook coincides with the Islamic sanctions which were out of practice due to the dominance of tradition. Thus education is reinforcing Islamization and with the development of rational outlook Islamic values are gaining strength. It is also important to point out that those favouring inter-caste marriage are mostly in favour of establishing marital relations with the families of high caste. It suggests that the concepts of superiority and inferiority are still persisting and the change in the attitude is not fully rationalised. But a trend of change has definitely started in respect of marital relations and inter-caste marriages.

The institution of purdah was a major obstacle in the Muslim society blocking the way of female education. The religious sanctions in respect of purdah were made extremely rigid in traditional Indian Muslim society, which resulted not only in complete seclusion of women but also in the confinement of women within the four walls of the house. The women were allowed to go out only on specific occasions like marriage or death in the families of relatives. But this outside movement was possible only with complete purdah. This traditional practice of purdah system supported by the Islamic sanctions regarding purdah alway created hindrances in the education of women.

It was a common belief in the traditional Muslim society that the women do not need high level education because they are not to earn the livelihood. Their main education should remain confined to the learning of Qur'an and other elementary books on religion and culture for offering prayers and observing Islamic sanctions. Hence arrangements were made inside the house for this elementary religious education in some of the Muslim families belonging to upper stratum of the society. When in the early decades of the present century the Indian National Congress and social workers started a campaign in favour of female education and non-observance of purdah, the Muslims in general reacted against it. Due to poverty and economic hardships it was also not possible for low caste Muslims to educate their wards. At ideological level they were opposed to female education. Only a few middle-class Muslim families living in urban areas gave a positive response to the call for female education. But in those days the Muslims living in rural areas were completely opposed to the idea of female education.

When the views of the Muslims living in the village are taken into consideration it is found that significant changes are taking place in attitudes and practices in respect of general as well as female education. The data analysed in Chapter 5C suggest that the majority of the people are now in favour of educating their girls. This favour is not only at ideological level rather in actual practice also. The girls in their early ages, i.e., before the age of 11 or 12 years, are sent to village Maktab or madrasa and then modern schools for education. As there is no provision for separate education of girls in the high schools, the Muslims do not allow their girls to continue education in higher classes in such a school. They are opposed to co-education. This opposition may be either due to the concept of purdah or due to the idea of maintaining a distance between the two sexes. Consequently, the girls do not complete their education in the school up to secondary level. Those who can afford, manage for private coaching of their girls at their own houses. After coaching. these girls appear privately at secondary school examination. A number of girls have passed matriculation examination in the village. This reality shows that the idea and attitude have considerably changed in respect of girls education. Only in two cases the girls of the village were sent to the town for college education, where they were not kept in the hostels, rather with their relatives living there. Moreover, these two girls receiving college education were admitted in girls college and in this way co-education was unacceptable even at this stage to the guardians. These facts clearly indicate that the traditional values are not completely vanished. But a complete domination of tradition also is not found and the process of tradition-rationality continuum has started. The idea of girls education is being gradually liberalised, and, in actual practice also, changes are taking place in the village life.

Moreover, these facts also reveal that the changes in attitudes of the people are not uniform. The educated people are more liberal and rational than the illiterates and semi-literates. The illiterates are completely opposed to co-education whereas a smaller section of educated people favours the idea of co-education. In the same way, the favour for girls education is in a higher degree among educated people than the illiterates and semi-literates. It means that the factor of education is in itself a force of liberalisation contributing to the development of rational outlook. Hence, with the increase in literacy and education, a trend of change is found in respect of female education in the village.

Changing are also taking place in the observance of purdah in the village. The complete seclusion of women within the four walls of the house practised in traditional society is not favoured by majority of the people in the village. Moreover, the Islamic sanctions of purdah are also not criticised or opposed by the people. Even those families where purdah is not strictly observed or where deviations from Islamic sanctions are found in purdah observance, the religious sanctions were not made the object of criticism or opposition. The people feel that in the changing circumstances purdah observance has been liberalised. On the other hand, they interpret this liberalisation as reaction against the strict traditional purdah and thus blame the extreme rigidity for the present changes in observance of purdah system. In this way the traditional outlook is gradually becoming insignificant and the idea of complete seclusion has become a talk of the past.

The facts lead to draw the inference that among lower caste families observance of purdah is not so strict. The women of these families move freely and work as maid servants, agricultural labourers and wage earners in other jobs inside and, in some cases, outside the village. Hence, the economic reason stands in their way of observing purdah. They are to earn for the family and hence are compelled by the circumstances to move unveiled and to go outside for earning livelihood. In the past also low caste Muslim women did not observe purdah so strictly and worked as maid servants or agricultural labourers. Hence among them purdah was not rigid even in the past. But in the present age a new trend is emerging among low caste Muslim families. The families in which economic condition has improved and whose members are earning in towns or cities or one or two male members are employed after receiving education, purdah is being observed. The women of such families do not move outside freely. When they come outside they wrap a chadar or shawl around their body and remain semi-veiled by using the shawl for covering their faces partially. Thus with the improvement in social and economic conditions some of the low caste families also have started purdah.

In the traditional society purdah was strictly observed by high caste Muslim families. The traditional ties are weakening but observance of purdah has not been abandoned. Purdah is still being observed in such families but in a liberal manner. The women are allowed to move in the village during day hours under a veil or burqa. In certain cases the faces are uncovered where in other cases the faces are also veiled. Moreover, the women also go from village to the town for attending any function in the house of relatives, or for shopping on the occasion of marriage in the family, or for medical treatment. In a few cases young girls have also been sent to the town for receiving college education. The villagers employed in towns sometimes take their wives and children to their places of job where the contact with urban society results in the liberalisation of purdah. In this way the purdah observance is changing and has entered a phase of transition in which varying degrees of purdah observance are found. It was also gathered that the attitude towards purdah has significantly changed. Many of the women and girls belonging to younger generation do not favour purdah, but still they are to observe purdah under social pressures. The fear of community criticisms compels them to observe purdah. In case they are permitted to behave on their own accord, many of them would not favour purdah observance. Thus a wind of change is blowing in respect of purdah observance, and both Islamic and traditional sanctions are becoming less operative.

Changes in economic relations are also taking place in the village community. The facts collected about their present economic life, the attitudes towards different occupations, the level of satisfaction or dissatisfaction with income and profession have been analysed in Chapter VI. This interpretative analysis shows the persistence of a changing trend in rural economy.

In the past, the villagers were generally engaged in cultivation. Excepting five or six zamindar families, all the families in the village lived on cultivation or were associated with agriculture. The lower section of the village community did not possess sufficient plots of land for cultivation and, hence, the members of this section worked as agricultural labour for land owners. The families having adequate plots of land either did cultivation themselves or gave the land to landless farmers for share cropping. In spite of this engagement in agricultural occupation, the villagers were inclined to receive education. The persons belonging to the upper stratum of the society received school or college education in the past also. As a result of this education teachers, lawyers and doctors were also produced in the village. These doctors and lawyers earned money out of their professions as well as through the cultivable lands they possessed in the village. In this way the main basis of economic life was cultivation.

But today the situation is different from the past. Zamindari has been abolished and the members of ex-zamindar families are also adopting occupations of agriculture or service or business. Mostly these people are service holders. A new trend has now developed in the present age in the economic life of the village community. A considerable number of villagers have taken up business occupation in urban areas where they are engaged in different types of business activities like embroidery work, truck and taxi transport and shop keeping, etc. These businessmen mostly belong to the traditional middle stratum of the society. A considerable number of persons belonging to the lower status are also working in cities and towns as manual workers and wage earners. With this income they are not only supporting their families in the village but also purchasing plots of cultivable land. Relatively there is a decline in the economic condition of the upper stratum and many families of upper stratum are disposing of parts of their cultivable land. These lands on the other hand are being purchased generally by the families of middle or lower strata of the past. In the recent past the traditionally low ranking families are purchasing lands in a higher frequency. Hence a considerable number of the low ranking families in the village had now become cultivator. It has definitely brought a significant change in the economic relation among the families in the village. There are still a few poor families in the lower stratum who are landless and whose members work as Kamia or agricultural labourer. These agricultural labourers are not only employed by high caste families but also by low caste families possessing landed property.

Due to the spread of education a higher percentage of village population is engaged in receiving college and university education. In the past this modern education was an exclusive privilege of the upper caste but now the low caste people are also receiving general and technical education and are preferring to some job. Consequently a considerable number of persons are employed as clerks, teachers and officers in different departments of the public and private concerns. This trend of getting employment after receiving education was not found in the traditional society; and, hence, with the employment of people, economic relations have also significantly changed. Those who are employed in towns and cities do not have the same relation with the landed property as do the cultivators have. They manage the cultivation of their land either through share cultivators or they have handed over their family members residing in the village and engaged in cultivation. In this way their economic relations with the family members, kins and villagers have changed.

The facts also suggest that, on the whole, the economic condition is not satisfactory. Due to the rise in prices and higher cost of living, most of the people are dissatisfied with their present economic condition. This expression of dissatisfaction is not in the lower income group only but in all income groups; and, hence, a general dissatisfaction prevails. Moreover, the satisfaction with the present occupation is also not at an adequate level. Most of the people desire to change their occupation. This desirability of change is in a higher percentage among agricultural labourers and small cultivators. Those who are in business are not much in favour of change in occupation, and those who are in service also desire to remain in service but with better emoluments and service conditions. In the past also the economic condition of lower section was not satisfactory, nor all members belonging to upper caste were rich or economically satisfied. But the people were generally contended and hence there was no expression of dissatisfaction in a higher intensity. Today contentment is absent and materialistic outlook has become dominant. It has resulted in the development of dissatisfaction.

The facts further lead to draw the inference that the villagers are aware of agricultural innovations and the facilities given by the government for increasing land output. But they are not in a position to avail or utilise these facilities in full because of poor economic condition. It means that the facil ties concerning agricultural innovations are not being fully utilised by the cultivators. Consequently the increase in the agricultural output is not up to the mark. It is, therefore, affecting the village economy adversely. The fact has also come to light that the villagers do not like to set up cottage industries. They are not much inclined towards enjoying the facilities extended for the development of cottage industries. Hence it may be concluded that the villagers are not much exposed to the modern facilities of cultivation and cottage industries. Consequently they have not derived full benefits from these governmental schemes. Under the impact of various forces and factors changes in occupational composition, economic relations, attitude towards different types of economic activities and standards of living are changing resulting in the change of economic relations and the structure of the village community.

The rise and development of political awareness and political consciousness among the villagers are found these days as analysed in Chapter VII. This rise of political consciousness is an index of changing political relations and thus the change in the structure of the village community. The data gathered and analysed suggest that the people in the village are participating in the parliamentary system of democracy, not only as a voter but also as sympathizers of candidates and parties contesting the election. It was informed that the villagers become quite active at the time of election and participate in campaigning in favour of one candidate or the other. They also attend election meetings and work as polling agents. Moreover, two or three persons of the community also hold some posts in one political party or the other. These facts reveal that the political participation of the people is of considerable degree.

The facts further reveal that the people not only participate in political activities and elections but also have liking for one party or the other. The majority of the villagers is inclined towards rightist political forces and a relatively smaller section supports the leftist parties. It is also important to keep in mind that the present village is situated in naxalite belt, but in spite of this political feature of the region the village is more inclined towards rightist forces. It may be due to the fact that the village is inhabited by the Muslims, whereas the naxalite activities are mostly confined to the scheduled castes of the society. The villagers are harassed by such violent activities of the naxalites. This may be the reason for a higher degree of favour for the rightist political parties. The facts also reveal that the uneducated working class has shown a higher degree of favour for rightist parties, whereas relatively a higher degree of favour for the leftist parties is found among the educated section of the village. It suggests that the arousal of a higher degree of political consciousness tilts the balance in favour of the leftist forces. Moreover the facts lead to draw the inference that the reactionary political parties are not liked by the villagers in a considerable percentage.

The villagers have also the knowledge of different forms

of government and have also expressed their liking or disliking for them. The majority shows a greater degree of favour for the parliamentary system of democracy and a considerable percentage has also favoured presidential type of government. A very small section has supported authoritarian system of government. This favour has come from the weaker section of the society. It may be perhaps due to the exploitation of this section under democratic system.

Panchayati Raj system is also known to the villagers and they are conscious of the ways and means adopted in the panchayat election. In general, the villagers declared that physical power, wealth and caste factors played vital roles in the panchayat elections. They have also stated that as a result of adopting wrong means in these elections, the persons elected to the village panchayat are not worthy and good. On the other hand, undesirable elements have been elected who have failed to do any positiv eservice to the village community. In other words, the villagers are neither satisfied with the ways in which panchayat elections are held nor with the persons contesting and winning these elections. The views expressed by the villagers about their favour or disfavour for political parties, their liking or disliking for different forms of government and their frank comments on gram panchayat's elections, both the procedure and the outcome lead to draw the inference that the villagers are undergoing the process of political socialization. Thus both political participation and political socialization are found in the village community. These two aspects constitute the basis of political consciousness and political awareness. Hence it may be concluded that politically the villagers are conscious of the facts and are aware of the political happenings around them. Thus political consciousness or political awareness are not only confined to upper stratum or wealthy or to educated section of the society, rather found in the whole of the village community. But the degree of political awareness is not uniform. It is in high degree among the educated section than in the less educated or unducated section. As the service holders are by and large educated and those in business, agriculture or in wage earning occupation are less educated or uneducated, the degree of political awareness is higher in the category of service holders than in other occupational categories. Thus persistence of political awareness and political consciousness has contributed to the development of new patterns of political relations in the community life. The traditionally lower and exploited section is aspiring for a better place in the society and is expecting a just treatment from the traditionally dominant section. This rising consciousness in the weaker section and the realization of changing political climate of the country by the dominant section are instrumental in changing political relations and in the patterns of interaction with each other. Hence the emergence of new dimensions in the village politics have contributed to the change in the patterns of political socialization and degree of political consciousness. Thus with the change of political relations, the structure of the village community is also changing.

As the people living in the Pinjrawan village are Muslims, their beliefs, rituals and festivities show an imprint of Islamic sanctions. They are believers in Islam and hence they have a faith in God, the Almighty. But at the same time it is found that the profound impact of Islamic sanctions found in the past is not existing today. Moreover, in the traditional society the behaviours and observances were not influenced only by religious sanctions but also by customary rules and traditions. In the present age these customary rules and traditional obligations are becoming less effective due to the development of rational outlook under the impact of modern forces like education, democratic system of government and exposure to urbanism, industrialism and media of mass communication. In the traditional society superstitions also played a vital role in the community life. The constituents of superstitious beliefs like ganda, taweez, tona, jadu and evil spirits of bhut, witch and the like are no more significant in the life of the people. In the past when a person suffered from small pox, the superstitious belief in the 'mata' stood in the way of taking any step for the cure of the disease. During the period of ailment certain observations were also essential in the house. Cooking of certain commodities was prohibited and traditional as well as superstitious means were adopted for the treatment. But in the present age the outlook is totally changed. People do not regard the appearance of small pox as an act of evil spirit, rather as a physical disease. Doctor is consulted and medical treatment is given to the patients. The restrictions on cooking and other such observations are also not found. In the same way the belief in the existence of witch or ghost (bhut, parit and churail, etc.) has also almost disappeared and the persons showing abnormal behaviours are not believed to be in the grip of these evil spirits, rather they are regarded as persons suffering from some mental disease. The neuro-surgeons and psychiatrists are consulted for the treatment. These facts suggest a change in the superstitious beliefs of the people. The facts suggest that a very small section still has some belief in superstition and this smaller section belongs to the lower stratum of the society. The lack of education and social backwardness of this section is responsible for the persistence of superstitious beliefs. In the upper stratum of the society where education is relatively higher, the approach is rational.

But the faith in Islamic sanctions is still persisting, and the people do not oppose the Islamic sanctions concerning prayers and other religious congregations. In actual practice, there appears to be a change because the observance of faith is not up to the mark. The loyalty to the Islamic sanctions is complete in words but partial in action. Nobody is opposed to namaz, but 100 per cent of the people do not offer namaz five times a day regularly. Friday prayers are offered by a large number of people but the offerers of panjgana are much less in number. In the same way, 100 per cent of the people believe in keeping fast but a smaller section is not particular. The payment of zakat is in practice but not in cent per cent of the cases. Offering sacrifices on the day of Baqr-Id and the performance of haj pilgrimage require heavy expenses and hence majority of the families do not afford to it. But even those families which can afford the performance of haj, did not perform it in cent per cent of the cases. It has also come to light that many of the people offer qurbani not primarily because it is a religious obligation, but because it is a symbol of social prestige and status. The facts further reveal that the religious gatherings like milad, waaz, tabligh and urs are organized from time to time in the village. But the participation in such gatherings is not in 100 per cent of the cases. It is true that from Islamic point of view the participation in such religious gatherings is not obligatory (wajib) but this participation definitely shows devotion to faith and religion. The lesser degree of participation in these gatherings is definitely an indicator of declining importance of religion in the practical life of the village community. In addition to these facts the views of the people in respect of the occurrence of miseries, calamities and mishappenings suggest that the people no more exclusively believe in divine decree for such happenings rather they also interpret these happenings in terms of their own misdeeds, miscalculations and the factors operating around them. In this way, alongwith a faith in divine decree, the rational explanation is also being given by these people. These facts clearly suggest that the religious dominance is weakening in actual life and the people are becoming more and more reason oriented. A complete faith in fate (taqdir) is not found rather the faith in fate co-ordinated by personal deeds (tadbir) is also quite strong. In this way the importance of reason is gradually gaining ground and a synthesis of faith and reason is found in the explanations of the events, understanding situations and interpreting calamities and mishappenings.

The changes are also taking place in rituals and festivities in the present age. In the past people observed the rituals of maktab, aqiqa, circumcision, roza-kushai and the like in a luxurious form, but now these functions are being simplified and the rituals are observed in a different way. The basic aspect of religion, i.e. 'aqida' (faith), remaining the same, the socio-cultural superstructure is changing fast. Instead of folk songs, film songs are played on loudspeakers. Moreover, the dress patterns of traditional style are being replaced by modern dresses. A child in the past wore silken shirwani, cap and pajama on the occasion of his aqiqa or circumcision or maktab, and, now-a-days, in most of the cases pants and shirts are used. Thus the impact of modern outlook and modern living is explicit in the observance of rituals.

In the same way, in respect of festivities also changes are taking place. On the occasion of Shab-e-baraat, for example, prayer for the whole night was a religious obligation which was observed by most of the people in the past. But these days only a few elderly persons spend their nights in prayers, while the rest celebrate this festival as a merry-night. They enjoy 'atashbazi' and bread and halwa on this occasion. On the occasion of Id and Baqrid the people go for namaz not as performing a religious duty but attending a socio-cultural gathering. The dress and styles on these occasions is no more traditional, rather modernized. In the past people spent the day of Id or Baqr-Id in meeting people and in offering sewai and milk to the visitors. But during these days many youths of the village go to the town to see films. Moreover, instead of atar, perfumes of modern styles are used. Modern amenities have been used for a greater degree of enjoyment in lieu of maintaining the pure and pious mode of life exercised during Ramazan for a greater degree of social and moral order. On the occasion of Muharram the akhara procession is still taken out but the religious sanctity is not maintained. Instead of mourning the Great Shahadat and demonstrating the main theme of daring 'Qurbani' in the way of Allah, most of the akhara processionists create ugly scenes. Thus it is apparent that pious rituals have been coloured in the festivities of joy and pleasure more than a religious sanctimony.

The institution of waqf is an important aspect of Muslim community life. Most of the religious works are performed out of waqf income. Maintenance of sanctuaries like mosque, Imambara, karbala, musafirkhana; running of the media of religious instructions like madrasas, zikr-o-majalis, milad; and feeding the institutions of 'khairat' and help to the helpless constitute the main aspects of 'Awqaf'. In Pinjrawan altogether five waqfs were created and do exist. The purpose of creating the waqf was the same as mentioned above. There is a properly elected body known as Village Waqf Committee which looks after the affairs of all the five waqfs in the village. But due to certain sectarian differences among the members of the Waqf Committee, all the awqat have become victim of gross mismanagement and uncare. The people of the village know the importance and utility of the waqf institution, but are highly dissatisfied with the management. Still they are not ready to hand over the waqfs to government; as they do not foresee any tangible improvement in getting another Waqf Committee appointed by government; and as such the majority of the respondents have opposed any change in the management. They want to take the Committee above factionalism. Thus, it will be seen that in this respect the attitude of the villagers is quite rational and constructive.

In the conclusion it may be stated that the social structure of the village community is changing in all aspects of life under the impact of changing socio-cultural climate. With the spread of education and a higher degree of exposure to the general mass media as well as confrontation with the realities of life, the outlook and attitude of the villagers is changing from tradition-oriented to reason-oriented and they are ready to accept the hard facts of life in replacement of the superstitious and orthodox traditions of the past. As a result of the development of rational outlook many of the Islamic practices, which were dominated by traditions, are undergoing a change or reform thus bringing them close to the realities of Islam and human life. General rationalization of approach among the youth creates a hope for the future of the village people. Changes are also found in the patterns of entertainment, hobbies, attitude towards education in general and female education in particular and inter-caste relations. These changes in inter-caste relations are a manifestation of changes in economic relations, beliefs and rituals and the changes in orientations. In this way the roles of the people, cultural values, status pattern and other aspects of social structure of the community as a whole.

Glossary

Aangan	Courtyard.
Abu Zaid	An Arabian traveller historian.
Ahle Hadis	Muslim sect following Abdul Wahhab Najdi as their spiritual guide.
Ajlaf	Low caste Muslims.
Akhara	Moharram procession.
Alif	The first letter of Urdu alphabets.
Alim	Islamic theologist.
Amarat Sharia	Muslim Court of Jurisprudence.
Ameer	Leader of the Muslim community.
Anchar	Pickles.
Ansari	A Muslim community of weavers.
Aqiqa	An Islamic ritual pertaining to the first removal of hair from the head of a child.
Arab Sarai	An inn for dignitaries.
Ashraf	Dignified people of the community or upper Muslim caste.
Atashbazi	Fire-ware played at happy occasions.
Atraf	Low caste Muslims.
Awqaf	Plural of 'waqf' = religious trust.
Bailghara	Oxen house or cattle house.

Baithka	A male apartment of a house.
Bait-a-Mal	Islamic treasury.
Barhi	Carpenter.
Basant	Spring season.
Basia	Not fresh.
Be'	The second alphabet of Urdu language.
Bhai-band	Co-sectarians.
Bhut	Ghost, evil spirit.
Bihari	Of the Bihar province.
Biradari	One's own sect.
Biri	Smoking candle.
Bismillah	To begin, By the name of God.
Bohra	A Shi'ite sect.
Brahmin	The super-most Hindu caste.
Burqa	Female veil, used by purdah-observing ladies.
Buzurg	Elderly person of family/community.
Caliphate	Successorship to the Prophet of Islam.
Caste	Sect.
Chatni	Sauce.
Chaupal	An agricultural programme on radio.
Churail	Female evil spirit.
Churihara	Bangles seller.
Dai	Maid servant, One who invites persons towards God.
Dargah	Grave of a pious soul.
Darul-Uloom	University of Islamic Learning.
Dasehra	A Hindu festival.
Dastar-bandi	The ceremony of making successor to a priest.

Dhimmi	A non-Muslim subject under a Islamic rule.
Diwali	A Hindu festival of joy, performed in autumn season.
Diwan-e-Waqf	Ministry of Religious Trust.
Dupatta	Scarf for women to cover head and upper parts of her body.
Dusadh	A menial Hindu caste.
Dwij	Twice-born.
Falah	Betterment.
Faqir	Beggar, A priest leading secluded life.
Fiqah	Islamic Law.
Gaushala	Cattle-shed or cow shed.
Gair-mahram	One before whom appearance is prohibited.
Gharara	A petticoat for women, used as garment.
Ghee	Ghee.
Ghunghat	A covering of face.
Habs	Confinement.
Hadis	Tradition, Sayings of the Prophet.
Hadith	Hadis, as produced in English language.
Haj	A pilgrimage of Khana-e-Kaaba, Mecca.
Halal	Permissible.
Hakim	A Unani physician.
Hat	A rural market place.
Hambalite	Followers of Imam Ahmad-bin-Hambal.

Hanafite	Followers of Imam Abu-Hanifa.
Hejab	Veil, purdah; To feel shame.
Hiba	Gift.
Hindi	Indian.
Holi	A Hindu festival celebrated in spring.
Hookah	An Indian smoking device, hubble-bubble.
Iddat	Confinement period for widows after the death of one's husband.
Idgah	Place of mass prayers on the eve of Id.
Idul Fitr	An important Muslim festival celebrated on the first day of the tenth Lunar month.
Idul Zoha	Another important Muslim festival celebrated from 10th to 12th of the twelfth Lunar month.
Ijma	A consensus of Islamic Jurists.
Ilm	Knowledge.
Imam	Spiritual leader.
Islam	Religion brought by Prophet Mohammad.
Ismaili	Followers of Mohammad-bin-Ismail.
Istehsan	To make one gracious.
Jadu	Sorcery.
Jagir	A property gifted to one in acknowledgement of his loyal services.
Jagirdari	The system of having jagir.
Jamaat Islami	An association formed for service of Islam.
Jamia Millia	An Anglo-Islamic University (Delhi).
Jamaat-ul-Ulema	An Advisory Committee formed of the Muslim Jurists to advise government of India on Islamic issues.

Jehad	Fight against evils/excesses/for safety of religion.
Jehl	Ignorance.
Jin	A rare parallel to man living of the earth.
Kaba	The Islamic sanctuary situated at Mecca, towards which Muslims throughout the world face at the time of prayers.
Kachcha	Earthen construction/mud-built.
Kalal	A low occupational Muslim caste dealing in desi wine.
Kamin	Indignified, filthy,
Khairat	Alms.
Khan	Pathan sect.
Khanzada	Descent of Pathan.
Khatna	Circumcision.
Khalifa	Spiritual leader.
Khilafat	Successorship to Prophet Mohammad.
Khanqah	Sufi hospice.
Khira	A summer vegetable fruit.
Khoja	Follower of the Eastern Wing of the Ismaili School of Islamic Law.
Khula	Divorce of a bridegroom (male) by his wife.
Kichin	An evil spirit.
Krishi Mela	Agricultural Fair.
Krishi Samachar Patra	Agrieultural Information Magazine.
Lungi	A cloth generally used by weavers and Madrasis in place of pantaloon.
Madkotha	Mud-built upper storey.
Mahram	One who is permissible to face another.

Majalis	Plural of 'Majlis'= religious gathering.
Majlis-e-Awqaf	Council of Religious Trusts.
Maktab	Primary school of ethics.
Mallah	Fisherman.
Mallick	An upper Muslim caste.
Masjid	Mosque.
Mata	Small pox (mother).
Maulvi	Religious teacher.
Mauza	A big-sized village.
Mazar	Tomb of a Muslim saint.
Mehr	The consideration money of Nikah, payable to the bride.
Mela	Fair.
Memon	A Gujrati Muslim sect.
Milad	Ceremony in memory of Prophet.
Mulezada	A mixed low caste.
Mulla	Priest and teacher.
Musafirkhana	An inn.
Nabvi	Pertaining to the Prophet.
Nafqa	Subsistence to a wife (Same a Naan-o-Nafqa).
Namahram	One prohibited to face by another.
Namaz	Prayer.
Nazrana	Gratification.
Nikah	The central cite of marriage.
Ojha	Blower and whiffer.
Oraon	Name of a scheduled tribe.
Paijama	Trousers.
Pan	Betel.
Pathan	An upper Muslim caste.
Pir	A saint.

Pukka	Brick-built/metalled (road or building).
Panchayat	A village court/ statutory society.
Purdah	Seclusion.
Qazi	A jurist.
Qiyas	Speculation.
Qurbani	Sacrifice.
Ramzan	Muslim's fasting month, 9th month of lunar year.
Rangrez	A lower Muslim occupational caste—dyer and printer.
Rauza	A construction erected on the grave of a pious.
Re-Islamization	The process of re-vitalization of Islam.
Roza-kushai	Fast-breaking ceremony.
Sahar	A light meal at dawn during Ramzan.
Sakna	Residential holding.
Samjukta Parivar	Joint family.
Sari	A long cloth worn round the body by Indian women.
Se	6th alphabet of Urdu language.
Shab-e-Barat	A Muslim festival on 15th Shaban (8th lunar month).
Shafi'ite	A follower of Imam Shafei.
Shaikh	The descent of the three Caliphs.
Shalwar	A loose trouser type dress worn by ladies.
Sharara	A loose dress used by females.
Sharbat	A sweet drink.
Sharia	The Law of Islam.
Sharm	To feel shy of.

Shia	One of the five religious sects of Islam.
Shikar	Prey.
Shirvani	Long coat, mainly used by Indian Muslims.
Shorfa	Dignitaries.
Siwai	An Indian type of sweet marcony.
Sufis	Muslims who believe every good/bad to be action of God.
Suhagin	A married woman whose husband is alive.
Sunnah	Practices and sayings of Prophet.
Syed	Uppermost Muslim caste.
Tabligh	Propagation of Islamic teachings.
Tadbir	Action, Deed.
Talaq	Divorce.
Talib Ilm	Student.
Taqdir	Luck.
Tari	Toddy.
Tarawih	Recitation of Qur'an during Ramzan Prayers.
Taweez	A tablet containing Qur'anic Ayats.
Tazkia	Purification of thought and belief.
Te'	4th alphabet of Urdu language.
Tola	Small settlement beside a village.
Tona and Totka	Superstitious actions to damage others for one's own gain.
Ulema	Plural of 'Alim' = religious teacher.
Umayyad	Descent of Umayya, twin-brother of Hashim, ancestor of the Prophet.
Unchi Zat	Upper caste.
Urdu	A well-known Indian language.

Urs	A ceremony in the memory of a pious soul.
Vazir	Minister.
Waaz	Preaching.
Wajib	Religious obligations.
Waqf	A religious trust.
Worldly medicine	Drugs.
Zakat	Islamic tax (2½ % of the annual savings).
Zamindar	Landlord.
Zat	Caste.
Zena	Illegitimate sexual behaviour.
Zikr-o-Majalis	Religious gathering for remembering the champions of Islam.

Bibliography

BOOKS

Ahmad, Aziz, Studies in Islamic Culture in the Indian Environment, London, Clarenden Press, 1964.

Ahmad, Imtiaz, Ed., Caste and Social Stratification among the Muslims, Delhi, Manohar Book Service, 1973.

Ahmad, Imtiaz, Ed., Family Kinship and Marriage among Muslims in India, New Delhi, Manohar Book Service, 1976.

Ahmad, Saghir, Class and Power in Punjabi Village, New York, Monthly Review Press, 1977.

Ali, A. Yusuf, The Making of India, London, A. & C. Black, Ltd., 1925.

Ali, S. A., Economic Foundation of Islam, Calcutta, Orient Longmans, 1964.

Ali, Syed Amir, The Spirit of Islam, Calcutta, S.K. Lahiri, 1902.

Ali, Hazrat, Nahjul Balagha (Urdu), Unknown, Ahbab Publication, 1970.

Ali, Syed Nausha, Musalman-e-Hind-o-Pakistan ki Tarique-e-Taleem (Urdu), Karachi, Sulman Academy, 1963.

Ammer-ul-Hassan, Islamic Shi'ite Encyclopaedia, Vol. II.

Anderon, Walfred, A. and Parker, Fredrick, B., An Introduction to Sociology, New Delhi, Affiliated East-West Press, 1966.

Ansari, Ghaus, Muslim Castes in Uttar Pradesh, Lucknow, 1959.

Ashraf, K. M., Life and Conditions of the People of Hindustan, New Delhi, Munshiram Manohar Lal, 1970.

Azimabadi, Maulvi Fasihuddin Balkhi, Tarikhe Magadh (Urdu), Delhi, Anjuman-e-Taraqui-e-Urdu, 1944.

Azimabadi, Shaad, Tarikh-e-Bihar (Urdu), Subhe Sadiq, Patna, 1893.

Beteille, Andre (Ed.), Social Inequality, London, Richard Clay, 1972.

Bihar, Public Relation Department, Bihar, 1958-59 : Facts and Figures.

Broom, Leonard and Selznick, Philip, Sociology, A Text with Adapted Readings, Evanston, Ill., Row Peterson & Co., 1955.

Brown, A. R., Structure and Function in Primitive Society, London, Cohen and West, 1964.

Buchanan, Francis Hamilton, An Introduction to the districts of Bihar and Patna in 1811-12, Vol. I.

Choudhry, P. C. Roy, Bihar District Gazetteers, Gaya, Patna Secretariat Press, 1957.

Choudhury, P. C. Roy, Gaya District Gazetteer, 1957.

Diwakar, R.R., Bihar through the Ages, Bombay, Orient Longmans, 1959.

Dube, Leela and Kutty, Abdul Rahman, Matriliny and Islam, Religion and Society in the Lacadives (University of Saugar Monograph in Anthropology and Sociology), Delhi, National, 1969.

Durkheim, Emile, Elementary Forms of the Religious Life, trans., J. W. Swain, Paris, Free Press, 1947.

Eister, Allan W., A Dictionary of Social Sciences, Edited by Julius Gold William D. Kolb, New York, The Free Press, 1967.

Firth, R., Elements of Social Organisation, London, Watts 1951.

Fyzee, A. A. A., Outlines of Muhammadan Law, London, 1964.

Gerth, H. H. and Mills, C. W. (Ed.), Essays in Sociology, New York, Oxford University Press, 1964.

Heffing, Encyclopaedia of Islam, Vol. II.

Hiller, E. T., Social Relation and Social Structure, New York, Harper and Bros., 1947.

Hitti, Philip K., History of Arabs, London, 1940,

Hussain, S. Abid, The Destiny of Indian Muslims, Bombay, Asia, 1965.

Imam, Zafar (Ed.), Muslims in India, New Delhi, Orient Longman, 1975.

India, Census of India, 1981, Series A, Bihar.

India, Ministry of Irrigation & Power, Waqf Section, Waqf Administration.

Johnson, H. M., Sociology, Bombay, Allied Publishers, 1967.

Karandikar, M. A., Islam in India's Transition to Modernity, Bombny, Orient Longmans, 1969.

Karim, A.K. Nazmul, Changing Society in India and Pakistan, A Study in Social Change and Social Stratification, Dacca, Oxford University Press, 1956.

Karna, M. N. (Ed.), Bihar Economy and Society, New Delhi, Concept Publishing Co., 1981.

Khalid, Rashid S., Waqf Administration in India, New Delhi, Vikas, 1978.

Lari, S. M. R. N., Western Civilization Through Muslim Eyes, Britain, Biddles Ltd., 1977.

Levy, Reuben, The Social Structure of Islam, U. S. A., Cambridge University Press, 1962.

Madan, T. N. (Ed.), Muslim Communities of South Asia, New Delhi, Vikas Publishing House Pvt. Ltd., 1976.

Mahajir, Ali Musa Raza, Tenets of Islam, Bangalore, Islamic Literature Publishing House, 1963.

Mahmood, Tahir, Muslim Personal Law, New Delhi, Vikas, 1977.

Martindale, Don, Nature and Types of Sociological Theory, London, Routledge and Kegan Paul, 1961.

Marx, Karl, Capital, Vol. 3, Chicago, Kerr, 1909.

Misra, S. C., Muslim Communities in Gujrat, Bombay, Asia Publishing House, 1964.

Mulla, D. F., Principles of Mohammadan Law, Bombay, 1968.

Mujeeb, M., The Indian Muslims, London, George Allen & Unwin, 1967.

Naumani, Shibli, Seerat-un-Nabi, Vol. II, Azamgarh, 1352 A.H.

Naqi, Maulana Syed Ali, Islam ki Hakimana Zindagi (Urdu), Lucknow, Naaz Publisher, 1932.

Nehru, Pandit Jawahar Lal, Discovery of India, 6th Edition, Calcutta, Signel Press, 1956.

Nazami, K.A., Some Aspects of Religion and Politics in the 13th Century, Bombay, Asia Publishing House, 1961.

O'Malley, L.S.S. (Ed.), Philosophy of Education, Calcutta, 1941.

Qutb, Muhmmad, Islam the Misunderstood Religion, Delhi, The Board of Islamic Publications, 1968.

Rashid, A., Society and Culture in Medieval India, Calcutta, Firma K.L. Mukhupadhayay, 1969.

Rashid, S. Khalid, Waqf Administration in India, New Delhi, Vikas Publishing House, 1978.

Raz, S.M., The Process of Socialization—A Multi-Ethnic Study, New Delhi, Chetna Publications, 1976.

Shukla, N.K., The Social Structure of an Indian Village, New Delhi, Cosmo Publications, 1976.

Shushtery, A.M.A., Outlines of Islamic Culture, Bangalore, Bangalore Publishing Co., 1937.

Siddiqui, M.K.A., Muslims of Calcutta, Calcutta, Anthropological Survey of India, 1974.

Siddiqui, N.A., Population Geography of Muslims of India, New Delhi, S. Chand, 1976.

Singh, Harjinder (Ed.), Cast among non-Hindus in India, New Delhi, National Publishing House, 1977.

Sorokin, P.A., Social and Cultural Mobility, London, Harper and Brothers, 1927.

Tarachand, Influence of Islam on Indian Culture, Allahabad, Indian Press, 1954.

Yasin, Md., A Social History of Islamic India, Lucknow, Upper India, 1958.

JOURNALS

Ahmad, Zeyauddin, Marriage and Family among the Muslims of Bihar, in Family in India—A Regional View (ed.), George Kurian, Paris, Monton, 1974.

Ansari, Ghaus, Muslim Caste in Uttar Pradesh—A Study in Culture Contact, Eastern Anthropologist, 1959.

Hoda, Najmul, Universal Brotherhood and Islam, Annals of Oriental Research of the University of Madras, Vol. 31, Part I.

Ibrahim, Hafiz Muhammad, Waqf Administration, New Delhi, The Muslim Waqf Section, Ministry of Irrigation and Power, Government of India, 1961.

Karna, M.N., Etiology of Disease, A Sociological Study in the Rural Context, Man in India, Vol. 56 (1), March, 1976.

Khan, Hasan Ali, Twarikh-e-Daulat-e-Sher Shahi, Medieval India Quarterly, Vol. I, July, 1950.

Nasiruddin-al-Bafi, Mohammad, Islam Aur Asre Jadid (Urdu), Vol. 5(1), 1973.

Nooruddin, Saleema, Purdah no bar to Progress. Muslim Review, Vol. XII (5), 1933, p. 9.

Ojha, Pandit Gauri Shanker, History of Medieval Civilization, Journal of the Aligarh Historical Research Institute, 1941.

UNPUBLISHED SOURCES

Raza, S. Musi and Ahmad, Sarfarazuddin, Para-bonded Labour in Ramtari Village, Seminar on Rural Sociology in India (U.G.C.), Patna, 1978.

Raza, S. Musi, Changing Pattern of Muslim Community in Bihar, Ph. D. Thesis, Patna University, 1976.

Index